MW00568607

Romantic Women Poets

Genre and Gender

39 DQR STUDIES IN LITERATURE

Series Editors

C.C. Barfoot - A.J. Hoenselaars
W.M. Verhoeven

Romantic Women Poets

Genre and Gender

Edited by
Lilla Maria Crisafulli
Cecilia Pietropoli

Amsterdam - New York, NY 2007

Cover image: Jean-Honoré Fragonard, *A Young Girl Reading*, oil on canvas, c.1776. Gift of Mrs. Mellon Bruce in memory of her father, Andrew W. Mellon, Image © 2007 Board of Trustees, National Gallery of Art, Washington.

Cover design: Aart Jan Bergshoeff

The paper on which this book is printed meets the requirements of 'ISO 9706: 1994, Information and documentation - Paper for documents - Requirements for permanence'.

ISBN-13: 978-90-420-2247-8
©Editions Rodopi B.V., Amsterdam - New York, NY 2007
Printed in The Netherlands

ACKNOWLEDGEMENTS

We would like to thank Cedric Barfoot who has followed the development of this book with unfailing support and precious advice. Our gratitude also goes to Keir Elam who has given us assistance with his invaluable suggestions, corrections and additions, as well as by reading different drafts of the manuscript. We also thank Mariarita Ferretti for her essential help with editorial and graphic-related matters.

CONTENTS

INTRODUCTION

LILLA MARIA CRISAFULLI AND CECILIA PIETROPOLI

> A century ago – notwithstanding we had never been altogether without female attempts, and those occasionally successful – it was still thought wonderful in England that a woman should versify …. her poems were ushered into the world under the patronage of the great, and prefaced by the praise of the learned. She acquired fame equal to her wishes, and it perished with her. The female of our own age claim a more just and durable celebrity. Miss Seward, Mrs Barbauld, Charlotte Smith, will take their place among the English poets for centuries to come.[1]

Between the end of the eighteenth and the beginning of the nineteenth century, as the epigraph from *The Critical Review* (1802) suggests, women poets started to gain a considerable position in the literary market. The success of Barbauld's, Seward's, and Smith's volumes of poetry, the anonymous reviewer notes, helped to change the way women poets were considered by contemporary readers. Only a century earlier, not only was it "still thought wonderful in England that a woman should versify", but her fame was not expected to last. At the beginning of the nineteenth century, instead, women poets could supposedly acquire lasting fame, even if, in reality, this fame did not go much beyond the early nineteenth century itself.

[1] *Critical Review*, XXXVI (1802), 413.

As Marilyn Butler has underlined, however, after 1800 periodicals such as *The Edinburgh Review* and *The Quarterly Review* started a process of inclusion and exclusion of writers that was to influence the construction of the Romantic literary canon.[2] This selection had the effect of banishing some among the most authoritative women writers of the period from the literary canon, although not from the literary scene.

The critical neglect that followed such a successful and influential literary output by women poets is well documented. In his Introduction to *The Female Poets of Great Britain, Chronologically Arranged: with Copious Selections and Critical Remarks* (1848), Frederic Rowton regretfully remarks “the fact that this is almost the first book expressly devoted to the poetical production of the British female mind”, a fact that “tends strongly to prove that women's intellect has been overlooked, if not despised by us hitherto”. “It is high time”, Rowton adds, “we should awake to a sense of our own folly and injustice”.[3]

Rowton had in fact foreseen the erasing of women's poetic voice from the literary canon. The process of marginalization of women's poetry led first to the creation of a secondary market, a sort of literary ghetto in which women's poetry could be confined, and eventually to their complete disappearance from traditional literary critical attention. An arbitrary canon, rooted in rigid literary and gender assumptions, sealed women's silence for more than a century.

Even at the end of the eighteenth and in the early years of the nineteenth century, women were often in practice marginalized in the literary market, restricted by their gender to the writing of specific genres or to addressing specific subjects, but despite this restriction they dared in practice to venture into politically engaged verse as well as into the formulation of poetic theory, even though these were traditionally considered masculine fields. When writing poetry, women were aware of defying this artificial and arbitrary confinement, and they actively promoted and pursued a transition from being the object to becoming the subject of poetry.

---

[2] Marilyn Butler, “Culture's Medium: the Role of the Review”, in *The Cambridge Companion to British Romanticism*, ed. Stuart Curran, Cambridge, 1993, 141-42.

[3] Quoted in *Romantic Literature*, eds Jennifer Breen and Mary Noble, London, 2002, 144.

Forced to write with a limited publishing market in mind, women poets astutely elaborated a rhetoric of modesty, which only apparently complied with traditional assumptions regarding female writers, while, at the same time, they addressed a much wider audience and more substantial issues. In this way, their rhetoric of self-restriction and their aesthetics of inadequacy became a sort of poetic self-discipline, an indirect way of exercising personal and artistic self-assertion, negotiating authorial subjectivity and the demands of the literary market, so that, through their poetry, women's vulnerability evolved from mere social condition to self-conscious poetic style.

In the last two decades of the twentieth century, British and American criticism has fully re-evaluated the position of women within the Romantic literary canon. The works of writers such as Anna Laetitia Barbauld (1743-1825), Matilda Betham (1776-1852), Felicia Hemans (1793-1835), Letitia Elizabeth Landon (1802-1838), Mary Russell Mitford (1787-1865), Hannah More (1745-1833), Mary Robinson (1758-1800), Anna Seward (1742-1809), Charlotte Smith (1749-1806), Mary Tighe (1772-1810), Dorothy Wordsworth (1771-1855), Ann Yearsley (1756-1806), have been recognized as fundamental to a complete understanding of British Romanticism.

This volume aims to contribute to the process of re-evaluation of the role that women poets played within English Romanticism and to retrace their participation in the construction of Romantic sensibility and poetics, thereby shedding new light on the importance of their contribution to the making of British culture in this period.[4] In particular, our volume intends to re-evaluate women's rhetoric of modesty and their aesthetics of inadequacy, and recognize the intrinsic ambiguity and ironic implications involved. Irony and ambiguity in women's poetry are at the origin of a more or less conscious revision of traditional poetic modes and techniques. Paradoxically, women's marginalization leads to a newly acquired liberty of expression, which opens up new literary perspectives, and allows women to confront public subjects from an unusual point of view, thereby challenging conventional assumptions. The woman poet occupied the position, in

---

[4] The essays included in this volume are the result of a four-year research project on "Women and Europe", run by the members of the *Centro Interdisciplinare di Studi Romantici* at the University of Bologna, in collaboration with other Italian, American and British scholars.

Julia Kristeva's words, of "a perpetual dissident in respect of social and political consensus, in exile in respect of power".[5]

At the same time, the essays in this collection aim to analyse the interaction between women poets and those usually considered to be the "major Romantic poets". Our intention is to demonstrate how women poets contributed to the creation of the literature and culture of the Romantic period as much as better-known male poets such as Wordsworth and Coleridge. It was indeed the reciprocal influence of male and female poets that helped to shape the literary network of what later became known as British Romanticism. The impact that Mary Tighe's *Psyche, or the Legend of Love* (1805), for example, had on the young John Keats is well known. The young William Wordsworth was deeply influenced by the works of Joanna Baillie (1762-1851), Helen Maria Williams (1761-1827) and Charlotte Smith. Particularly striking is the influence of Joanna Baillie's "Introductory Discourse" to her *A Series of Plays in Which It Is Attempted to Delineate the Stronger Passions of the Mind* (the first volume, 1798) on Wordsworth's Preface to the *Lyrical Ballads* (1800) but also, in a different way, on P.B. Shelley's *A Defence of Poetry* (1821). Similarly, Dorothy Wordsworth's journals and diaries helped to shape William's *Lyrical Ballads* and, more generally, his poetics, a fact that is still largely unacknowledged. The magical, surreal and melancholic atmosphere suggested by Mary Robinson's *Lyrical Tales* (1800) deeply influenced S.T. Coleridge's fascination with the uncanny. Byron's debt to Anne Louise Germaine de Staël (1766-1817), Sydney Owenson (Lady Morgan 1776-1859) and Ann Ward Radcliffe (1764-1823), although evident, is still largely overlooked by contemporary scholarship.

In order to tackle all the questions raised by such an important and complex issue, the essays included in this volume have pursued four different, though strictly interconnected, critical paths, which are mirrored in the four sections of the book itself.

The first section, **Modes of Women's Verse and Voice in the Romantic Period**, considers women poets' re-vision of traditional poetic forms and the creation of a new poetics of Romanticism. Despite their anxieties about self-exposure, women achieved a

[5] Julia Kristeva, "La Femme, ce n'est jamais ça", in *Polylogue*, Paris, 1977, 519.

successful balance between psychological introspection and poetic expression.

In “Anna Seward and the Dynamics of Female Friendship”, Stuart Curran analyses the literary and sociological aspects of Romantic friendship between women. In particular, he focuses on the literary trope whereby the poet transposes her friend into the spirit of a particular place, casting her within an aura of timeless myth. Curran shows the recurrence of this trope in many of Anna Seward’s poems, from those dedicated to her half-sister Honora Sneyd to her long poem dedicated to the Ladies of Llangollen, in which Lady Eleanor Butler and Sarah Ponsonby incarnate the myth of female friendship.

Jane Stabler’s “‘Know me what I paint’: Women Poets and the Aesthetics of the Sketch 1770-1830” examines the ways in which Romantic women poets use painterly techniques, particularly the sketch, in order to make themselves appear decorously hesitant and at the same time ambitiously bold in the act of publishing their works. The wide circulation of pictures and portraits gave women poets the opportunity to articulate their anxieties about self-display and to find a sympathetic audience.

Lilla Maria Crisafulli’s “Within or Without? Problems of Perspective in Charlotte Smith, Anna Laetitia Barbauld, and Dorothy Wordsworth” once more discusses the traditional gender-based (and gender-biased) distinction between the universal vision of traditional Romantic poets and the domestic dimension of much poetry produced by women. Through her analysis of Smith’s, Barbauld’s and Wordsworth’s poetry, Crisafulli shows how women escape the male objectifying gaze and become observers themselves. Women’s vision spans from within to without, from microcosm to macrocosm, going far beyond that horizontal perception that has traditionally been though to characterize women’s poetry.

In “Helen Maria Williams: The Shaping of a Poetic Identity”, Lia Guerra analyses Williams’ Introduction to her *Poems on Various Subjects* (1823) and other textual sources in order to trace the different stages of the author’s self-conscious development as a writer. In 1823, Williams’ self-portrait combines the emerging poet of her youth with the more mature subjectivity of an experienced writer.

The second section of the volume, **Creating a Public Voice,** examines the negotiation of the boundaries between domestic affections and public sphere, too often considered as separate. Women poets were actually concerned with topical public issues, such as the problem of the alarming expansion of the cities, and with important political problems, such as the construction of national cultural identity.

Timothy Webb's "Listing the Busy Sounds: Anna Seward, Mary Robinson and the Poetic Challenge of the City" focuses on women poets' response to industrial growth and expansion of the urban world, a subject rarely addressed by modern criticism. Webb considers poems in which the conventional representation of the city-versus-country trope gives way to the use of innovative techniques, such as cataloguing and impressionistic descriptive brush-strokes.

Dorothy McMillan's "Joanna Baillie's Embarrassment" discusses how Baillie's works enter the contemporary debate on the representation of Scotland and Scottishness. In particular, they suggest an image of Scotland that contrasts with Scott's definition of it as "romantic Caledonia". Besides a Romantic and sentimental present, Baillie's Scotland reveals a problematic past, often represented as violent and wild.

The third section, **Genre Crossing: Verse versus Prose and Drama**, focuses on the interaction between form and cultural complexity in women's poetry. By stressing the generic fluidity and hybridism of many poetical works, the essays grouped in this section show how women's texts eschew easy categorizations and simplistic taxonomies.

Beatrice Battaglia's "The 'Pieces of Poetry' in Ann Radcliffe's *The Mysteries of Udolpho*" analyses the poetical sections interspersed in the novel, such as "The Sea-Nymph", "The Glow-Worm", "The Butterfly to His Love", and "The Song of the Evening Hour", thereby foregrounding the lyrical dimension of Radcliffe's Gothic fiction. The main function of these lyrics is to endow the romance with a peculiar musicality, which creates a suggestive atmosphere and evokes the subconscious and the irrational.

Diego Saglia's contribution, "Ending the Romance: Women Poets and the Romantic Verse Tale" studies two of the most representative verse tales of the Romantic period: Felicia Hemans's *The Abencerrage* and Letitia Landon's *The Improvisatrice*. These long poems exemplify women's engagement with verse romance in comparison with the narrative poems of Byron, Southey and Scott.

Hemans and Landon seem to absorb the tradition of narrative poetry, but in reality they re-elaborate it into a new poetical form, one that disrupts the traditional romance plot.

Serena Baiesi's "Letitia Elizabeth Landon's *The Improvisatrice*: the Fatal Combination of Gender and Genre" describes Landon's poem as a hybrid literary genre – a meeting-point between poetry and prose – with specific gender implications. In particular, Baiesi refers to the private-versus-public dichotomy and to the complex relationship between romantic subjectivity and objectivity, self-inscription and observation, experienced and expressed through the art of improvisation.

Donatella Montini's "Anna Laetitia Barbauld's Ethics of Sentiment" scrutinizes Anna Laetitia Barbauld's critical discourse. In particular, Montini focuses on Barbauld's edition of Richardson's *Letters* (1804) and on her *British Novelists* (1810). Barbauld's belief that a good novel is "an epic in prose" seems to suggest a process of hybridization of a well-established literary genre. To the novel, Barbauld applies the Addisonian principle of the "pleasure of imagination", which she considers to be likewise an essential ingredient of poetic composition.

The fourth and final section of the volume, **Romantic Female and Male Poets: Dialogue and Revision**, deals with the interaction between women's poetry and established male poetic norms. This section shows the original and experimental quality of women's re-visionary approach to traditional poetic forms, and reveals the important influence that this approach exerted on the "canonical" poets.

In "Women Romance Writers: Mary Tighe and Mary Hays", Cecilia Pietropoli examines the revival of medieval romance in Romantic women's poetry. Pietropoli examines two paradigmatic examples: Tighe's Spenserian poem *Psyche* and Hays' Gothic tale *A Fragment, in the Manner of the Old Romances*. These two texts represent different but complementary ways – one more aristocratic and conservative, the other more radical and subversive – of absorbing and re-visioning the traditional world of romance.

In "Felicia Hemans, Letitia Landon, and 'Lady's Rule'", Richard Cronin reveals how in his juvenile poems the young Tennyson assumes a female persona that clearly shows similarities with the poetic icons personified by Felicia Hemans and Letitia Landon. Cronin underlines that in the 1820s and 1830s Hemans and Landon played such a dominant role in the literary scene that Tennyson was drawn to imitate their poetic works and personas.

Gioia Angeletti's "Women Re-writing Men: The Examples of Anna Seward and Lady Caroline Lamb" looks at how some of Seward's and Lamb's works appropriate and re-elaborate stylistic, linguistic and thematic aspects of earlier and contemporary male poetry. Some of Seward's lyrics, for example, are undoubtedly indebted to the rhetorical style of her friend and mentor Erasmus Darwin, while the eponymous heroine of her *Louisa* resembles Pope's, Prior's and Rousseau's female heroines. Lamb's *Glenarvon* and her parody of *Don Juan*, "A New Canto" are clearly haunted by Byron and his stylistic idiosyncrasies. Angeletti underlines how both writers do not simply imitate existing models, but also re-elaborate them, thereby producing original and innovative texts.

The essays in this collection, therefore, aim to establish the crucial role that women played in the construction of Romanticism, enriching it with cultural diversity and informing it with new vitality. As such, they offer a timely contribution to the on-going critical reassessment of Romantic literature.

MODES OF WOMEN'S VERSE AND VOICE IN THE ROMANTIC PERIOD

ANNA SEWARD AND THE DYNAMICS OF FEMALE FRIENDSHIP

STUART CURRAN

Romantic friendship between women is a significant cultural formation of the eighteenth and nineteenth centuries in Britain, but what it actually signifies has been a subject of considerable debate. Although this interrogation has uncovered much previously unknown documentary evidence, its interpretation has depended on exclusionary premises. The process began with Lillian Faderman's *Surpassing the Love of Men*, a study that saw these friendships as essentially platonic and, in their safe removal from the realm of adult sexuality, enjoying the support of men as well as of women.[1] Emma Donoghue, on the other hand, in *Passions between Women*, accumulates documentation to support her contention that in the eighteenth century active genital relations were possible under the cover of female friendship.[2] A third approach has been advanced by Betty Rizzo, in *Companions without Vows* (1994), who fixes her attention on the psychological and sociological pressures that existed within the somewhat separate cultural institution of female companionship.[3]

Donoghue's gathering of the spotty evidence there is in the eighteenth century to support the existence of what we would think of today as lesbian relationships, along with Rizzo's broader focus on companionship and Faderman's treatment of passionate friendship,

---

[1] Lillian Faderman, *Surpassing the Love of Men: Romantic Friendship and Love between Women from the Renaissance to the Present*, New York, 1981.

[2] Emma Donoghue, *Passions between Women: British Lesbian Culture, 1668-1801*, London, 1993.

[3] Betty Rizzo, *Companions without Vows: Relationships among Eighteenth-Century British Women*, Athens: GA, 1994.

then, provide us at this juncture with a map of the terrain. It is, however, curiously limited by the premises of the investigation and the intrinsic concerns of the genres most commonly consulted. The sources on which the arguments are based are, typically, legal records, anecdotal accounts from periodical literature, correspondence, and the renditions of female behaviour extractable from popular novels of the eighteenth and early nineteenth centuries. These have been ably treated as sociological documents or as vicarious field explorations in cultural anthropology, allowing us centuries later to discriminate how it was that people, whom in our retrospect we conceive along the line of fictional characters, lived their lives and pursued their loves or other such emotional attachments. That is certainly necessary and important as a historical recovery of lost dimensions of human experience. But it lacks something as literature. What it lacks, in broad terms, is what Shelley called "the poetry of life". Hence the subject of this particular investigation. Whatever the spectrum of attachment, in other words, how did it figure itself? How did it reflect upon its dynamics? We know it existed, but what did it mean? What did it mean to mean?

Hovering over this entire formation was the public celebration of one particular female couple, known popularly as the Ladies of Llangollen, Lady Eleanor Butler and her once-tutor Sarah Ponsonby, who had "eloped" (this is how it was universally described) in 1778 and lived together just outside the Welsh town of Llangollen in a magnificent house called Plas Newydd for a half century, until Butler's death in 1829. As they were on the high road to the Welsh port of Holyhead, from which crossings to Dublin were made, their retirement was regularly invaded by curiosity-seekers among the well-placed, with the result that their fame was constantly renewed by the reports of their visitors. These ranged from prominent writers like Scott to the future George IV, even to the young Felix Mendelssohn. The major eighteenth-century celebrant of the Ladies of Llangollen in verse was Anna Seward, and since her deep investment in passionate female friendship is my subject here, I wish to begin with her treatment of this renowned friendship.

Seward's volume, *Llangollen Vale, with Other Poems*, went through three editions in 1796, the third involving a major expansion of the miscellaneous verse accompanying the celebratory title poem. Seward's encomium is generally dismissed as over-elaborated with fustian, a not-infrequent characteristic of her style, but beneath its orotund façade lies a carefully measured tribute. The poem begins in the valley of the River Dee during the Middle Ages, scarred by the spread of plague and the bloody quashing of Owain Glyndwr's rebellion by Henry IV: if there are redeeming qualities to this bleak fourteenth-century scene, they are confined to the passionate but doomed love of the Bard Hoël for Lady Mifamwy Vechan. This early culture of Llangollen Vale is epitomized near the end of the poem with a description of the Abbey of Valle Crucis whose ruins overlook the valley, to Seward a beacon not of devotion but of superstition and bigotry. Past records of a dominant, life-hating male culture thus surround, but are transcended by, a new cultural entity embodied in Plas Newydd, which is presided over by "sacred Friendship", "graceful arts", "Obedient Science", and "strains Æolian".[4] Notwithstanding what may seem the predictability of these abstractions, they testify at length (in fact, over four pages) to the effect of feminizing this rude and remote valley.

In another tribute, "A Farewell to the Seat of Lady Eleanor Butler, and Miss Ponsonby", only published in the three-volume posthumous works edited by Walter Scott in 1810, Seward offers an elaborate tour of the Valley landscape that centres on the hard labour of improvement by which the Ladies have enabled trees to be planted on the river banks so as to withstand the spring floods of the Dee. Here, again, violence is tamed; nature is methodized; good works ameliorate the commonweal. Tellingly, the poem ends with an invocation whose private admonition subsumes a public extension:

> Haste to the scene, benignant powers of life,
> Mild Lachesis, and gay Hygeia, haste,
> From day to day propitious ...[5]

That apostrophe perhaps needs some translation: the basic wish is that the Ladies continue to live their happy and healthy lives, but the larger recognition is that they have brought both happiness and health to the valley over which their mansion presides like a tutelary presence.

---

[4] Anna Seward, "Llangollen Vale", ll. 75, 76, 77 and 78, in *The Poetical Works of Anna Seward; with Extracts from Her Literary Correspondence*, ed. Walter Scott, New York, 1810 (Edinburgh and London, rpt. 1974), II, 31.

[5] *Ibid.*, III, 349-50.

These two poems, dating from 1796 and 1802 respectively, perhaps reflect the settled views of a relatively older woman. But their essential trope, that the Ladies of Llangollen have infused the valley in which they reside with their vital presence, is one that can be discerned in a number of poems by the younger Seward, poems that are themselves more vital in their consciousness of the dynamic energy involved in such an infusion. One might, indeed, wish to credit Seward with the widespread diffusion of this trope, except that, with only a few exceptions, the poems in which one finds it at its fullest intensity were carefully held back and remained unpublished upon her death. But, before turning to these poems in which Seward's heart is so deeply invested than one detects a radiance uncommon in her verse, in order to introduce its basic terms we might consult a much simpler poem of genuine charm, "An Epistle" we find in Elizabeth Hands' single collection of verse, *The Death of Amnon ... and Other Poetical Pieces*, published by subscription in 1789.

Appropriately, Anna Seward was one of the twelve hundred subscribers. "An Epistle" credits the absent Maria with being a kind of Ceres to the small world in which her friend lives. Although the interchange between human and natural worlds is continuing, nature has lost its meaning without the presence of its tutelary spirit; most important, the writer has lost her own sense of presence. The poem ends with the terms for renewal:

> 'Tis you, Maria, and 'tis only you,
> That can the wonted face of things renew:
> Come to my groves: command the birds to sing,
> And o'er the meadows bid fresh daisies spring:
> No! rather come and chase my gloom away,
> That I may sing like birds, and look like daisies gay.[6]

Maria's return will vivify not only nature but its poet Belinda, who will once again be able to function as poet laureate of her small realm.

Hands began to be noticed a decade ago when Roger Lonsdale published a small selection of her verse in *Eighteenth-Century Women Poets*. The title poem of her collection, "The Death of Amnon",

[6] "An Epistle", ll. 39-44, in Elizabeth Hands, *The Death of Amnon ... and Other Poetical Pieces*, Coventry, 1789, 92 (reprinted in Emma Donoghue's anthology, *Poems between Women: Four Centuries of Love, Romantic Friendship, and Desire*, New York, 1997, 28-29).

recounts an Old-Testament story involving incestuous rape, hardly the usual subject for an unknown woman to render into verse. Conscious of her brashness, Hands writes two remarkable poems forecasting the reception of her miniature biblical epic: “A Poem, On the Supposition of an Advertisement appearing in a Morning Paper, of the Publication of a Volume of Poems, by a Servant-Maid” and “A Poem, On the Supposition of the Book having been Published and Read”. In her knowing class-exposé, Hands wittily satirizes the pretensions of upstairs philistinism. Actually, by the time her volume was published, Hands was no longer a servant-maid: she had moved up in the world by marrying a local blacksmith. That, then, is the context against which to read “An Epistle”. Its author is not Hands, but Belinda, an outdoorsy version of the urbane, cloistered, virtually enamelled heroine of Pope’s *Rape of the Lock*. By contrast, at least presumably, Hands tends to the kitchen, as her husband does the forge. She would have little sense of Belinda’s “tedious hours” (l. 10) because she is generally busy, would have to forego the luxury of “walk[ing] forth to take the morning air” (l. 13), or “At sultry noon retiring to the groves” (l. 17) because she must work, and most likely would lack both the “painted chair” of line 21 and the “couch” of line 29. “An Epistle”, then, however single-mindedly passionate is its troping, is, like those poems in which she mimicked her own reception, rather a put-on, or a send-up, of upper-class refinements and gentleladies’ friendships. By late in the eighteenth century it would seem that the tutelary presence can be understood as a cultural *donée*, even, perhaps, something of a cliché.

With Anna Seward it begins early with her poetry and is associated, in a complex pattern, with her relationship with Honora Sneyd, an orphan brought into the household at the age of five, when the poet was in her early adolescence, fourteen years old. Functioning as an older sister, Anna Seward became deeply attached to Honora, and the bonds were only strengthened after the early death of her blood sister, Sarah. In her adolescence Honora was courted by the unfortunate Major André, who, when he was spurned, became a British officer in the American war and, as Benedict Arnold’s associate, was shot as a spy. In her widely diffused *Monody on Major André* of 1781, Seward has a remarkable vignette of André’s concealing a miniature portrait of Sneyd in his mouth to avoid its being taken from him after his capture. Without taking liberties with the text, one can suppose this an instance of poetic license, and less the truth than a remarkable projection of Seward's own inner compulsion, extending the process of internalization – truly incorporation – she enacts through her many poems centring on her own affection for Sneyd. By this point Honora Sneyd was herself dead and Seward, by her own report, consumed by grief.

The tributes to Sneyd begin in 1769, when Seward was twenty-seven and her friend eighteen: there is none that does not convey a sense of anxiety beneath its expression of affection.[7] "Honora, an Elegy", written in the spring of that year, begins with an immediate identification between Honora and the environs of the Bishop's Palace of Lichfield, where the Sewards lived:

> This bowery terrace ...
> That tower, that lake, – yon willow's ample shade,
> All, all the vale her spirit seems to breathe …
>
> (ll. 5-8)

But those surroundings close in on the poet with a sense of sudden vacuity, "I bend on vacancy an earnest gaze" (l. 11), and her recourse, at least figuratively, is to attempt to sketch a portrait. To render Honora into art, however, is to lose her variety of mien and meaning, the full spectrum of her disposition, her emotive range, the play of her mind, her signification. Seward's shifting accents in the last stanzas, as she limns the changes in Honora's face, capture a protean vitality that cannot be fixed.[8]

Whatever the case, in Scott's chronological presentation of Seward's career, from the point of "Honora, An Elegy" on through a number of poems written over the next several years, Seward is almost obsessed with Honora Sneyd's presence within an anxiety-laden

---

[7] *The Poetical Works of Anna Seward*, I, 65. Scott seems to have understood the personal and poetic significance of these previously unpublished poems, grouping them prominently in the first volume of his 1810 edition.

[8] It might be noted here that one of the abiding figures of Seward's poetry is of sketching, either portraits or landscapes, and this trope deserves study for the way it translates one art form associated with feminine domesticity into another as a more intellectualized understanding of space and structure. It could be argued, indeed, that the profound sense women poets evince of a tutelary presence within their spatial circuit entails exactly such an elaboration. This kind of cultural understanding conspicuously informs the argument of Richard C. Sha's insightful study, *The Visual and Verbal Sketch in British Romanticism*, Philadelphia, 1998.

absence, whether it is in the reflexive "Anniversary" of the month after, a poem celebrating Honora's centrality to a family from whom she has been absent during this intervening time, or the fearful timbres, a year later, of an "Epistle to Miss Honora Sneyd, written Sept, 1770" (with this ominous explanatory footnote: "Miss H. Sneyd was then in Bristol, on account of a consumptive complaint"), to her "Epistle of May 1772. Written in a Summer Evening, from the Grave of a Suicide", to "Time Past. Written Jan. 1773", in which the recollection of winter enclosure as a space of intense female bonding is intensified by its sudden loss, as Honora leaves the Bishop's Palace to accept the marriage proposal of Richard Lovell Edgeworth and become, improbable as it may seem, stepmother to Maria Edgeworth. The poem ends thus:

> Affection, – Friendship, – Sympathy, your throne
> Is winter's glowing hearth; – and ye were ours,
> Thy smile, HONORA, made them all our own.
> Where are they now? – alas! their choicest powers
> Faded at thy retreat; – for thou art gone,
> And many a dark, long eve I sigh'd alone,
> In thrill'd remembrance of the vanish'd hours,
> When storms were dearer than the balmy gales,
> And the grey barren fields than green luxuriant vales.
>
> (ll. 28-36)[9]

In other words, what Seward now experiences is also what she sees as her prospect for the future: internalized storms and a flat landscape of "grey barren fields" extending in all directions. The brief "Elegy Written at the Sea-side and Addressed to Miss Honora Sneyd", written the year before, takes on significance from our recognition that Honora's marriage and permanent displacement are soon to transpire. However Seward attempts to inscribe her friend, she lacks the power to circumscribe her: every poem in this long sequence seems an attempt to stop time and render permanent the emotional axis binding the two women friends and sisters, yet each seems only to repeat the action of this short poem, as Seward writes Honora's name in the sand, only to watch it be wiped clean by recurrent, mundane, uncontrollable circumstantiality.

---

[9] *The Poetical Works of Anna Seward*, I, 88.

The climax comes with "Lichfield, An Elegy. Written May 1781", in Seward's thirty-ninth year. This tribute begins deceptively as a celebratory loco-descriptive poem, for six pages surveying the town's geography, its richness of culture, and its legacy of friends, culminating in an exclamation of devoted tribute to Honora Sneyd:

> And O! blest days of pleasure's soft increase,
> That rose in gladness, and that set in peace,
> Ye saw Honora, loveliest of the maids
> That deck'd our winter dome, our summer shades!
> O'er that light form what animated grace!
> How did that mind's warm energies disdain
> Whate'er allures the haughty and the vain!
> How spurn the tinsel claims of wealth and birth!
> How cherish every gleam of wit and worth!
> What varying charms, in turn, ascendance gain'd,
> And in her voice, her air, her glances reign'd!
> Ninon's gay spirit, gladness to inspire,
> Lucretia's modesty, Cornelia's fire;
> O! Of all hours was she![10]

At this point, with shattering suddenness, the poem veers into lament, virtually donning mourning as Seward recounts her solemn journey to Weston in Shropshire to visit Sneyd's grave. Yet, slowly and in an uncanny way, we are made to realize that what we thought was enunciated as a prelude to Seward's lament is also its postlude. The last pages, in which Honora Sneyd's image dominates the Lichfield to which the poet returns, enact a total reversal of its opening celebration. Now the dead has triumphed over the living, the past over either the present or future, as the tutelary spirit, with a kind of platonic perfection, at once infuses the landscape – "Waft her remember'd voice in every gale!/ Wear her etherial smile, thou lovely vale" – and shadows it with its insufficiency: "Yet here the spirit of departed joy/ Shall chain my step."[11]

The construction of this figurative and emotional oxymoron seems to be a turn in the development of Seward's posthumous attachment to Honora Sneyd, preparing the way for a remarkable literary text, a work whose explosive passion is intensified by its formal craft, her

[10] *Ibid.*, 94.
[11] *Ibid.*, 98 and 99.

"Invocation to the Genius of Slumber. written Oct. 1787". In this poem Seward manages to conflate a whole series of contraries around the meeting point of death and life: reality and illusion, the profane and sacred, even, it would appear, the sexual and spiritual. I suspect the poet herself would protest over the last of these binary pairings, but her representation of intense, undeviating, yet frustrated desire and its climactic invocation, "Come to my dreams, my lost Honora, come",[12] convey a powerful sense of a longing that transcends whatever spiritual affinity it recognizes as sustaining it. At the same time, by drawing us into a realm beyond the real where its longing can alone be fulfilled, the poem also transcends the physical and, therefore, the merely sexual.

If "transcend" seems a verb with too many mystified associations, then a slight shift of the linguistic root may reveal the inherent dynamic animating this poem. What Seward invokes here so disturbingly is a wholly transgressive power: for Honora Sneyd to "step across" the boundary separating life and death, for Seward to "step across" whatever conventional barriers the mundane world would erect to forestall the satisfaction of insistent desire. The world of dream is unpoliceable either by social constructions or private inhibitions: indeed, it is even beyond the terms of conventional representation. In the interiorized space of Seward's bedroom stands the silhouette of Honora, two-dimensional, merely profiled, a "shadowy form", she calls it, suggesting its mere adequacy to the "lone musing of the joyless day".[13] Even if not filled in with black like the conventional silhouette (and the poem is ambiguous on this point), it nonetheless cannot be "Freed from that sense which shrouds with dire controul / Volition's image in a cypress stole".[14] In the world of dream, however, volition is wholly liberated: Honora's fully-dimensional and animated image confronts and impels Seward's own imagining in an intercourse pure of conceptual definition, one that steps across all conventional boundaries, that seems not to recognize their existence, and is wholly permeating:

> Now strikes the midnight clock; – the taper gleams
> With the faint flash of half-expiring beams,

---

[12] *Ibid.*, 103.

[13] *Ibid.*, 102 and 100.

[14] *Ibid.*, 101.

And soon that lovely semblance shall recede,
And Sleep's dim veils its thrilling powers impede.
I feel their balmy, kind, resistless charms
Creep o'er my closing eyes, – I fold my arms,
Breathing in murmurs thro' the paly gloom,
"Come to my dreams, my lost HONORA, come!
Back as the waves of Time benignly roll,
Shew thy bright face to my enchanted soul!"[15]

This is as purely "queer" a poem as the early modern period offers us, whatever might be thought its status in a lesbian history.

Among the finest of Seward's many sonnets are those addressed to Honora Sneyd within the traditionary complex of platonic love, dating both from the time of Sneyd's death and, like the "Invocation to the Genius of Slumber", later in the ongoing acts of Seward's memory. Yet, their artistry reminds us that there is more than mere desire at work in this complex. Seward, who finally published her sonnets as a totality in 1799 to stake a claim to her command of the sonnet form, here recreates her relationship with Honora Sneyd within an enclosed, interiorized, condensed space. It is a counterpart to and an enactment of the relationship two women may hold outside the normative social structures defined by patriarchy. Each of these sonnets replays the themes we have been observing in Seward's poems. In Sonnet 30, "That song again! – its sounds my bosom thrill",[16] a reheard song re-establishes a lost language not only for the poet but for the natural world surrounding her; where there was disruption there is suddenly continuity, total interchange, recommunion with Honora as tutelary presence. In Sonnet 33, "Last night her form the hours of slumber bless'd",[17] we are given access to the precincts of a dramatically charged prayer for the return of that communion experienced in dream the previous night, a cry for "bliss" as the object of unslakeable desire, a claim to it as her right, a sense of the insufficiency of anything less:

Bliss, in no waking moment now possess'd,
Bliss, ask'd of thee with memory's thrilling tears.
Nightly I cry, – how oft, alas! in vain …

(ll.7-9)

---

[15] *Ibid.*, 103.
[16] *Ibid.*, III, 151.
[17] *Ibid.*, 154.

In Sonnet 44, "Rapt Contemplation, bring thy waking dreams",[18] Seward retreats to a forest bower where, in writing her sonnet, she communes with its subject as she recreates her in reverie: the "dear, persuasive, visionary form" (l. 12) of her communion is, in one sense, Honora Sneyd, in another sense, a limning of her, and in yet a third sense, its formal embodiment, a sonnet.

In these poems Honora Sneyd functions with curious propriety as the Muse whose afflatus impels Seward into verse. But what is generally understood as merely a figure of convention in this dynamic takes on a startling immediacy of power, and the poet responds with something like neurotic compulsion to her insistent demands. In the realm of a British eighteenth-century male poetics, the equivalent might be the way both Gray and Collins break down before the spectre of Milton, so that "The Progress of Poesy" and the "Ode on the Poetical Character" do not so much reach closure as sputter into self-questioning silence. But that is the anxiety-fraught poetics of male competition, and it has no place in a woman's poetics, however that, too, may be haunted with anxiety.

Yet, Seward's intense consciousness of the Other as an unattainable object within a closed field of desire is by no means unique, even if it issues in one of the most moving and anguished series of poems in women's literature. The field in which this permeability functions, however, has other, more public manifestations that circumscribe the intense privacy of Seward's focus on Honora Sneyd and that perhaps, indeed, legitimate and liberate her right to so concentrated a fixation. This public representation of women's friendships as a model for community, or even, with the Blue-Stocking movement, for advancing the interests of civilization, is highly significant for the history of an emerging feminism. Yet, it somehow pales before the remarkable interiority of Seward's exploration of the dynamics of female friendship. There she confronts a love that will not allow displacement, a second self that hovers over her as a ghostly, almost demonic, spectre, and a muse who is most forcefully a presence in her unrecoverable absence.

---

[18] *Ibid.*, 165.

"KNOW ME WHAT I PAINT": WOMEN POETS AND THE AESTHETICS OF THE SKETCH 1770-1830

JANE STABLER

Lord Byron flaunted his attack on Robert Southey in "The Vision of Judgment" as "my finest ferocious Caravaggio style".[1] Women writers, however, usually selected more discreet painterly models. Think of Jane Austen's definition of her own "little bit (two inches wide) of ivory" on which [she] work[ed] with so fine a brush, which was echoed in Walter Scott's review of her Flemish minuteness and Charlotte Brontë's assessment of Austen's "Chinese fidelity". But painting allowed women poets to be bold and decorous so it may be a mistake to see the metaphor of the sketch only as expressive of feminine modesty. When the sketch is invoked as a disclaimer – in, for example, Anna Barbauld's bowing out of a poem with the admission that she lacks "A master's pencil" and that her Muse's colours are "too weak" and her lines "too faint" – there almost always seems to be a degree of self-conscious irony, a sense that this gesture is expected and is completed for form's sake.[2]

In this essay I shall be looking mainly at first generation women romantic poets and tracing the different ways in which they found the aesthetics of painting and sketching to be liberating rather than constricting launching their flights on the "viewless wings of poesy" and anticipating many of the claims of some of the second generation male romantics. Richard Sha and Jacqueline Labbe have recently examined the way in which women writers invoke visual arts. Both of

---

[1] George Gordon Lord Byron, *Byron's Letters and Journals*, ed. Leslie A. Marchand, London, 1973-1994, V, 240.

[2] "The Invitation" (11. 184-88), in Anna Letitia Barbauld, *The Poems of Anna Letitia Barbauld*, eds William McCarthy and Elizabeth Kraft, Athens and London, 1994, 9.

them focus on the connections between sketching, drawing, painting and the decorous arts of the "proper lady" – what Barbauld calls "the pencil's task, the needle or the quill" ("[Martha Jennings]", l. 8). Sha sees sketching as "an ideological ploy to keep leisure-class women attached to the home", an occupation denned by "privacy, utility, morality, application, and industry". This domestic activity, he argues, is subverted unexpectedly by the prose travel writers Helen Maria Williams and Lady Morgan.[3] Jacqueline Labbe also defines painting as a discourse of closure.[4] On the other hand, scholars like Wenderlin Guenter have continued to work on the "sketch" as a Romantic mode akin to the fragment. Guenter sees the *"non finito"* as a marker of spontaneity, roughness, energy, liberty. This mode of indeterminacy was appreciated by Burke because it invited the imagination to supply what is not there.[5]

For Romantic writers, I would like to suggest, painting and sketching always had the potential either to be free or bounded, and that it is women writers who realize this doubleness most effectively.[6] While some male Romantic writers specialized in creating hybrid or compound genres – lyrical ballads, dramatic poems, visions in dreams – women writers explored the possibility of doubleness within a particular form or "bounded sphere".[7] This tendency represents a desire to do two things at once, a tendency which we might recognize in many modem feminist attempts to reconcile competitive or mutually exclusive demands. The attraction to contraries might explain the frequent celebrations of technology which we find in first generation Romantic women poets like Barbauld and Seward, or Barbauld's love of riddles and paradox. Technology brings together

---

[3] Richard C. Sha, "Expanding the Limits of Feminine Writing: The Prose Sketches of Sydney Owenson (Lady Morgan) and Helen Maria Williams", in *Romantic Women Writers: Voices and Counter Voices*, eds Paula R. Feldman and Theresa M. Kelley, Hanover, 1995, 195.

[4] Jacqueline M. Labbe, "Every Poet Her Own Drawing Master: Charlotte Smith, Anna Seward and ut pictura poesis", in *Early Romantics: Perspectives in British Poetry from Pope to Wordsworth*, ed. Thomas Woodman, London, 1988, 200-14.

[5] Wenderlin A. Guenter, "The Sketch, the Non Finito, and the Imagination", *Art Journal*, LII/2 (1993), 40-47.

[6] For theoretical exploration of feminism's "in between" status, see Alice Jardine "Opaque Texts and Transparent Contexts: The Political Difference of Julia Kristeva", in *The Poetics of Gender*, ed. Nancy K. Miller, New York, 1986, 96-116.

[7] "To Dr Aikin on his Complaining that she neglected him" (*The Poems of Anna Letitia Barbauld*, 60).

invention (often artful improvement on nature) and service to the community. So, when Barbauld writes about an umbrella or a canal, it is not just the quotidian which is of significance. In "The Invitation", the canal channels and controls, but it is also fanciful and magical. Sails passing through the landscape are seen by the traveller as:

> Now, like a flock of swans, above his head
> Their woven wings the flying vessels spread;
> Now meeting streams in artful mazes glide,
> While each unmingled pours a separate tide.
>
> (ll. 71-74)

These flying vessels with "woven wings" are barges full of coal. Building on Stuart Curran's essay "The I Altered",[8] I would like to look now at ways in which women poets move between careful visual representation and the imaginative prospects of thought's "bold career". In "Flora" Charlotte Smith invokes the "magic pencil" (l. 9) of Fancy to describe "each hybernacle" (l. 27) – that is, the bulb or protective covering around the shoot of a flower. In other poems, however, she is dismissive of "the slight botanic pencil's mimic powers", and her dissatisfaction with "the mimic pencil" is, I think, shared by her female contemporaries.[9] Extending the art of botanical drawing in her poem In "To Mrs. P[riestley], with some Drawings of Birds and Insects" Barbauld celebrates the ways in which "painting and poetry are near allied" (l. 5). Painting supplies precise "form", "a gayer brighter world" (l. 10), and poetry, a "deeper art" (l. 11), tracing the transformative movement of "mind" (l. 18). Both arts are linked because they enable fantasies of flight. Barbauld is fascinated by the eagle's control over "the wide waste of air" (l. 37), by the movement of emigrating songbirds "In dusky columns o'er the trackless sea" (l. 66); or by the hatching insects that "high in Ether sail" (l. 84) and "shoot like living stars, athwart the night / And scatter from their wings a vivid light" (ll. 110-11).[10] In this poem the exactitude and

---

[8] Stuart Curran, "The I Altered", in *Romanticism and Feminism*, ed. Anne K. Mellor, Bloomington and Indianapolis, 1988.

[9] "To Dr Parry of Bath, with some botanic drawings which had been made some years", 1. 8; Charlotte Smith, "Sent to the Honourable Mrs O'Neill with painted flowers", 1. 9. (*The Poems of Charlotte Smith*, ed. Stuart Curran, New York and Oxford, 1993, 57, 37).

[10] Richard Cronin has argued that the shift to prepositional meaning rather than

discipline of "mimic" botanical drawing become the occasion for the most ambitious of romantic visionary modes.

I think in the cases of Smith and Barbauld, we should pause before classifying a woman's way of seeing solely with modes of botanical precision and matters of fact. The dissenting science taught by Joseph Priestley at Warrington Academy, where Anna Barbauld spent a formative period, connected scientific observation with sublime speculation and in many ways her poetry develops this paradigm. In 1777 Barbauld's brother, John Aikin, published "An Essay on the Application of Natural History to Poetry". He argued that the "insipidity of modern poetry" was due to "a scarcity of original observations of nature" and he advocated the reform of poetry by "accurate and Attentive observation".[11] "The flowing line" of both poetry and painting connects "accurate", "scientific" attention with imaginative expansion in Barbauld's poetry. So, for example, she writes to Mrs Priestley,

> Thy friend thus strives to cheat the lonely hour
> With song, or paint, an insect, or a flower:
> Yet if Amanda praise the flowing line,
> And bend delighted o'er the gay design,
> I envy not, nor emulate the fame
> Or of the painter's, or the poet's name:
> Could I to both with equal claim pretend,
> Yet far, far dearer were the name of FRIEND.
>
> (ll. 121-28)

In this case, the flowing line becomes a medium of communication and connection, reminding us of the way that Susan Wolfson and Susan Levin and have located women Romantic writers in the domain of community and communality. But it is the possibility of a varied inventiveness which seems equally important here – the repeated use of "or" and the weighing of different possibilities. A similar openness characterizes Dorothy Wordsworth's poem "A Sketch" in her commonplace book:

---

aggregative meaning is Romantic as is the tendency of a Romantic poem to "contain parts which seem designed to shock the reader's aesthetic sense"(see Richard Cronin, *Shelley's Poetic Thoughts*, Basingstoke and London, 1981, 15-16).

[11] John Aikin, *An Essay on the Application of Natural History to Poetry*, London, 1777, I, 9-10.

There is one cottage in our dale,
In naught distinguished from the rest,
Save by a tuft of flourishing trees,
The shelter of that little nest.
The public road through Grasmere vale
Winds close beside that cottage small,
And there 'tis hidden by the trees
That overhang the orchard wall.
You lose it there – its serpent line
Is lost in that close household grove;
A moment lost – and then it mounts
The craggy hills above.[12]

The serpent line is, of course, the English artist William Hogarth's line of beauty – the model of "weakness, fragility or delicacy" which "leads the eye a wanton kind of chase".[13] Hogarth's influential *Analysis of Beauty* (1753) announced that it was written "With a view of Fixing the Fluctuating Ideas of Taste", but Dorothy Wordsworth emphasizes the line's fluctuating doubleness, its ability to combine uniformity and variety. The curving line is a "public road" which temporarily vanishes in domestic space. It connects the beautiful, singular "little nest" or "close household grove" with "craggy hills". Again there is the suggestion of upward movement, like flight, as the road emerges from the trees and "mounts / The craggy hills above". It is a brief poem, but its "moment" holds and then releases a sense of energy and potential. The quotidian is embraced "In naught distinguished from the rest", but the poet then reaches for the sublime.[14] Hogarth's "line of beauty", the "sinuous track" (l. 31) that

---

[12] *Romanticism: An Anthology*, ed. Duncan Wu, 2nd edn, Oxford, 1998, 438.

[13] The "flowing line" with all its potential for deception features in Anna Seward's Sonnet to Smith: "Let not or foreign taste or tales enchain / The genuine freedom of thy flowing line; / Nor the dark dreams of suicide obtain / Deceitful lustre from such tones as thine" (ll. 9-12; *Romantic Women Poets*: *An Anthology*, ed. Duncan Wu, Oxford, 1997, 4-5). See also Seward's "Verses to the Celebrated Painter, Mr Wright, of Derby": "What living lights, ingenious Artist, stream, / In mingling mazes as thy pencil roves! / With orient hues in bright expansion beam, / Or bend the flowing curve that beauty loves!" (ll. 17-20), in Anna Seward, *The Poetical Works*, ed. Walter Scott, 3 vols, Edinburgh, 1810, II, 141-42.

[14] Another example of the juxtaposition of public and private spheres occurs in Barbauld's "To a Lady, with some painted Flowers". This poem was singled out for criticism by Mary Wollstonecraft as a senseless reiteration of the lesson men wish to teach women, condemning them to a life of "sensual error". If we look at where the

"curves with capricious wantonness" (footnote) in Anna Seward's "Ode to William Boothby, Esq.", was advanced still further by picturesque theorists from the second half of the eighteenth century onwards. Despite theoretical bickering about whether the effect of the picturesque was physiological or associative, there was general agreement about its vitality. For William Gilpin it offered "variety" and "bold, free negligent strokes";[15] Richard Payne Knight detected "a playful and airy kind of lightness" and a "loose and sketchy indistinctness";[16] Uvedale Price found "intricacy"[17] and J.G. MacVicar "animation and expression".[18]

Following satirical accounts of the picturesque, which created a simplified and reduced version of the genre in order to destroy it, the picturesque has been seen as codified and restrictive – as it appears in Jane Austen's *Northanger Abbey* and *Sense and Sensibility*. But critics like Martin Price are more alert to the multiplicity of picturesque. It is, according to him "a phase of speculation" incorporating "a degree of arbitrariness and play fullness". "The sense of play", Price suggests, "finds exercise both in fancifulness and in those acts of abstraction

---

poem placed in the 1773 collection, however, we see that it comes in a group of songs and classical imitations that use a male voice and offer masculine meditations on "Beauty's Empire". In this context (and especially after the Virgilan epigraph), it may be more reasonable to treat "To a Lady" (in which the addressee is called "my fair" [l. 17]), as a further act of ventriloquism. The division of labour described in l. 9: "To loftier forms are rougher tasks assign'd", knowingly invokes the masculine public world of "invading foes" (l. 11) and "future navies" (l. 12) in order to highlight the regressive, impossibly Edenic situation of the "soft family ... born for pleasure and delight alone" (ll. 13-14). When Barbauld wants to celebrate real women, such as Amanda Priestley or Mrs Jennings, she always mentions intellectual and moral qualities. If "To a Lady" is a knowing masculine celebration of an "unformed mind", the idea of "copying" in the penultimate line becomes as ironical as Wollstonecraft could have wished (*The Poems of Anna Letitia Barbauld*, 77).

[15] William Gilpin, *Three Essays: on Picturesque Beauty, on Picturesque Travel and on Sketching Landscape*, London, 1792, 37; and *Observations on Several Parts of England, Particularly the Mountains and Lakes of Cumberland and Westmoreland, relative to Picturesque Beauty*, London, 1792, I, xiv.

[16] Richard Payne Knight, *An Analytical Enquiry into the Principles of Taste*, 4th edn, London, 1808, 150.

[17] Uvedale Price, *Essays on the Picturesque ... for the Purposes of Improving Real Landscape,* London, 1810, I, 22.

[18] J.G. MacVicar, "On the Beautiful, the Picturesque, the Sublime", in *The Picturesque: Literary Sources and Documents*, Mountfield, 1994, III, 280.

which call attention to the arbitrariness of all the mind's creations".[19] Because the picturesque combined the sublime and the beautiful, it allowed women writers to question those cultural binaries, licensing an element of playfulness within a bounded perspective. Picturesque landscape poetry, therefore, offered another "doubled" form of expression that uses a frame, but reaches beyond it. I shall now look at a landscape poem to see how this apparently stable mode incorporates the possibility of flight and fancy.

Ann Radcliffe's "Scene on the Northern Shore of Sicily"[20] begins from an elevated picturesque perspective – "Here from the castle's terraced site" – and celebrates a "varied scene" (l. 2) in the intermediate time of "coming night" (l. 5). Radcliffe adds to the picturesque "hamlets, woods and pastures green" (l. 3) a catalogue of sounds blending the sublime "ocean's roll" (l. 32) with softer bucolic or household noise: the shepherd's reed, village bells, the bleat of wandering sheep, and the feeble bark of a dog.[21] The poem presents an enigmatic occasion with the mention of "the buried friend" (l. 23), but its instability or lack of definite focus is emphasized by many participles and gerunds: "stretching", "coming", 'twinkling", "glancing", "stealing", "trembling", "wandering", "pacing", "closing", "streaming", "glimmering" and "flitting". The poem gradually moves towards closure as the music through "long, long galleries die[s]" (l. 41), but then – rather like Dorothy Wordsworth's flowing line – Radcliffe signs the picture with a flourish:

> Once more I stand in pensive mood,
>   And gaze on forms that truth delude;
> And still mid Fancy's flitting scene,
>   I catch the streaming cottage-light
> Twinkling the restless leaves between,
>   And ocean's flood, in moonbeams bright.
>
> (ll. 46-51)

[19] Martin Price, "The Picturesque Movement", in *From Sensibility to Romanticism: Essays Presented to Frederick A. Pottle*, eds Frederick W. Hilles and Harold Bloom, New York, 1965, 262-72.

[20] *Romantic Women Poets*, 268-69.

[21] *Gaston de Blondeville* composed 1802, published 1826. Radcliffe's glimpse of a sail is another standard picturesque attribute, see Gilpin's *Observations on the River Wye*, section IV: "In this part of the river, which now begins to widen, we were often entertained with light vessels gliding past us. Their white sails passing along the side of the hills were very picturesque."

Radcliffe positions herself between the homely "cottage-light" and the sublime "ocean's flood, in moonbeams bright". Her vision is indeed "restless" undoing the closure of the previous passage and leaving the reader irresolute "mid Fancy's flitting scene". This aesthetic of indeterminacy is not limited to Radcliffe and may be found in many of the landscape poems by first generation women Romantic poets. In these works picturesque variety allows women to become mental travellers, celebrating the prospect of liberty as, for example, Anna Barbauld does in "Corsica", or the sublime potential of new industry Anna Seward discovers in "Colebrook Dale".[22] Just as much as Byron, these poets were interested in frame-breaking, opening-up rather than conforming to aesthetic boundaries.

A creative indeterminacy also characterizes Charlotte Smith's sonnet "To the insect of the gossamer" (1797) which follows its subject from the territory of natural history up into the air on a "hue" which "floats buoyant":

> Small, viewless. Aeronaut, that by the line
> Of Gossamer suspended, in the mid air
> Float'st on a sun beam – Living Atom, where
> Ends thy breeze-guided voyage; – with what design
> In Aether dost thou launch thy form minute,
> Mocking the eye? – Alas! before the veil
> Of denser clouds shall hide thee, the pursuit
> Of the keen Swift may end thy fairy sail! –
> Thus on the golden thread that Fancy weaves
> Buoyant, as Hope's illusive flattery breathes,
> The young and visionary Poet leaves
> Life's dull realities, while sevenfold wreaths
> Of rainbow-light around his head revolve.
> Ah! soon at Sorrow's touch the radiant dreams dissolve![23]

Likened to gossamer woven on the breeze – another "flowing line" – the flight of Fancy is described as a form of inventive freedom. Smith borrows the new word "Aeronaut" (1784) from the new technology of hot-air ballooning, but Fancy's line proves ephemeral and, we

---

[22] Seward's view of the smouldering landscape (*c.* 1790) may owe something to her appreciation of Joseph Wright's painting of Vesuvius (1783).

[23] *The Cambridge Companion to British Romanticism*, ed. Stuart Curran, Cambridge, 1993, 66-67.

discover, bound to fragment or "dissolve" on contact with "dull realities". In this way the sonnet's exploration of technological optimism and tragic inevitability offers a different formulation of double or "twinned" vision characteristic of first generation women poets.

Although Smith's Preface to the "Elegiac Sonnets" asks her readers to respond to the sonnet as a vehicle of "a single sentiment", we find that rather like the sketch, the touch of the artist leaves lines the reader has to complete from his or her own imagination. As we have seen in the examples from Barbauld, Smith, Wordsworth and Radcliffe, the roles of Fancy in painting, sketching and drawing are complex. Women were encouraged to draw from life and to add colouring from fancy, but not too much. To draw wholly from fancy was to run the risk of delusion or "Frenzy", the madness which in high Romantic terms shadowed poetic genius.[24] Burkean theory famously construed feminine beauty as a "deceitful maze, through which the unsteady eye slides giddily, without knowing where to fix, or whither it is carried".[25] In response to this, women writers were particularly aware of the allure of the visual image and the danger of false representation. When Barbauld writes "On a Lady's Writing" it is to praise a line, "Correct though free, and regular though fair" (l. 4) which openly shows the moral virtues of the author:

> And the same graces o'er her pen preside
> That form her manners and her footsteps guide
>
> (ll. 5-6)

A similar awareness informs Barbauld's warning to the young Coleridge about "vistas lengthening into air" and wayward "webs / Of floating Gossamer" (ll. 24, 14-15). But such caution co-exists with her ability and her desire to sail on "fancy's wild and roving wing" (l. 72) in the elevated prospects of "A Summer Evening's Meditation". Fancy, John Keats' "deceiving elf", therefore, becomes for women Romantic poets a focus of desire for liberation and anxiety about

---

[24] Jane Eyre's surrealist paintings appeal to Rochester alone, her art of portraiture is appreciated by the Reed family.

[25] Edmund Burke, *A Philosophical Enquiry into the Origin of our Ideas of the Sublime and Beautiful*, ed. Adam Phillips, Oxford, 1990, 105.

disappointment; effectively, therefore, Fancy is the expression of their consciousness about the possibilities and perils of literary ambition.[26]

Painting and poetry have always been rival attempts to embody thought with distinguished advocates on both sides to dispute the relative values of the "sister arts".[27] Anne Finch had argued for the superiority of painting over poetry, "the pen traces where the pencil speaks", but in later eighteenth-century poetry, the pen finds a more suggestive power. In Anna Seward's "Epistle to Mr. Romney being presented by him with a picture of William Hayley, Esq.", it is impossible to choose between the two. Seward celebrates the "aerial Beings" of poetic imagination and then envisages them in terms of the spirits of different painters:

> Poetic Fancy o'er the shape and face
> Breathes Michael's force and Guide's flowing grace
> Nor to one image, nor one scene confin'd
> Successive pictures rise before the mind.
>
> (ll. 53-56)

To Seward, poetry surpasses painting in its power of movement, but Painting excels in its ability to summon up the presence of an absent lover or friend. The portrait, therefore, combines ambitious invention and faithful reproduction offering us another combination of fancy and the "mimic pencil". As critics are now discovering, there exists a whole sub-genre of women's poetry written on the back of pictures or portraits, poems which allow an intimate exchange of art across a space which is neither fully public, nor wholly private. Amelia Opie's "To Mr Opie, on his having painted for me the picture of Mrs Twiss" celebrates the portrait's ability to make the absent present and to embody what is "on [the] heart". The poem describes a fascinating conflict of aesthetic and affective responses:

---

[26] In its negative and positive aspects Fancy is allied with the visual arts. In Smith's sonnet "To fancy", she asks why she should "love the scenes thy sportive pencil drew ... Which shew'd the beauteous rather than the true!" (ll. 2-4). The "false medium" (l. 9) epitomizes delusive hope, which is always contrasted with harsh reality in the *Elegiac Sonnets.* In Smith's "Ode to Despair" she accuses Hope of being "a faithless flatterer ... whose pencil gay, / Pourtrays some vision of delight, / Then bids the fairy tablet fade away" (ll. 10-12). See, for example Sonnet XLIII "The unhappy exile" and XLVIII "To Mrs. ****" (*The Poems of Charlotte Smith*, 44, 79, 41, 45).

[27] For a view of the debate between male voices, see Morris Eaves, "The Sister Arts in British Romanticism", in *The Cambridge Companion to British Romanticism*, 236-69.

> But in my breast contending feelings rise,
> While this loved semblance fascinates my eyes;
> Now pleased, I mark the painter's skilful line,
> Now joy, because the skill I mark was thine:
> And while I prize the gift by thee bestowed,
> My heart proclaims I'm of the giver proud.
> Thus pride and friendship war with equal strife,
> And now the friend exults, and now the wife.
>
> (ll. 9-16)

We find inflections of the "skilful line" of aesthetic pleasure with the dynamics of human relationship in Anna Barbauld's poem "On a Portrait" of her brother which allows her "line by line, the well-known face [to] peruse" (l. 10), in Seward's poetic responses to portraits of herself and her father, in Mary Robinson's "Stanzas to a Friend who wished to have my Portrait". In all of these poems, the painting's ability to fix a moment is contrasted with the flux of time and the mobility of viewer and subject. The poems might look like dutiful celebrations of household objects, the quotidian and domestic relationships, but they allow the poet to cast forward in time, to picture future years, to imagine.[28]

The last poem I shall consider is one that was addressed to Anna Barbauld by Mary Scott. In *The Female Advocate* of 1774 Scott set out to counter the "contracted" opinions of men on the subject of female education. She selected Barbauld as a muse and an example of female Fancy: "How fair / how beauteous to our gazing eyes / Thy

---

[28] In a poem to a friend about the possibility of future meetings, Barbauld depicts the prospect of years passing as the ephemeral tincture of water colours:

> Who knows within so long a space
> What scenes the present may efface,
> What course thy stream of life may take,
> What winds may curl, what storms may shake,
> What varying colours, gay or grave,
> Shall tinge by turns the passing wave;
> Of objects on its banks what swarms –
> The loftier or the fairer forms –
> Shall glide before the liquid glass,
> And print their image as they pass.

("To the Baron de Stonne", ll. 45-52, in *The Poems of Anna Letitia Barbauld*, 109-110.)

vivid intellectual paintings rise!"[29] (ll. 425-26). But the poem is not just a celebration of Barbauld's "harmonious line" (l. 421) and "richest colouring" (l. 423). Scott projects Barbauld's influence on other women as a succession of flights: "Teach them", she urges, "with thee on Fancy's wing to soar" (l. 433) and crucially, she sees women as able to combine "Nature's minuter works" (l. 455) with "arduous flight" (l. 457) in "realms of intellectual light" (l. 458). Rebelling against the masculine "Salic Law" (l. 439), which excludes women from science and art, Scott envisages the possibility of women freely exploring and inhabiting multiple frames, "Lost in the boundless wonders of the sky" (l. 451). With this vocabulary of "glowing fire" "panting desire" and "rapture" (ll. 227, 428, and 445) we can see how the first generation Romantic women anticipated that liberal and impetuous disruption of the poetic line that would define later male writers and how they created their own "fine" and "ferocious Caravaggio style".

---

[29] *Romantic Women Poets: An Anthology*, 135-36.

Within or Without? Problems of Perspective in Charlotte Smith, Anna Laetitia Barbauld and Dorothy Wordsworth

Lilla Maria Crisafulli

Space and vision

This essay addresses the question of the place within literature occupied by that numerous group of women poets at the end of the eighteenth and at the beginning of the nineteenth centuries who spoke out, wrote, published and claimed their own artistic space and their own vision of the world. The opposition between "within" and "without" mentioned in my title can be given two different semantic interpretations, with reference to these women writers: either "inside or outside", or "being part of or deprived of". The poets in question may be seen to be part of the world of words and of power, or on the contrary excluded from it, kept on the outskirts, mere apprentices on the threshold of language, deprived of the Logos that God gave man. Yet was not Prometheus himself, the damned hero of Olympus who made a gift of the Logos in the form of fire, marginalized and enchained for this inopportune gift? Is the gift of the word a guarantee of a place in the world? And if so, does occupancy of that place mean being at its centre, "within", or alternatively at its margins, "without"? It follows that the within/without opposition that I intend to discuss here in relation to women's Romantic poetry implies not only a reassessment, namely whether they were at the centre (of the literary scene) or on the outskirts, but also whether they necessarily belonged to their own sex or, rather, if they were "unsexed, trans-sexed or even out-sexed"?[1]

---

[1] See Julia Kristeva, "L'autre du sexe", *Sorcières*, 10 (1978), 37.

Anna Laetitia Barbauld, Charlotte Smith, Jane Taylor, Anna Seward, Dorothy Wordsworth, Mary Tighe, Mary Lamb, Hannah More, Joanna Baillie, Mary Robinson, Felicia Hemans, Letitia Elizabeth Landon, and many others too numerous to be mentioned here, are the female poets who have been censured or forgotten within the canon of Romanticism. Even in today's reappraisal, notably the historical research that has been carried out in recent years, and in the re-elaboration of a canon that is no longer such – being, as it is, changeable and multifaceted – risks confining women poets to reassuring, private spaces. Despite themselves, women poets are sooner or later taken back to the domestic scene, to restricted areas and a horizontal outlook, such as the house, homely affections, the community, in brief that ethic of love, which, however humane and valuable it may be, undermines another type of perspective, which is also the basis of a whole aesthetic view, namely that of Romanticism itself.

Therefore, the conventional categories that define Romanticism – such as the infinite, the subversive, the symbolic, the individual, the universal, the subconscious, the struggle for freedom and fame, the destructive drives of *eros* and *thanatos*, the secular stance – would appertain solely to what has been called, not merely by chance, "high" Romanticism (a definition that has been used by analogy with "high culture").[2] This has to do with the canonical Romantic aesthetics that rises and stands vertical ("high"), and hence has been traditionally associated with male/masculine culture. But if this is so, to "high" Romanticism and culture there must also be a corresponding horizontal ("low") Romanticism, whether we like it or not, that it may be easily associated with women's Romanticism. In this case the perspective can only be biological, tied to the body, inscribed in the corporeal and psychological DNA with its everlasting castration complex, a genetics "without" rather than "within". "Horizontality is simply flowing over the surfaces, remaining flat in the field of appearances, the very mark of female passivity."[3]

---

[2] Lucy Newlyn, *Reading, Writing and Romanticism: The Anxiety of Reception*, Oxford, 2000, 141 and 223.

[3] Laura Kreyder, "Una donna banale. Il soggetto nella scrittura femminile", *Nuova Corrente – Donne/Letteratura*, 86 (1981), 500. In her highly interesting article focussing on subjectivity in women's writing, although it is now somewhat outdated but still significant today, Laura Kreyder takes as her starting point the traditional

However, for Julia Kristeva, who also advanced a theory of the female biological cage, woman is "a perpetual dissident in relationship to social and political power, in exile, therefore always single, divided, demoniac and a witch" even if she is "less inclined to anarchism, and more concerned with ethics" so that "hers is not the Nietzschian sort of anger".[4] It is, moreover, Julia Kristeva who also recalls how the function of love, while learning to be modest, is also a continual questioning: "far for being an all-encompassing Mother-Goddess, she is rather a place of vulnerability, of questioning herself and the use of language." And it is precisely this questioning that I want to take as the starting point in the present discussion since it completely overturns the place and the vision within which a woman moves, lives or creates by the way she looks and enquires into it. In her *Héretique de l'amour* Kristeva furthermore affirms that:

> When it happens that a woman worries about space, she does so in order to reconstruct the origin, to reshape her original space and create another space, like her own mother … or against, in the place of, or better than her own mother. But she never leaves the space as it is: she models it, annihilates it, breaks it up, weaves it, tranforms it. It is thus a criticism and contestation of other spaces, whatever they may be, but

---

assumptions that saw the equation between the categories of male as being vertical and female as horizontal in order to subvert them and to show how questionable, and even impossible, it is to make rigid and compromising generalizations, which are inadequate particularly as far as women are concerned. Kreyder, therefore, suggests using the metaphor of the veil because: "a woman's characteristic is, on the other hand, that of making it impossible to recognize her, almost impossible to define. It belongs alternately to all individual dimensions …. This capacity never to find an individuality seems to me a crucial point. How can we account for this? I should like to do so by borrowing Nietzsche's metaphor of the veil. First of all, because, if we wish to remain within the field of spatial metaphors, it is the very threads of material that are vertical and horizontal, the threads of the veil. The veil that delimits the surface and the depths, the hidden and the obviousness, the real and the illusionary. In this unusually polysemic word lies the knot of oppositions: it reconciles the vertical and the horizontal, the surface and the depths, the hidden and the obvious, the real and the illusionary. And it is not merely by chance that its other meanings bear a female connotation …." The metaphor of the veil used here to signify the very essence of female nature seems particularly useful to this discussion since, as is well-known, in the field of male Romantic poetry (but not only) it is the veil itself that is one of the most frequent poetic symbols and is always associated with figures of women that may, or may not, be real. It is a symbol that foresees and reveals the liminal, the ambiguous and the mysterious.

[4] Julia Kristeva, "La Femme, ce n'est jamais ça", in *Polylogue*, Paris, 1977, 519.

> always aiming at going back to the imaginary origin and setting her own stamp on it.[5]

Therefore, alongside a female, social, ethical and maternal protective being, there also exists a non-being, a woman born hostile, dissident, divided and solitary. It is, then, in this caesura, this *aporia*, that my essay will be situated in order to work out a critical position that includes, rather than excludes or dismisses, and that allows us to see a female poet as something permanent yet fluid, present yet fleeting, liminal yet influential, with the aim of recapturing lost visions and perspectives, hidden objects and poetic subjects buried beneath credible but restrictive labels.

I want to bring into the discussion at this point Harriet K. Linkin's article dedicated to Mary Tighe and Letitia Landon: "How Women Poets Recuperate the Gaze."[6] This study poses the question concerning the ability of women poets to turn from being perceived objects into being perceiving subjects, and thus enquires into both the observing and the observed "I".

The problem of viewpoint is, of course, essential to all forms of literature, founded as they are on perspectives, reflections and deflections, and on the characterization of individuals who perceive and are perceived from a particular angle of vision, whether it be that of the author, or of the narrative or poetic voice, thereby defining the reality and constructing the ideology of the text. A woman is shaped and determined by being viewed, since she is traditionally the object of perception. Moreover, poetry, particularly Romantic poetry, calls for a vision that returns to the self; it is self-reflexive and therefore jeopardizes femininity which, according to traditional canons, is not narcissistically self-centred. The Romantic sublime, masculine and egocentric, is inevitably an element of rupture for the female poetic "I" because, in order to claim any right to membership of this aesthetic category, the woman poet has to shake off the atavistic, patriarchal role of being an object and not a subject.[7] The woman

[5] Julia Kristeva, "L'autre du sexe", in *ibid.*, 39.

[6] Harriet K. Linkin, "Romantic Aesthetic in Mary Tighe and Letitia Elizabeth Landon: How Women Poets Recuperate the Gaze", *European Romantic Review*, VII/2 (Winter 1997), 159-88.

[7] Isobel Armstrong, "The Gush of the Feminine: How Can We Read Women's Poetry of the Romantic Period?", in *Romantic Women Writers: Voices and Countervoices*, eds Paula Feldman and Theresa M. Kelley, Hanover: NH and London, 1995.

incorporated, cannibalized and colonized by Romantic aesthetics becomes, in female Romantic poetry, an observer in her own right.[8]

Hence, if Romantic women's vision is acute, as Stuart Curran suggested[9]– accustomed as it is to scrutinizing gardens and observing flowers, studying the faces and expressions of those dear to them and dedicating time and attention to the careful tasks of needlework and embroidery – which direction can their view take and with what perspective? Harriet Linkin maintains that, according to conventional criticism, the Romantic woman "lacked voice for her own visions, much less sight upon which to gaze, trapped in a mirror stage that could only reproduce the male Romantic aesthetics".[10] In Linkin's opinion, however, recent new historical criticism, in examining the work of Romantic poets, has uncovered "a plenitude of women who did not suffer such paralysing anxiety". There remains the question of the stance that female Romantic poets adopted towards male Romantic aesthetics, and of how their own aesthetic view elaborated its own vision, challenging and in many ways even influencing that of men. We shall thus discover that female Romantic poetry affords extraordinarily diverse perspectives: far from being horizontally pacified, their vision suddenly and unexpectedly takes vertical and vertiginous turns. At other times, while following this outlook, we shall come across an ambiguous, intriguing and evasive sensitivity. In order to show this, I shall briefly speak of three woman poets, Anna Laetitia Barbauld, Charlotte Smith and Dorothy Wordsworth.

Anna Laetitia Barbauld: a new form of dissent

Anna Laetitia Barbauld (1743-1825) was an exemplary, cultured, bourgeois, intellectual radical. She taught, travelled and wrote poems, children's stories and literary criticism; after this, she became an editor, contributing first to the *The Monthly Magazine*, and then becoming its co-editor. She moved around London, animated the meetings of the bluestockings in their salons, yet refused to be

---

[8] Anne K. Mellor, *Romanticism and Gender*, New York and London, 1993, 16.

[9] I refer to the fundamental, innovative article by Stuart Curran, "The I Altered", in *Romanticism and Feminism*, ed. Anne K. Mellor, Bloomington: IN, 1988, 185-207. In particular, Curran states that "The actual vision might be said to be the province ... of women poets, whose fine eyes are occupied continually in discriminating minute objects or assembling a world out of its disjointed particulars" (189).

[10] Linkin, "Romantic Aesthetic in Mary Tighe and Letitia Elizabeth Landon ...", 160-61.

identified with the aristocratic ladies who were independent and influential. To Lady Montague, who asked her to establish an academy for young girls because she had had experience as a tutor, Anna firmly but politely declined because she was sure that women had to be educated first at home, within the family, in order to acquire their female role as mother and wife, and later gain the cultural one as intellectuals. Barbauld believed in the family as a political and behavioural model and in the nation as a family: she sees them reflected in each other in harmonious correspondence. This harmony was appreciated even by the notorious Reverend Richard Polwhele, who in his short satirical poem "The Unsex'd Female" of 1798, written to condemn the followers of Mary Wollstonecraft, partly praised Barbauld for her lines which he judged "chaste and elegant". The harmonious rapport between family and nation is reflected in the themes of her poems, and yet her brilliant career was disrupted by one of her poems, "1811", dedicated to her mother-country, which in effect accuses England of excessive consumerism, with its consequent decadence. The accusation is precise and offers neither pardon nor any extenuating factors to those who have led the country, after seventeen years of war with France, to a "ghastly want", that is to devastation and extreme poverty.

Even the history of English culture is relived from an innovative point of view: as far as literary history is concerned, Barbauld sets Shakespeare alongside Joanna Baillie; in political history, she associates the Magna Charta with the abolitionist commitment, and so on. This was enough to arouse ferocious criticism on the part of several reviewers, among whom John Wilson Croker stood foremost when, in the pages of the *Quarterly Review*, in 1812, he advised the poet not to show any interest in political matters because they were men's business, but rather to concern herself with the more feminine "shagreen spectacles" and "knitting needle", that had been unwisely set aside "in the magnanimous resolution of saving a sinking state".[11] We do not know whether in the following thirteen years Barbauld took Croker's advice seriously, but we certainly do know that, while she continued to write up till her death in 1825, nothing that she wrote in that period was ever published. It was her niece, Lucy Aikin, who sent a posthumous edition of her works to the printers (1825).

[11] *Romantic Women Poets: An Anthology*, ed. Duncan Wu, Oxford, 1979, 8.

To return to the theme of female perspective within the field of Romanticism, my interest here is her view and the space that her poetic vision dilates or circumscribes. Let us start with a fiercely ironic poem, such as "Washing-Day". The brief poem transforms this peaceful, female weekly ritual into a gigantic epic, into a day of apocalyptic terror, when the silence of the house is interrupted by an army of ill-tempered women with clothes to wash and who break up the tranquillity of family life like a pack of wolves:

> Come, Muse, and sing the dreaded Washing-Day….
>
> …. for to that day nor peace belongs
> Nor comfort; – ere the first grey streak of dawn,
> The red-armed washers come and chase repose.
> Nor pleasant smile, nor quaint device of mirth,
> E'er visited that day: the very cat,
> From the wet kitchen scared, and reeking hearth,
> Visits the parlour; – an unwonted guest.
> The silent breakfast-meal is soon dispatched;
> Uninterrupted, save by anxious looks
> Cast at the lowering sky, if sky should lower.
> From that last evil, oh preserve us, heavens! ….
>
> I well remember, when a child, the awe
> This day struck into me; for then the maids,
> I scarce knew why, looked cross, and drove me from them:
> Nor soft caress could I obtain, nor hope
> Usual indulgencies; jelly or creams, ….
> … so I went
> And sheltered me beside the parlour fire ….[12]

The clamour of arms and the first signs of war are delightfully recorded by a poetic self that is revealed through the eyes of the smallest girl in the house from her hiding-place, in a part of her home that has suddenly become alien and threatening. However, there are two further examples that subvert all expectations more delicately: "A Summer's Evening's Meditation'" and "The Mouse's Petition".

---

[12] Anna Laetitia Barbauld, "Washing-Day" (ll. 8, 12-22, 58-62, 66-67), in *Eighteenth-Century Woman Poets: An Oxford Anthology*, ed. Roger Lonsdale, Oxford, 1989, 308-309 (see also *Antologia delle Poetesse Romantiche Inglesi*, ed. Lilla Maria Crisafulli, Rome, 2003, I, 126-30).

In the first, "A Summer's Evening's Meditation" (1773), the eye of the poetic persona scrutinizes creation in the warm air. The self abandons itself to the firmament and wonders – but could a woman wonder? – where God is:

> …. Seiz'd in thought,
> On fancy's wild and roving wing I sail,
> From the green borders of the peopled earth,
> And the pale Moon, her duteous fair attendant;
> From solitary Mars; from the vast orb
> Of Jupiter, whose huge gigantic bulk
> Dances in ether like the lightest leaf;
> To the dim verge, the suburbs of the system,….
>
> ... fearless thence
> I launch into the trackless deeps of space,
> Where, burning round, ten thousand suns appear,
> Of elder beam, which ask no leave to shine
> Of our terrestrial star, nor borrow light
> From the proud regent of our scanty day;
>
> .... Here must I stop,
> Or is there aught beyond? What hand unseen
> Impels me onward thro' the glowing orbs
> Of habitable nature, far remote,
> To the dread confines of eternal night,
> To solitudes of vast unpeopled space,
> The desarts of creation, wide and wild;
> Where embryo systems and unkindled suns
> Sleep in the womb of chaos? fancy droops,
> And thought astonished stops her bold career.

The encounter between the self and creation takes place, the poetic, wholly female persona is reborn into the world, while at the same time, as if it were a spell, the universe itself becomes female, and God is reborn from her womb with a slightly daring touch:

> But oh, thou mighty mind! whose powerful word
> Said, Thus let all things be, and thus they were,
> Where shall I seek thy presence? how umblamed
> Invoke thy dread perfection?
> Have the broad eye-lids of the morn beheld thee?

Or does the beamy shoulder of Orion
Support thy throne? O look with pity down
On erring, guilty man; not in thy names
Of terror clad; not with those thunders armed ....
.... thou hast a gentler voice,
That whispers comfort to the swelling heart,
Abash'd, yet longing to behold her Maker.

But now my soul, unused to stretch her powers
In flight so daring, drops her weary wing,
And seeks again the known accustomed spot ... [13]

The bold flight ceases here, the wings are folded and the poetic "I", having abandoned the "ravished sense" that had accompanied the vision, starts to wander back to more familiar places, only a little intimidated and embarrassed.

If we consider this confrontation carefully, however, while being totally dissident, it is one between equals. The self and God give rise to an intense encounter on a higher plane, yet it is at the same time in many aspects simple and direct. The poetic imagination, enthralled by the vision that the evening meditation offers her, takes to her wings in the fullest, soaring in the most vertiginous Romantic tradition, in order to meet the Creator, a "thou" at first male, cosmic and terrifying, but then gently, almost female. Here the questioning of the poetic self reduces the terrifying divine vertical to a mild, horizontal integrity. It is a confrontation that is dramatic and sublime yet imbued with a knowing, almost irreverent, gaiety. It is a *vis à vis* that not even William Blake would have dared, because it is marked by that one ingenious trace of human fragility, by that "thou" – written with an initial lower case letter – addressed to God. The choice of an open, colloquial poetic language seems almost a provocation. God is called upon to respond for his responsibilities and for clemency by means of a voice and a look that are clearly within, at the centre of the world created.

This surprising aspect of Barbauld, in the second poem cited, "The Mouse's Petition Found in the trap where he had been confin'd all Night by Dr Priestley", is reduced to small details, and the space is

[13] "A Summer Evening's Meditation" (ll. 71-78, 81-86, 89-107, 109-14), in Anna Laetitia Barbauld, *Poems* (1792), Woodstock facsimile edn, London and New York, 1993, 141-44 (see also *Antologia delle Poetesse Romantiche Inglesi*, I, 112-14).

that of the microcosm, in this way overturning the vision and perspective, but not the final message to the reader. In this case, too, the viewpoint moves along a horizontal plane. But the aerial view, the eye looking down from the universal flight in "A Summer's Evening's Meditation", willingly gives way to the perspective seen in fear, which, as in the case of "Washing-Day", comes from below. The persona becomes a guinea pig, crying with, and like, a laboratory mouse shut up in a cage by a scientist for his experiments. It is an insignificant victim, a victim possessing no background, a body and flesh lacking sanctity. Yet the mouse observes the scientist, who is lord and master of its fate as a merely biological creature, and claims the right to live:

> If e'er thy breast with freedom glow'd,
> And spurn'd a tyrant's chain,
> Let not thy strong oppressive force
> A free-born mouse detain.
>
> Oh! do not stain with guiltless blood
> Thy hospitable hearth;
> Nor triumph that thy wiles betray'd
> A prize so little worth ….
>
> The well-taught philosophic mind
> To all compassion gives;
> Casts round the world an equal eye,
> And feels for all that lives ….
>
> Beware, lest in the worm you crush
> A brother's soul you find;
> And tremble lest thy luckless hand
> Dislodge a kindred mind.
>
> Or, if this transient gleam of day
> Be *all* of life we share,
> Let pity plead within thy breast
> That little *all* to spare.[14]

[14] "The Mouse's Petition" (ll. 9-16, 25-28, 33-40), in Anna Laetitia Barbauld, *Poems* (1792), 38-39 (*Antologia delle Poetesse Romantiche Inglesi*, I,102-104).

Stuart Curran comments that "it is a poem whose considerable charm masks a studied self-reflexiveness".[15] And further on:

> Like all fables, "The Mouse's Petition" has its interior shades of meaning. Even if addressed with youthful affection to an admired family associate, the poem is a direct assertion of the claims of feminine sensibility against male rationality .... In the clarity and delicacy of its style, it challenges the male universe exemplified by Priestley's scientific experiments.

Therefore, the poem elaborates two different perspectives of the world, the male and female, and turns them into metaphors, and the poetic "I" reveals a particular compassion for all living beings, unlike the rationality of the male scientist who considers how the world can be used.

The one question that remains to be answered is whether this poetic persona is not also expressing an interesting variation on the ideology of those dissenters, such as Price, Priestley himself and Thomas Paine, who called for an international brotherhood opposed to that of the slave/master relationship that dramatically characterized the age-old conflict between social classes, sexes and races, in which case Barbauld's choice seems clear: she wishes to include every single creature, even the least significant, in the democracy of universal rights and of individual feelings.

Charlotte Smith and the poetics of exile

The case of Charlotte Smith (1749-1806) is equally intriguing. Born into a wealthy family, she lost her mother and was married off by her father to an immature, dissolute young man at the age of sixteen. Together with her numerous children, she was imprisoned, along with her husband, Benjamin Smith for the debts he had incurred by betting. She then began to write and publish in order to keep both herself and her children and to obtain her husband's release from gaol. She fled with her family to France and, on her return to England, separated from her husband, without, however, managing to curb his requests for money. One by one, she witnessed the death of some of her children, while others emigrated in search of fortune. All her life she fought to claim the inheritance of her father-in-law, which according

---

[15] "The I Altered", in *Romanticism and Feminism*, 196-97.

to the patriarchal system was denied to her directly, since in the seventeenth and eighteenth centuries women had no legal rights. For twenty-three years, the inheritance was refused to her and her children and conceded only a few months before her death.

The frantic publication of her works, the vast number of them and her fraught correspondence with publishers and the subscribers of her works bear witness to the fact that for her writing was a serious matter, a question of survival. As a radical thinker, a poet of sensibility, journalist, prolific writer of sentimental novels, dramatist, and translator, Smith also provides the reader the image of an intellectual with far-ranging interests. However, her poetic voice seems to revolve so much around mourning and grief that another poet, Anna Seward, was irritated by it, and in a sonnet, "Advice to Mrs Smith. A Sonnet", reproved her for offering such a negative view of women to the reading public. Equally Mary Wollstonecraft, in her own reviews published in Joseph Johnson's *Analytical Review*, while recognizing her talent as a poet, accuses her of being over-sentimental in her novels.

Yet Charlotte Smith sold well and was successful. There were eight editions of her *Elegiac Sonnets* in the years from 1784 to 1800; in 1793 she published *The Emigrants* and a year after her death, in 1807, *Beachy Head, Fables and Other Poems* appeared. She seemed to have an unlimited source of inspiration: she wrote ten novels from 1788 to 1798, while at the same time children's books, histories of England, a rich epistolary, and so forth, were printed.

Charlotte Smith's *Elegiac Sonnets* became so important as to obtain, several years later in 1833, the praise of William Wordsworth, who was to say that she was "a lady to whom English verse is under greater obligations than are likely to be either acknowledged or remembered".[16] Charlotte challenged the male canon courageously: after sonnets, she successfully dedicated herself to the use of blank verse and competently quoted Petrarch, Shakespeare, Milton and Goethe; when accused of plagiarism, she replied with closely-written, erudite notes at the bottom of the pages of her poems, wherein she occasionally begged pardon for having dared to attempt so much. Her poems are imbued with the profound melancholy resulting from all the afflictions life had reserved for her, while her novels are tinged with

---

[16] *Ibid.*, 202.

autobiographical elements. Her friend William Cowper bears witness to the exhausting work Smith undertook in order to keep her family: "Chain'd to her desk like a slave to his oar, with no other means of subsistence for herself and her numerous children, with a broken constitution, unequal to the severe labour enjoined by her necessity, she is indeed to be pitied ... she will and must 'ere long die a martyr to her exigencies."[17] Smith herself remarked:

> I wrote indeed under much oppression of Spirit from the long and frequently hopeless difficulties in which my children's affairs continue to be involved .... For two three or four years, the burthen of such large a family whose support depends entirely upon me ... might be undertaken in the hope that at the end of that period their property might be restored to them ... now the worn out pen falls from the tired hand, and the real calamities of life press too heavily to allow of the power of evading them by fictitious detail.[18]

It is significant that such a personal confession of what is lacking in fiction should be given in the very introduction to a novel, and in which Smith not only presents herself as a mother-cum-martyr, the archetypical example of a woman's condition at the beginning of the nineteenth century, but that she herself should reject any consolatory function of art. This attitude becomes even more explicit in her poetry, where the tone of denunciation is clear and strong. This position is clearly evinced in the graveyard sonnet "Written in the church-yard at Middleton in Sussex" (*Elegiac Sonnets*, XLIV):

> Press'd by the Moon, mute arbitress of tides,
> While the loud equinox its power combines,
> The sea no more its swelling surge confines,
> But o'er the shrinking land sublimely rides.
> The wild blast, rising from the Western cave,
> Drives the huge billows from their heaving bed;
> Tears from their grassy tombs the village dead,
> And breaks the silent sabbath of the grave!
> With shells and sea-weed mingled, on the shore
> Lo! Their bones whiten in the frequent wave;

---

[17] *The Letters and Prose Writings of William Cowper*, eds James King and Charles Ryskamp, Oxford, 1984, IV, 87.

[18] Loraine Fletcher, *Charlotte Smith: A Critical Biography*, London and New York, 1998, 179.

> But vain to them the winds and waters rave;
> *They* hear the warring elements no more:
> While I am doom'd – by life's long storm opprest,
> To gaze with envy on their gloomy rest.[19]

Consolation, typical of the elegy, does not follow on from the melancholic tone of loss and grief.[20] The aesthetics of mourning and loss break loudly, like waves against a cliff, against an alienated and estranged viewpoint. The bodies' lack of feeling is a metaphor for the detachment of the beholder, who from the height of solitude and inner suffering is not regenerated by any metaphysics.

Such a secular attitude, unusual in a female poetic voice of the Romantic era, disconcerted her contemporary readers and was severely reproached by critics and early biographers. *The British Critic* attacked the immorality of her *Elegiac Sonnets*, whereas in 1861, almost half a century later, Jane Williams, portraying Charlotte Smith in *The Literary Women of England*, stated:

> Untaught in her infancy to pray to Our Father who is in Heaven, the sacred fire of devotion was never enkindled upon the alter of her heart to shed its healthful warmth and gladdening light from within, and transmute all evils into good .... Discontent was the bane of her happiness, Viewing this world only as a day for enjoyment, the next world merely as a night for repose, she rebelled against troubles and trials as unjust inflictions, not discerning their probationary use, in the preparation of human character for an immortal and heavenly life.[21]

Smith's elegiac sonnets reveal – just like those white, drifting bones – solitude and frustration, but also the ability to shout out a denunciation to the world. The same vertical, empowered viewpoint can be found in the long poem, "The Emigrants", in which the poetic *persona* observes the exiles fleeing from the war in France, who reach England, and identifies itself with them:

---

[19] *The Poems of Charlotte Smith*, ed. Stuart Curran, Oxford, 1993, 42.

[20] See Judith Hawley, "Charlotte Smith's Elegiac Sonnets: Losses and Gain", in *Women's Poetry in the Enlightenment: The Making of the Canon, 1730-1820*, eds Isobel Armstrong and Virginia Blain, New York, 1999, 184-97, for a convincing article on how Charlotte Smith articulated and renewed the genre of the Elegy. Hawley writes: "Smith felt that her readers owed her pity just as she was owed money, security, status" (190).

[21] Jane Williams, *The Literary Women of England*, London, 1861, 223-24.

Slow in the Wintry Morn, the struggling light
Throws a faint gleam upon the troubled waves;
Their foaming tops, as they approach the shore
And the broad surf that never ceasing breaks
On the innumerous pebbles, catch the beams
Of the pale Sun, that with reluctance gives
To this cold northern Isle, its shorten'd day.
Alas! how few the morning wakes to joy!
How many murmur at oblivious night
For leaving them so soon; for bearing thus
Their fancied bliss (the only bliss they taste!),
On her black wings away![22]

Along with the exiles and fugitives, the poetic "I" beaches among the foamy waves of a distant homeland, where the boats, a traditional symbol of high Romantic imagination, are lost or wrecked. It is the inhospitable coast of a land that has never been one's own, consisting of sharp rocks and men who speak an incomprehensible tongue. In this society of strangers, nature itself is indifferent, buffeted by ceaseless storms. The eye closely observes the chasm from the top of a rock; rejecting any type of natural or social integration, the creatures it describes are outsiders and exiles, scattered and empty. Not even the sympathy that the lyrical "I" articulates for the destiny of those women, children and men who land on the British coast, having lost everything, seem able to mitigate the melancholic strain of the poem.

The reader stands behind the observer, seeing only the dark figure and the silhouette, following the gaze cast towards infinity, and from this viewpoint encounters a hint of another, subsequent estranged image, that of an unredeemed self. In this case, the vision is without, that is on the outside and in exile, but it is also within, being indeed the founding moment of the grand tradition of Romantic meditative subjectivity.

But Charlotte Smith's gaze becomes particularly intriguing when we come to *Beachy Head.* Smith has been called "the muse of the botanic" for the increasingly scientific nature of her poetry at the end of her literary career. Works such as *Rural Walks: Dialogues Intended for the Use of Young Persons*, *Rambles Farther*, *Minor Morals*, *Conversations Introducing Poetry: Chiefly on Subjects of Natural*

[22] *The Poems of Charlotte Smith*, ed. Curran, 135 (the opening lines).

History, and the posthumously published *Beachy Head, with Other Poems* show her keen interest in the natural world and the sharp attention of her scientific eye towards the organic process. In this regard Judith Pascoe remarks "Smith's earth-bound aesthetic provides an intriguing rejoinder to the more transcendent one that we know as 'the' Romantic, the central and normative mode. In addition, the scientific eye she casts over the natural world in her botanical poetry makes these poems intriguing points of reference in the ongoing critical debate over the female gaze."[23] Her poem, however, seems dominated by two distinct modes of gazing. The incipit of *Beachy Head* is unequivocally cosmic, offering to the reader a wide-angle view. Here we see through a panoptic eye, while we hear a poetic person standing on the summit of a cliff overhanging the ocean revoking the origin of the world:

On thy stupendous summit, rock sublime!
That o'er the channel rear'd, half way at sea
The mariner at early morning hails,
I would recline; while Fancy should go forth,
And represent the strange and awful hour
Of vast concussion; when the Omnipotent
Stretch'd forth his arm, and rent the solid hills,
Bidding the impetuous main flood rush between
The rifted shores, and from the continent
Eternally divided this green isle.
Imperial lord of the high southern coast!
From thy projecting head-land I would mark
Far in the east the shades of night disperse,
Melting and thinned, as from the dark blue wave
Emerging, brilliant rays of arrowy light
Dart from the horizon; when the glorious sun
Just lifts above it his splendid orb.
Advances now, with feathery silver touched ….

(ll. 1-18)

Afar off,
And just emerging from the arch immense
Where seem to part the elements, a fleet
If fishing vessels stretch their lesser sails;

[23] Judith Pascoe, "Female Botanists and the Poetry of Charlotte Smith", in *Re-visioning Romanticism: British Women Writers, 1776-1837*, eds Carol Shiner Wilson and Joel Haefner, Philadelphia, 1994, 193.

While more remote, and like dubious spot
Just hanging in the horizon, laden deep,
The ship of commerce richly freighted, makes
Her slower progress, on her distant voyage,
Bound to the orient climates, where the sun
Matures the spice within its odorous shell,
And, rivalling the grey worm's filmy toil,
Burst from its pod the vegetable down;
Which in long turban'd wreaths, from torrid heat
Defends the brows of Asia's countless casts.
There the Earth hides her glowing breast
The beamy adamant, and the round pearl
Enchased in rugged covering; which the slave,
With perilous and breathless toil, tears off
From the rough sea-rock, deep beneath the waves.
These are the toys of Nature; and her sport
Of little estimate in Reason's eye:
And they who reason, with abhorrence see
Man, for such gaudes and baubles, violate
The sacred freedom of his fellow man –
Erroneous estimate!

(ll. 36-60) [24]

This poetic eye/"I" scrutinizes the horizon and the universe discussing the geological eras and the signs they left behind; facing past and present history, the colonizing and colonized worlds and the exploitation of the one over the other; contrasting natural and artificial values, the stars and the diamonds. The second half of the poem is ordered instead by a more intimate and domestic eye/I whose universe is centred on a country cottage and its surroundings. In its progression the persona gets to know and to describe more and more circumscribed scenery, smaller and smaller objects to the point of reaching the tiniest detail of shape and describing the slightest shade of colour. Thus we familiarize ourselves with the invisible and the unnoticeable, which consequently acquire relevance and significance, beauty and splendour:

Where woods of ash, and beech,
And partial copses, fringe the green hill foot,

---

[24] *The Poems of Charlotte Smith*, ed. Curran, 217-19 (*Antologia delle Poetesse Romantiche Inglesi*, I, 240-44).

The upland shepherd rears his modest home,
There wanders by, a little nameless stream
That from the hill wells forth, bright now and clear,
Or after rain with chalky mixture gray,
But still refreshing in its shallow course,
The cottage garden; most for use design'd,
Yet not of beauty destitute. The vine
Mantles the little casement; yet the briar
Drops fragrant dew among the July flowers;
And pansies rayed, and freak'd and mottled pinks
Grow among balm, and rosemary and rue
There honeysuckles flaunt, and roses blow
Almost uncultured: Some with dark green leaves
Contrast their flowers of pure unsullied white;
Others, like velvet robes of regal state
Of richest crimson, while in thorny moss
Enshrined and cradled, the most lovely, wear
The hues of youthful beauty's glowing cheek. –
With fond regret I recollect e'en now
In Spring and Summer, what delight I felt
Among these cottage gardens, and how much
Such artless nosegays, knotted with a rush
By village housewife or her ruddy maid,
Were welcome to me; soon and simply pleas'd.

(ll. 320-45) [25]

Smith masterfully controls both perspectives, shifting from the infinite and the grand (a sublime, however, consciously deprived of the Burkean dimension of the awful and fearful), to the aesthetic of the invisible and the minute.[26] The binary opposition between within and without also becomes a journey of knowledge and self-awareness: while the joys and fulfilment of a subjective past experience are retraced in nature by memory, the individual experience of the world troubles throws a shadow over the present and more universal history of mankind.

---

[25] *Ibid.*, 230-31.

[26] D.R. Ruwe, "Charlotte Smith's Sublime: Feminine Poetics, Botany, and 'Beachy Head'", *PRISM(S) Essays in Romanticism*, Special Issue in Honor of Jean-Pierre Barricelli, American Conference on Romanticism, VII (1999), 117.

Dorothy Wordsworth "a violet ... half hidden from the eye"
Far-removed from Charlotte Smith's egocentric, all-inclusive vision, which filters the world through the eye of grief and melancholy, and equally far-removed from Anna Laetitia Barbauld's political, libertarian outlook, Dorothy Wordsworth has been praised by critics for her ability to establish a relationship of equality between people and things: in her journals, letters and poems things seem to live on a horizontal plane of humble acceptance. Dorothy's perspective is, therefore, an objective one, of flowers, of turf and of the disinherited, who live for one day outside economic or historical time. Lauded by her brother as a domestic muse and custodian of family ties, Dorothy seemed to do nothing to refute the cliché attributed to her, namely that of a gentle but apparently ancillary female presence.

Her early childhood was happy, but at the age of six, when her mother died, Dorothy began a long period of moving around from one relative's house to another, often as an unwelcome guest. In those years, after her father's death, she created the dream of having a house for herself and her four brothers. The waiting period became agonizing, even maniacal. In her image of the house, Dorothy was in fact seeking not a place to settle but rather her origins, her own lost roots. The dream came true with great difficulty and in successive stages, until in 1799-1800 when, besides her brother William, with whom she had been reunited some years before, another brother, John, a sailor, also joined their small community for a brief period. The three finally settled in a cottage in Grasmere, in the Lake District. It was the ideal home in which to grow up and mature, being neither parental nor conjugal, but a democracy in which Dorothy could do many things denied to other women. She was permitted, not without the gossip of neighbours and relatives, to go for walks, read and travel, together with William, and in the same way as he did. Domesticity and culture were fused together with lack of law or order, in a desired (and studied) anarchy.

Meanwhile, she had already told her friend, Jane Pollard, how happy she was to be reunited with William. In a highly emotional letter of 16 February 1793, she described to Jane the occasion when another brother, Christopher, also came back for a while. However, what occupied her time was the delighted, meticulous description of the days spent with William, days that went by with endless conversations and books, interrupted only by meals so frugal that guests, such as the Hazlitts, reproved her for them. In this letter, Dorothy defined the house by quoting a line of William's "the central point of our joys".[27] In the letter, Dorothy hoped to convince Jane to spend a long holiday with them. This invitation, with its enthusiasm, hid perhaps the slightly vain desire to show off her domestic happiness but also her wish to have someone close who could witness it, almost as if she were afraid it might vanish like a dream.

William was the fulcrum of all this joy, indeed he administrated it and produced it; she was struck by the passion and energy he exuded:

> William has both these Virtues steady and sincere in his attachments in an eminent degree; and a sort of violence of Affection if I may so Term it which demonstrates itself every moment of the Day when the Objects of his affection are present with him ... a tenderness that never sleeps, and at the same Time such a Delicacy of Manners as I have observed in few men.

In short, William's affection and presence were associated with a refuge, the house itself, in which there was no corner that did not express the daily actions the brother and sister carried out and the attention they paid to each other. For Dorothy the house was William, and in it, and in him, she found self-realization and freedom:

> I look forward with full confidence to the Happiness of receiving you in my little Patronage, I hope you will spend at least a year with me .... When I think of Winter I hasten to furnish our little Parlour, I close the Shutters, set out the Tea-table, brighten the Fire. When our Refreshment is ended I produce our Work, and William brings his book to our Table and contributes at once to our Instruction and amusement, and at Intervals we lay aside the Book and each hazard our observations upon what has been read without the fear of Ridicule or Censure. We talk over past days, we do not sigh for any Pleasures beyond our humble Habitation "The central point of all our joys".[28]

At the same time, the image of the house, as a physical and emotional haven and refuge, either as a metaphor for the seclusion from the storms of life and sexuality, or as a projection of the fragility of the self, and thus a threatening imprisonment, can be found

---

[27] *Letters of Dorothy Wordsworth: A Selection*, ed. Alan G. Hill, Oxford, 1985, 13.
[28] *Ibid.*, 13.

everywhere in Dorothy's works according to her own poetics of space, to use Bachelard's appropriate definition. For Bachelard, both in literature and in dreams, we outwardly design what we bear within ourselves, thus poetry becomes in this way a sort of "literature of the depths", rendered such from the maps they design, from the places they create or narrate. Places and spaces are important because that is where our soul ceases to wander, where it resides for a long or short period in order to seek and/or elaborate, with the aid of memory, its own identity. Consequently, Bachelard notes:

> Topoanalysis would be the systematic psychological study of the sites of our intimates lives .... At times we think we know ourselves in time, when all we know is a sequence of fixations in the spaces of the being's stability – a being who does not want to melt away, and who, even in the past, when he sets out in search of things past, wants time to "suspend" its flights.[29]

Of these places, one of the most significant is one's own home:

> The house is a privileged entity for a phenomenological study of the intimate values of inside space .... For the house furnishes us with dispersed images and a body of images at the same time .... For our house is our corner of the world. As has been often been said, it is our first universe, a real cosmos in every sense of the word ... the house shelters daydreaming, the house protects the dreamer, the house allows one to dream in peace .... Without it, man would be a dispersed being. It maintains him through the storms of the heaven and through those of life. It is body and soul.[30]

In the image of the house, the analyst has to find "the original shell",[31] the primary involucre of being, interiority. For the dreamer it affords a proof, or illusion, of stability. Moreover, Bachelard writes, the house is imagined as a vertical entity: it rises. Yet it is also, in Jungian terms, a hybrid consisting of two poles and as such dramatizes a union of high and low, of rationality and irrationality, of light and fear, represented respectively by the attic (light and rationality) and the cellar (darkness and the subconscious).[32] This is what it turned out

---

[29] *The Poetics of Space*, ed. Gaston Bachelard, trans. Maria Jolas, Boston, 1969, 8.
[30] *Ibid.*, 3-4 and 6-7.
[31] *Ibid.*, 4.
[32] *Ibid.*, 17, and 18-19.

to be for Dorothy Wordsworth, an ambiguous place of contradictions, of unexpressed tensions that were never admitted.

We should not, therefore, be surprised that her brother's marriage to Mary Hutchinson, a friend from her childhood days, found her unprepared, causing her anxiety and worry, so much so that she wore her brother's wedding-ring all night on the eve of the wedding. This particular episode is recorded in her diary on 4 October 1802:

> I gave him the wedding ring – with how deep a blessing! I took it from my forefinger where I had worn it the whole of the night before – he slipped it again onto my finger and blessed me fervently.[33]

For Pamela Woof the episode has a deep significance: "this seems to be her sacramental benediction and his pledge of a continued shared life."[34] This was also a ritual, good-luck gesture that while sealing an almost incestuous tie demonstrates how the house as haven could be threatened by storms and how the "within" cannot ignore a "without" that is thickening around it. In her works, we can find examples scattered around almost everywhere of this inner awareness that the conquests of today are transient gifts and that the internal and external worlds are dangerously interchangeable, in particular, in her poem, "Address to a Child during a Boisterous Winter Evening":

> What way does the wind come? What way does he go?
> He rides over the water, and over the snow,
> Through wood, and through vale; and o'er rocky height
> Which the goat cannot climb, takes his sounding flight;
> He tosses about in every bare tree,
> As, if you look up, you plainly may see;
> ...
> As soon as 'tis daylight tomorrow, with me,
> You shall go to the orchard, and then you will see
> That he has been there, and made such a rout,
> And cracked the branches, and strewn them about;
> Heaven grant that he spare but that one upright twig
> That looked up at the sky so proud and big
> All last summer, as well you know,
> Studded with apples, a beautiful show!

---

[33] Robert Gittings and Jo Manton, *Dorothy Wordsworth*, Oxford, 1985, 138.
[34] Dorothy Wordsworth, *The Grasmere Journals*, ed. Pamela Woof, Oxford, 1991, 46.

Hark! over the roof he makes a pause,
And growls as if he would fix his claws
Right in the slates, and with a huge rattle,
Drive them down, like men in a battle:
– But let him range round; he does us no harm,
We build up the fire, we're snug and warm;
Untouched by his breath see the candle shines bright,
And burns with a clear and steady light.

Books have we to read, but that half-stifled knell,
Alas! 'tis the sound of the eight o'clock bell.
– Come now, we'll to bed! and when we are there,
He may work his own will, and what shall we care?
He may knock at the door – we'll not let him in;
May drive at the windows – we'll laugh at his din;
Let him seek his own home wherever it be;
Here's a *cozie* warm house for Edward and me.[35]

That this short poem should end with lines that seem to emulate Shakespearian sonnets in making fun of the blasts of the wind, with its destructive force that cannot harm the happiness of the inhabitants of the cottage, does not allow us to ignore the fact that there are so many threatening metaphors for the outer world beating against the walls, windows and doors – too many to be ignored.

In order to please William, Dorothy started to keep diaries recording in every minute detail the encounters and sensorial experiences of the day: she wrote down all the smells, colours and slight noises that somehow struck her, precious notes, the revelatory signs of a special daily event. What she wrote is fragmentary and tense, at times it dwells on things, or turns and goes back on itself in a curious form of stream of consciousness, restrained by her will-power and revealed by small graphic marks, pauses, silences. Yet neither her diaries nor her poems were to be published until after her death. Dorothy categorically refused to publish her works, except for a few short poems included in the Appendix to William's *Collected Works* that appeared in 1815 and 1840, saying "my sister's works". She herself admitted that she was afraid to reveal herself, or simply to show a pride that was not fitting for the image she had created for

[35] *Woman Romantic Poets 1785-1832: An Anthology*, ed. Jennifer Breen, London 1992, 128-29 (see also *Antologia delle Poetesse Romantiche Inglesi*, I, 606-608).

herself and her dear ones. "I should detest the idea of setting myself up as an Author",[36] she wrote to Catharine Clarkson in December, 1810, and confessed to Lady Beaumont "I have not those powers which Coleridge thinks I have – I know it. My only merits are my devotedness to those I love and I hope a charity towards all mankind."[37] But in her diaries and poems, once again, the female botanical eye is hard at work. Dorothy names plants and flowers with expertise, while her ear recognizes birds from their songs, and effortlessly her vision circumscribes her own space, dwelling in safety even within a whole valley, "An eye like a camera's", as Elizabeth Hardwick was to write.[38] In Dorothy's pages, nature itself seems to become a house, a place of integration of thought and imagination, the destiny of the interiority of the poetic "I", so much so that in the pages of her poems and her diaries all the confines between the micro – and macrocosm, between within and without, seem to have been suppressed:

> Friday May 14th 1802. A very cold morning – hail & snow showers all day. We went to Brothers wood, intending to get plants …. William teased himself with seeking an epithet for the Cuckow. I sat a while upon my last summers seat the mossy stone – William's unemployed beside me, & the space between where Coleridge has so often lain. The oak trees are just putting forth yellow knots of leaves. The ashes with their flowers passing away & leaves coming out. The blue Hyacinth is not quite full blown – Gowans are coming out – marsh marigolds in full glory – the little star plant a star without a flower. We took home a great load of Gowans & planted them in the cold about the orchard. After dinner I worked bread then came & mended stockings beside William he fell asleep.[39]

Elizabeth Hardwick once again notes:

> By writing her journal she spoke of her belief in the supreme value of their lives. The morning, the butterflies, the mists, the stops at lonely cottages, the views, the streams, were magnified and glorified …. She

---

[36] *The Letters of William and Dorothy Wordsworth*, ed. Ernest de Selincourt, Oxford, 1967, II, 454.
[37] *Letters of Dorothy Wordsworth: A Selection*, xiii.
[38] *Seduction and Betrayal: Women and Literature*, ed. Elizabeth Hardwick, London and New York, 1975, 151.
[39] Dorothy Wordsworth, *The Grasmere Journals*, 99.

> looked, she walked, she climbed; she returned home and with her pen looked and walked and climbed again.[40]

However, this natural world, this nature-house, was not to remain as uncontaminated as she desired, but was marked by a strange anxiety that Dorothy could not control. The following poem, "Floating Island (At Hawkshead: An Incident In The Schemes Of Nature)", is significant in this regard:

> ....
> Once did I see a slip of earth
> By throbbing waves long undermined,
> Loosed from its hold; – *how* no one knew,
> But all might see it float, obedient to the wind.
> ....
> Food, shelter, safety, there they find
> There berries ripen, flowerets bloom;
> There insects live their lives – and die:
> A peopled *world* it is; in size a tiny room.
>
> And thus through many seasons' space
> This little Island may survive
> But Nature, though we mark her not,
> Will take away – may cease to give.
>
> Perchance when you are wandering forth
> Upon some vacant sunny day
> Without an object, hope, or fear,
> Thither your eyes may turn – the Isle is passed away.
>
> Buried beneath the glittering lake!
> Its place no longer to be found,
> Yet the lost fragments shall remain,
> To fertilize some other ground.[41]

Here the poet is celebrating the natural cycles that traditionally stand for the perpetual renewal of life, yet the fragility of this floating island seems to overshadow quite another fate, one marked by death rather

---

[40] *Seduction and Betrayal*, 151.

[41] *Woman Romantic Poets 1785-1832*, 131-32 (see also *Antologia delle Poetesse Romantiche Inglesi*, 610).

than rebirth. We are struck, therefore, by the tone of this poetic voice that begins by celebrating the triumph of the presence and fertility of nature only to end by singing of a natural world which is overcome by arbitrary, absent and transitory factors. For Anne K. Mellor this poem is a metaphor of a fleeting self: a self that can be visible or invisible, appearing and disappearing in an instant, partly created by other people's gaze and deeply rooted in the ground of the surrounding natural world. It is in many ways the ambiguity that Susan Levin tracks down in another of Dorothy Wordsworth's poem, "A Winter's Ramble", whose central lines "My youthful wishes all fulfilled, / Wishes matured by thoughtful choice", and final line "How could I but rejoice" seem to insinuate the doubt that there is after all no complete happiness and absolute fulfilment for the speaking subject.[42]

However, what did Dorothy represent for William? Undoubtedly somewhat more than a silent presence, if we are to believe the famous lines he dedicated to her: "She, in the midst of all, preserv'd me still / A Poet, made me seek beneath that name / My office upon earth, and nowhere else."[43]

William Wordsworth did indeed draw direct poetic inspiration from Dorothy's *Grasmere Journals*, of which there are many examples: from the pages written on 27 May 1800, he wrote "Beggars"; from those of 3 October, "Resolution and Independence"; from 15 April 1802, "I wandered lonely as a Cloud" and from 29 July in the same year, "Composed upon Westminster Bridge", and so on. The gift of Dorothy's imagination, with all its details, while remaining creative and spiritual, was at her brother's disposal. William repaid this by immortalizing the fellowship in some famous poems, of which "Lines Composed a Few Miles above Abbey" (XXVI - ll. 114-122) and *The Prelude* (Book XIV, ll. 231-232) are just two of the more memorable examples. Still, for William himself, Dorothy was to remain a being in the shadows, like Lucy she was "A violet by a mossy stone / Half hidden from the eye", a presence that was beautiful but hidden to the eye of even the person who loved her. Who was, then, the true Dorothy?

---

[42] Susan M. Levin, "Subtle Fire: Dorothy Wordsworth's Prose and Poetry", *The Massachussets Review*, XXI/2 (1980), 345-63.

[43] William Wordsworth, *The Prelude* (1805 version), X, 919-21, ed. Ernest de Selincourt, Revised Impression, London, 1969, 202.

The impressions of Coleridge, a faithful member of this unusual community, present us with the traits of an intelligent, sensitive woman, but above all describe her artistic intuition and her magnetic gaze, ever attentive to all the slightest natural phenomena: "She is a woman indeed! – in mind, I mean, & heart – … her manners are simple, ardent, impressive – … her eye watchful in minutest observation of nature – and her taste a perfect electrometer …. "[44]

It is, however, De Quincey's acute, intriguing portrait of her that creates doubt and forces us to seek further. He writes:

> Immediately behind her moved a lady, shorter, slighter, and perhaps, in all other respects, as different from her in personal characteristics as could have been wished for the most effective contrast. Her face was of Egyptian brown, rarely in a woman of English birth, had I seen a more determinate gipsy tan. Her eyes were not soft, as Mrs. Wordsworth's, nor were they fierce or bold; but they were wild and startling, and hurried in their motion. Her manner was warm and even ardent; her sensibility seemed constitutionally deep; and some subtle fire of impassioned intellect apparently burned within her; which, being alternately pushed forward into a conspicuous expression by the irrepressible instincts of her temperament, and then immediately checked, in obedience to the decorum of her sex and age, and her maidenly condition, gave to her whole conversation, an air of embarrassment, and even of self-conflict, that was most distressing to witness.[45]

From this portrait emerges a woman who was restless, divided and passionate in search of rigour and a form of behaviour that she perhaps did not believe in or did recognize in herself. The violet hidden among the mossy stones was not, therefore, Dorothy, or was only one aspect of Dorothy. The other was mysterious, and fleeting, as is betrayed by her own gaze.

---

[44] *Collected Letters of Samuel Taylor Coleridge*, ed. Earl Leslie Griggs, Oxford, 1966, I, 330-31.

[45] Susan Levin, "Dorothy Wordsworth and the Women of Romanticism", in *Seduction and Betrayal*, 171-72.

HELEN MARIA WILLIAMS: THE SHAPING OF A POETIC IDENTITY

LIA GUERRA

When Helen Maria Williams edited her own *Poems on Various Subjects: with Introductory Remarks on the Present State of Science and Literature in France*, which was published in London in 1823, she was probably getting on, possibly over sixty, although the exact date of her birth is still a matter of debate. Her husband, John Hurford Stone, had died in 1818, and in 1819 she had issued her last effort of an historical-political nature, *Letters on Events Which Have Passed in France since the Restoration in 1815*. It comes as a surprise that it was as late as 1823 that Williams decided to go back to poetry after some thirty years of literary activity mainly dedicated to prose, the only exception being an "Ode on the Peace of Amiens", which in 1802 had provoked Napoleon's angry reaction and had cost her a day in prison. Apart from this, she had not published poetry since at least 1790, when she had introduced some poetical pieces, among them the famous "The Bastille, A Vision", into her first novel *Julia: a Novel; Interspersed with Some Poetical Pieces*.

Williams first visited France briefly in 1790, on the wave of her involvement with a young French couple who had been separated by law: Mons. du Fossé had been imprisoned and disinherited by a royal *lettre de cachet* because his father did not approve of his marriage out of the aristocracy. He was freed by the Revolution and could reclaim his patrimony. In 1791 she was back in Paris, where she turned into an almost permanent resident, taking part in that community of expatriates (made up mainly of members of the Dissenting and radical circles) that characterized in such a peculiar way the intellectual life in Paris in the last decades of the eighteenth century. These circles also fuelled the continuous swarming of people from England to France, a phenomenon that should be set in the proper context of a long tradition of radicalism, and not considered as the result of a sudden enthusiasm: radicalism had long been fostered in London, at 72, St Paul's Churchyard, the location of the bookshop of the Dissenter Joseph Johnson, who played host to people like Mary Wollstonecraft, Thomas Christie, Henry Fuseli, Joseph Priestley and other members of the Lunar Society. Williams was eventually forced to flee to Switzerland for six months when, in 1794, her political activity interfered with the Revolutionary authorities and the result of her short stay there took the shape of a travelogue, *Tour in Switzerland* (1798). In the meantime she had acquired a reputation for political engagement as an eyewitness reporter for English readers on the events of the Revolution in France, and also as a translator from French. For about thirty years, in fact, she had devoted herself mainly to writing non-fictional prose.

What therefore could be her motive for re-editing in 1823, at the end of a long career, some of her early youthful poems, together with some additions, and a very private dedication? Considering the fact that she had become famous during the 1780s for her poetry (her "Sonnet to Twilight" and her ode "To Sensibility", collected in the 1786 edition of *Poems*, are among her best works, in tune with that philosophy of Sensibility she was later to apply to the French Revolution), my suspicion is that she was trying to present her reading public with an image of herself that might conjure up images from the past, thereby simultaneously effacing the portrait of the passionate revolutionary lady she had been propagating in the meantime. Writing prose had meant, in a very peculiar phase of Williams' own history and of history at large, a revolution in her own personal style and an intrusion into masculine topics. And History was ready, by the 1820s, to influence change once more. The Restoration following 1815 and the general conservative political reaction which was its aftermath, certainly contributed to silence many bold voices, while at the same time witnessing the safe hold of the female poet on the literary world. As Stuart Curran maintains, discussing mid-eighteenth century female writing,

> … the rise of the novel threw starkly into relief the extent to which poetry had been sealed off as a male, upper-class fiefdom, requiring for its licence not simply birth and breeding, but a common education and exclusive standards of shared taste. That, of course, did not keep women from aspiring to it, whether like the Bluestockings by

> honoring the agreed terms or, like later women poets, by shifting the accepted grounds underneath generic expectations. By the 1820s, at the point that the term poetess attains common cultural currency, poetry too could be claimed to have become a woman's genre.[1]

Williams' career, characterized as it is by movements from poetry to prose and vice versa, seems to me to fit precisely into this scenario. In order to investigate the degree of her adherence to such a critical historical milieu, the following pages will attempt to explore the paratext – the complex side-phenomenon described by Genette and other authors[2] as being formed by the crossing of texts that move from and around a literary work – so as to outline the shaping of her identity as an author *tout court*.

Most of Williams' choices, between 1790 and 1820, in the political, literary and private spheres, had certainly irritated many of her English friends and prompted quite peevish reactions, especially among those groups of intellectual women in England who had previously appreciated her (Anna Seward, Mrs Piozzi). An improper lady, like many other female characters in History – one name, Mary Wollstonecraft, can stand for all – Williams, possibly spurred by necessity, was ready in 1823 to offer a portrait of herself in which she included glimpses of her early youth, texts that had appeared in earlier collections of *Poems*, lines included in other works, and many new compositions. The Introduction runs as follows:

> I feel that I have little to urge in behalf of these slight compositions, which I wish to preserve. They bear a character of melancholy that nature and early sorrows have made the habitual disposition of my mind; this is all I shall venture to say of them, for they scarcely deserve the honours of a grave defence. I have indeed endeavoured to correct some of their inaccuracies, yet I feel far more apprehension than usual at the publication of the present volume: this may be easily explained. I have long renounced any attempts in verse, confining my pen almost entirely to sketches of the events of the Revolution.[3]

---

[1] Stuart Curran, "Women Readers, Women Writers", in *The Cambridge Companion to British Romanticism*, ed. Stuart Curran, Cambridge, 1993, 182.

[2] Gérard Genette, *Palimpsestes: la littérature au second degré*, Paris, 1981; Philippe Lejeune, *Le pacte autobiographique*, Paris, 1975.

[3] Helen Maria Williams, Introduction to *Poems on Various Subjects: with Introductory Remarks on the Present State of Science and Literature in France*, London, 1823, ix.

In spite of its late date, this Introduction sounds surprisingly in tune with the expressions of anxiety and lack of assurance that had accompanied the publication of Williams' early works, perhaps in part because in 1823 her name did not elicit the same indulgent curiosity and respect that her early enthusiasm had provoked at the beginning of her French adventure. The renewed anxiety and uncertainty, connected with the return to poetry, might perhaps be read as an attempt to force the response of the audience, particularly the English audience, that had so promptly responded to her poetical writings, but had shown a less intense sympathy since the 1790s, when she had turned to political prose. Was she planning to refurbish her own identity with a safe varnish in order to put forward an image of herself more in keeping with that older self? However simplistic such an explanation might sound, it can be seen as part of a strategy of self-authorization that, by 1823, could more easily rely on new possibilities in the literary field and at the same time on decreasing political opportunities.

The question requires a careful analysis of the paratext accompanying her production, starting with her first published work, *Edwin and Eltruda. A Legendary Tale*, issued in 1782. The reading public was, at that first date, presented with a portrait of the author drawn by Andrew Kippis, one of the leaders of the Dissenter group to which the Williamses belonged and Helen's mentor for at least the first part of her career. The silhouette emerging from his "Advertisment by the Editor" is rather vague although certainly situated within the semantic area of reticence, timidity and, above all, anxiety. Williams, at the time a young girl, perhaps still in her teens, had recently moved to London with her mother and sisters from Scotland, and had received an irregular education, like many girls of her status. "Her sole instruction was derived from a virtuous, amiable and sensible mother", wrote Kippis, who also insisted on the elements of virtue and modesty that could win the sympathy of the readers. As to her previous years, Kippis tended to surround them with a halo of mystery: "[She] was removed, with her Family, in very early life, to a remote part of the kingdom .... In so a distant a situation, she had ... little access to books." As a conclusion, Kippis mentions young Williams' reluctance to publish, overcome only by the insistence of friends.[4]

Edwin and Eltruda heralded a poetical career characterized by enthusiastic adherence to the conventions of Sensibility: it is not surprising, therefore, that in the 1823 edition of *Poems*, Williams inserted immediately before the earlier *Edwin and Eltruda* her later text "Sensibility", which begins "In Sensibility's loved praise / I tune my trembling reed".[5] The portraits she draws of the characters of the legend correspond to those conventions, but the same is also true of the author's profile sketched by Kippis. His "Advertisment" seems to prompt a parallelism between the product of Williams' pen (the characters portrayed in the tale) and the producer, the writer herself, who is endowed with her own peculiar traits by analogy with the result of her poetic construction. The process of withdrawal, effected both in a metaphorical and in a literal sense by the presence of the voice of the Other – Dr Kippis' – places Williams within her own poetical objects, creating an effect of semantic redundancy. The immediate goal of Kippis' words was obviously to confer authority on Williams' entrance into the literary world and to acknowledge his own responsibility for the publication, thus taking away from her any suspicion of artistic presumption. His mention of Williams' incomplete education is part of a defensive strategy meant to justify any flaws in the text.

Dr Kippis is still involved in promoting the young female poet[6] on two further occasions: the first, when in 1783 she published an "Ode on the Peace" to celebrate the conclusion of the American Revolution, and subsequently in 1784 to introduce her *Peru. A Poem in Six Cantos*, a hymn to universal harmony dedicated to Mrs Montague. A seminal text for any understanding of her subsequent attitudes to the matter of history, this historical poem is centred on the European exploitation of South America, and was widely appreciated by her contemporaries. When she reissued *Peru* in her 1823 edition of *Poems*, she discussed her way of dealing with history in the Introduction:

---

[4] Quoted in Lionel D. Woodward, *Hélène-Maria Williams et ses amis* (1930), Geneva, 1977, 14.

[5] Williams, *Poems on Various Subjects*, 111-16.

[6] See Anne K. Mellor, "The Female Poet and the Poetess: Two Traditions of British Women's Poetry, 1780-1830", *Studies in Romanticism*, XXXVI/2 (1997), 261-76.

> I have not ventured to dignify [the Peruvian Tales in verse] with the appellation of historical, although they are chiefly composed of facts taken from Robertson's History of Spanish America .... In relating the adventures of that period, it was little necessary to seek to inspire interest by having recourse to fiction; misery and oppression have at all times composed the great materials of human history, and the fashion has not passed away; it may be traced from the fifteenth to the nineteenth century, from the invasion of Peru to that of Naples.[7]

What caught her attention in this reconstruction of some episodes of the *Conquest* was the fate of individuals, the misery of families disrupted by violence, in short, the breaking of family ties that she viewed as the immediate consequence of any project of usurpation. A parallel attitude led her to read anew a much-debated passage of English history first in the "Irregular Fragment", published in her Poems of 1786, and later on, in 1788, in her "Poem On the Bill Passed for Regulating the Slave-Trade", with which she took up a commonly-shared political interest (Hannah More and Ann Yearsley also wrote poems on the topic in the same year). The subject was deeply felt by the Dissenters, strongly affected by the debate on tolerance since Locke's *Epistola de Tolerantia* had appeared in 1689.

Thanks to the generous subscription of friends and admirers organized by George Hardinge, a new collection of *Poems* in two volumes was published in 1786, which Williams chose to introduce herself and dedicate to the Queen. Apparently she did not feel the necessity of a mentor, but the persona emerging from her words is once more the projection of her message – as the explicit reference to her first publication in the Preface seems to suggest:

> The apprehension which it becomes me to feel, in submitting these Poems to the judgement of the Public, may perhaps plead my excuse, for detaining the reader to relate, that they were written under the disadvantages of a confined education .... My first production, Edwina and Eltruda, was composed to amuse some solitary hours, and without any view to publication. Being shewn to Dr Kippis, he declared that it deserved to be committed to the press, and offered to take upon himself the task of introducing it into the world.

The process of shaping her own authorial identity continued

[7] Williams, Introduction to *Poems on Various Subjects*, x-xi.

therefore with acts of denial: the source of her strength seemed to lie in the admission of her weakness. This is true for her characters, as her already-quoted words on Peru seemed to imply, but also for herself, confirming that the boundaries between subject and object are still uncertain:

> When I survey such an evidence of the zeal of my friends to serve me, as the following honourable and extensive list affords, I have cause for exultation in having published this work by subscription. They who know my disposition, will readily believe that the tear which fills my eye, while I thank them for their generous exertions, flows not from the consideration of the benefits that have arisen from their friendship. It is to that friendship itself, that my heart pays a tribute of affection which I will not attempt to express – for my pen is unfaithful to my purpose.[8]

Anxiety and reticence are therefore the dominant topics. But the actual act of speaking – and the central position of the self in the utterance – allows for an evaluation of the degree of her artistic consciousness and a questioning of the supposed modesty explicitly worded by the author. Let us consider briefly some contemporary reactions to Williams' work. The image of her as author-character is further illuminated by Anne Seward's reaction to *Peru* in 1784, in a sonnet published in *The Gentleman's Magazine*: Williams is described as a "poetic sister" caught in the act of seizing "the epic lyre", as a "female bard" invited to guard "from obtrusive lyres my well-sung story"; or by Elisa Woolwich who, in the pages of the same magazine, caught a glimpse of the transgressive strength of a woman who had been able to give up a leisured life with its waste of intellectual capacities in order to impose the power of reason.[9] The figure of the author thus shifts readily from the role of subject to that of poetic object and the shaping of her poetic identity – initiated with acts of denial – is delegated to others.

In 1787 *The European Magazine* published a "Sonnet on Seeing Helen Maria Williams Weep at a Tale of Distress" by "Axiologus", pseudonym of the sixteen-year-old William Wordsworth. Once more

---

[8] Helen Maria Williams, Preface to *Poems in Two Volumes*, 1786 (also to be found on Project Gutenberg's Poems: http://www.gutenberg.org/files/11054/11054-8.txt, vol. 1).

[9] Quoted in Woodward, *Hélène-Maria Williams et ses amis*, 17.

the poet is subject and object at the same time, in a rhetorical exchange of a dramatic kind dominated by the beginning of the Wordsworthian sestet: "That tear proclaims – in thee each virtue dwells."[10] That tear immediately evokes the tear she had mentioned in the Introduction to her 1786 *Poems*, already quoted, but the echo sends us back to the "Sonnet to Twilight", in the same collection, which registers a melancholy bent to those "shadowy" moments of declining haze and sounds that call for the "luxury"[11] of tears. The sensibility engendered by one text can breed a new text: the tear becomes a sign of union between creator and object of the creation, thus giving rise to another redundancy – but of a dialogical, dramatic nature. This dramatic quality was also present in the Advertisment to the first edition of *Peru*, 1784, where Williams spoke of herself in the third person, confirming the strategy of inadequacy that draws on a denial to evaluate: "The author has only aimed at a simple detail of some few incidents that make a part of that romantic story, where the unparalleled sufferings of an innocent and amiable people, form the most affecting subject of true pathos."[12]

The point of contact between the poet and the prose writer can be found in the publication of her novel *Julia*, in 1790, a few months before her first visit to Paris. The contemporary reaction was largely positive, mainly on moral grounds, and the text was in keeping with the extremely rich production of novels of Sensibility, written mainly by women, in the 1780s. What interests us here is the fact that it contains "The Bastille, A Vision", a poem which marks the beginning of the process of destabilization – albeit temporary – of the rules of sentimentality, and which "briefly disturbs the otherwise impeccably private world of Helen Maria Williams' sentimental novel"; here we have, in the opinion of Vivien Jones, "the pervasive transgression of gendered ideological and generic boundaries which characterises her later writings".[13] In the Advertisement Williams proclaims her full

---

[10] [William Wordsworth] "Sonnet on Seeing Miss Helen Maria Williams Weep at a Tale of Distress", *European Magazine*, XL (1787), 202.

[11] Williams, "Sonnet to Twilight", in *Poems in Two Volumes*, I.

[12] Helen Maria Williams, Advertisment to *Peru. A Poem in Six Cantos*, London, 1784, quoted in Mark Ledden, "Perishable Goods", *Michigan Feminist Studies*, IX (1994-1995), 12.

[13] Vivien Jones, "Women Writing Revolution: Narratives of History and Sexuality in Wollstonecraft and Williams", in *Beyond Romanticism*: *New Approaches to Texts and*

adherence to the genre, but she adds some interesting words, in her final paragraph, which lend support to our metadiscursive interest: "I have been encouraged, by the indulgence which my former poems have met with, to intersperse some poetical pieces in these volumes; but the uncertainties of being able to engage the continuance of favour, leads me to offer these farther productions in verse, with as little confidence as this first attempt in prose."[14]

Williams arrived in France in July 1790, in time to witness the celebrations of the anniversary of the storming of the Bastille, imbued with the ideologies of the Bluestocking women and of the radical circles: a political background that was to remain virtually unaltered through the years.[15] That is to say, Williams reached Paris already inclined towards a deeply biased reading of events, anxious to test history from the point of view of the eyewitness, but above all driven by her involvement in a personal situation, the predicament of her friends, the du Fossés.

Her novel *Julia* had already underlined the function of Sensibility as a vital force in interpersonal relationships, and there was room now to see it actually at work. The Revolution set her in motion and prompted her to move on to prose. The only allusion, in the *Letters*, to her role as a prose writer suggests that she was impelled only by the mode of the expression, perhaps another mark of uneasiness: "What, indeed, but friendship, could have led my attention from the annals of imagination to the records of politics; from the poetry to the prose of human life?"[16] Three months later she returned to England and set out to prepare for the press what was to be the first volume of *Letters from France*, which would appear within the year and was to be followed by twelve more volumes covering some thirty years of French history.

The experience of travel therefore involved a shift in genre: in adopting the travelogue, Williams chose a socially legitimized genre,

---

Contexts 1780-1833, eds Stephen Copley and John Whale, London and New York, 1992, 178-79.

[14] Helen Maria Williams, Advertisment to *Julia, A Novel. Interspersed with some Poetical Pieces*, London, 1790, iv.

[15] A comparison of the imagery she employed in "The Bastille, A Vision", composed in reaction to the fall of the Bastille before her visit to Paris, and the description of the actual visit recorded in the first volume of *Letters Written in France* shows that the physical impact of the place did not substantially modify her attitude.

[16] Helen Maria Williams, *Letters Written in France, in the Summer 1790, to a Friend in England, containing various anecdotes relative to the French Revolution, and Memoirs of Mons. and Madame Du F-*, Oxford, 1989, 195.

and by the same token abandoned poetry. The renunciation sounds at times as if it had been forced upon her, for example in a passage in Letter XIII where the moonlit landscape is said to exceed the limits of the instrument of prose: "I will not attempt to describe, lest my pen should stray into rhyme."[17]

Letters Written in France presents the customary structure of the travel book "told in personal letters". There are twenty-six such letters, twelve of which relate to her Paris sojourn, the thirteenth being metaphorically and literally transitional (it acts as a point of conjunction between the first and the second part of the book and describes the transit from Paris to Rouen); the other twelve letters are set in Rouen. The latter include a highly significant core represented by Letters XVI-XXII, that tell the exemplary story of the du Fossés, a sort of *mise-en-abyme* of the whole book, intended to offer the reader an inferential and apologetic key for an understanding of Williams' stance with respect to the French Revolution and her political and emotional involvement in it. The argumentative purpose of the episode is accompanied by an emotional role intended to appeal to the reader's sympathy. The last letter, Letter XXVI, from London, acts as an Epilogue.

It has been rightly stressed that Williams in her writings on the Revolution repeatedly "painted herself as the English outsider/'spectatrice' of revolutionary events and politics, while simultaneously making a public spectacle of herself, her sentimental attachments, and the domestic virtues she espoused",[18] and this once again seems to point to the author's double function as subject/object.

Curiously enough, and against the usual practice of travel literature, neither Preface nor Advertisement is appended to the text to justify the rupture the trust previously established with the reader. Probably Williams is adopting a different strategy and it is therefore necessary for us to read between the lines, and see if we can unravel her writing project through an analysis of her rhetoric of enunciation.

First of all the choice of genre – and more precisely the use of the private letter as a vehicle for information – is perfectly in keeping with historically recorded choices made by women, which allow them as writers to smuggle forbidden messages under the cover of private

---

[17] *Ibid.*, 97.

[18] Mary A. Favret, "Spectatrice as Spectacle: Helen Maria Williams at Home in the Revolution", *Studies in Romanticism*, XXXII (1993), 275.

discourses with strong connotations of usefulness.[19] But the historical context in this case prompts further reflection: the perception of the unique moment, the urgent need to be there, to record one's presence – to be, as it were, in the floodlight of history – together with the certainty that the moment was well worth living, and particularly well worth telling, legitimizes even private writing. The simple human subject seems to receive extra light from a specific movement of history. Consequently the context itself turns any such writing into an authentic testimony and renders credible the subject of writing who is presented as the biographer of her own time.

Being private by definition, intimate writing escapes codification, eschewing rules that even revolutionary and radical contents impose on other genres. The choice of the epistolary register – that writing of the self that, historically, clears the path for the woman writer into the world of letters – leads to a full exploitation of the tension generated by the clash between a colloquial style and a heroic feeling of testimony. "I have seen what I relate, and therefore I have written with confidence; I have there been trading on the territory of History, and a trace of my footsteps will perhaps be left":[20] these words by Williams appeared in the 1823 Introduction but are a clear illustration of the intimate bond between enunciation and testimony. The physical presence of the writer on the site of the events is a guarantee of her authority, and her commitment to recording her experience testifies to the value of travelling as an instrument of knowledge, capable of leading one to the truth. In her *Letters* Williams programmatically narrates through anecdotes, as the long title suggests, using them as examples intended to strengthen personal impressions: sometimes she introduces characters, both anonymous and famous (for example, Madame de Sillery), with the result of making her own personality redundant: a less direct strategy to enact the same mechanism of identification and self-justification that had been expressed more explicitly in other works.

Epistolary writing obviously implies an addressee, but the instances of direct emotional appeal to the reader are rather rare in the text, where the maximum concentration is on the sender and the

---

[19] See Rosa Maria Colombo, "Donne e letteratura: da Aphra Behn a Jane Austen", *L'età di Johnson: La letteratura inglese del secondo Settecento*, ed. Franca Ruggieri, Rome, 1998, 259-61.

[20] Introduction to Williams, *Poems on Various Subjects*, ix-x.

message itself. The addressee appears as a vague "you", mentioned at the beginning of letters in just a few instances, and normally with a meta-narrative function. This happens for instance when Williams seems to hint at the writing of letters as a way of authenticating history and as the fulfilment of an inescapable social duty, defined before setting out (Letters I, VII, IX, XIV); only in two cases can we guess at a closer familiarity with a "you" that could be identified with a specific female addressee (Letters VII and XXIII). Only two instances refer to letters received and in these cases the answer tends to intensify argumentative matters in order to justify the enthusiasm exhibited: they therefore appear somewhat instrumental and tend to condition the writing register. The strategy of involving the readers from an emotional point of view is effected through the long narrative of the tale of misfortune of the du Fossés which serves a double function: not only does it justify the enthusiasm that might perhaps raise perplexity in the addressee; it also serves a purely phatic function, in the attempt to create a communion of feeling, even to guide the reading of the text in those instances that might constitute a cultural gap, as in Letter II. In the opening letter of the second volume the underlying meaning of the tale of misfortune is stated quite explicitly:

> I again take up the pen to write to you at the Chateau of Mons. Du F-, from which place I last year sent you the history of his misfortunes; those misfortunes which have led me to love, as well as admire, the revolution. For you know we are so framed that, while we contemplate the deliverance of millions with a sublime emotion of wonder and exultation, the tears of tenderness, the throbbings of sympathy, are reserved for the moment when we select one happy family from the great national group, and when, amidst the loud acclamations of an innumerable multitude, we can distinguish the soothing sounds of domestic felicity.[21]

The *Letters* of 1790 register many of the uncertainties experienced by Williams, for the first time trying her hand at reflexive prose, in the process of "authorizing herself": she frequently underlines the inadequacy of the written word to register a climate, an atmosphere, to transcodify the feeling, and also suggests that the reader – and the "you" in the first place – should actively participate in the

[21] Letter I, in Williams, *Letters from France*, London, 1792, II, 1.

construction of its sense. Reticence is also exhibited both in the suspension of a socio-political judgement ("My love for the French Revolution, is the natural result of sympathy, and therefore, my political creed is entirely an affair of the heart"[22]) and in renouncing any evaluation in the sphere of visual arts.[23] If we consider this attitude independently of the complex process of the shaping of an identity, it might appear in sharp contrast with the portrait of determinacy and courage that Williams' biographers have handed down to posterity. This apparent ambiguity can perhaps be illuminated when we notice how "as the Revolution unveils an Englishwoman's private theatrical, it also becomes her stage",[24] highlighting Williams' disregard of the conflict between the public sphere of print culture and the sociable salon: "Her published *Letters* open the salon onto the larger, less select stage of the reading public while at the same time exploiting the ideological force of domesticity, transparency and femininity."[25] The theatrical paradigm that determines the observer's point of view has been thoroughly analysed and is obvious to any reader who considers the number of terms that are connected with this specific semantic area (spectacle, theatre, spectators, amphitheatre, scene, vision). Popular response to the French Revolution was also fashioned by the language of the stage and even Edmund Burke, initially, tended to recognize the quality of performance in events in France. Wordsworth himself, visiting the ruined site of the Bastille, unable to feel emotionally transported, records having passed too abruptly "Into a theatre, of which the stage / Was busy with an action far advanced".[26] The metaphor survives in the critical idiom, as testified by the Preface to a book on the topic.[27]

A final consideration: the moment Williams, with her *Letters*, intruded into the sphere of competence traditionally ascribed to male authors, she tended to understate the role this publication had in reshaping her literary career by screening it with a sentimental façade, a façade which bore heavily on the events narrated. The progress of

---

[22] Letter IX, in Williams, *Letters Written in France, in the Summer 1790*, 66.
[23] Letter X, *ibid.*, 75.
[24] Favret, "Spectatrice as Spectacle", 278.
[25] *Ibid.*, 276, n.9.
[26] William Wordsworth, Book IX, ll. 94-95, in *The Prelude*, ed. E. De Selincourt, Oxford, 1959, 319-20.
[27] Anders Iversen, *The Impact of the French Revolution on English Literature*, Aarhus, 1990, 7.

literacy and social activity of eighteenth-century upper-and middle-class women has been widely investigated. Comparatively few women dared openly to challenge the accusation of biological and intellectual inferiority clearly meant to curb and play down their cultural awakening. However, Williams, in contrast, never chose to use pseudonyms, or to withdraw from the public world: she tested herself in all the aesthetic forms in which male writers excelled; she strove to work her way out of the female sphere to which she should have remained confined. Contemporary conservative female writers reacted rather aggressively to her daring shift to political engagement: in her *Letters on the Female Mind Addressed to Miss Helen Maria Williams* (1793) Laetitia Matilda Hawkins invited women to be "very careful to do nothing to provoke our superiors to take away the lamp they allowed us"[28] and masked her political dissent to the content of *Letters* with a full sexist assault. The French Revolution channelled a complex socio-political education into the path of fiction, and brought to light the necessity for empathy. The female poet became eyewitness and reporter but she derived this function from her sympathetic nature: to write and to publish *Letters* represents a necessary testimonial act. The shaping of a poetic identity has to go by way of history through the personal story of individuals.

[28] Quoted in Ledden, "Perishable Goods", 2.

Creating a public Voice

LISTING THE BUSY SOUNDS: ANNA SEWARD, MARY ROBINSON AND THE POETIC CHALLENGE OF THE CITY

TIMOTHY WEBB

The varied and complicated reception of the city, and the new pressures and experiences generated by the rapidly growing influence of the urban, left a mark on English writing whose full complexity has yet to be unravelled. Male poets, in particular, showed a tendency to be anxious and to compare the achievement and the experience of life in the contemporary city to earlier and more agreeable classical models, or to set the urban unfavourably against the comforting charms and pleasures of the country by resorting to the comparative register provided by the pastoral model. William Cowper, for instance, described the damaging effects of commerce in *The Task* where he eloquently attacked the "smoke, [and] … the eclipse / That Metropolitan volcano's make, / Whose Stygian throats breathe darkness all day long"; his exposure of the effects of "madness in the head / And folly in the heart" may have answered to a deeply personal need, to a timidity which was neurotic even at times paranoiac, yet Cowper's antithesis between the vices of the city and the virtues of the country articulated and in its turn influenced a social anxiety which was much more than merely personal.[1] Such difficulties continued to affect male writers, especially the poets, throughout the nineteenth century, so that G. Robert Stange could label them, with some justification, the "frightened poets". As he put it: "… most of the English writers in the time of Victoria repressed their knowledge of the city, just as they repressed their knowledge of sex – and for the

[1] *The Task*, III, 736-38, 741-42, in *The Poems of William Cowper*, eds John D. Baird and Charles Ryskamp, 2 vols, Oxford, 1985, I, 181.

same reasons: Puritanism had taught them the habit of repression, and they were afraid."[2]

Yet it might be argued that, even if this suggestive formulation is undeniably correct in many ways, it is all too easy to leave out of consideration several facts of central importance. In the first place, we must allow sufficiently for the force of British cities other than London. Within the equation, London is usually taken to define "city", as it grows in size and scope, and its very inclusiveness and multiplicity may seem amply to justify such an assumption; but this apparent inclusiveness does not allow adequately for the somewhat different experiences of the urban offered by, for example, Birmingham, Manchester, Leeds and Glasgow.

Secondly, such a reading of the city is essentially class-orientated and usually presents the perspective of the prosperous and the privileged, or the relatively privileged. While this perspective is often valuable, it tends not to admit, or not to admit sufficiently, that there may be other points of vantage that are equally valid. Characteristically, it imposes the perspectives of the polite, of "literature", while ignoring other approaches which are often less polished but which have a vitality of their own which should not be ignored in any account of attempts to come to terms with the possibilities of the urban.[3] Some interesting examples of these alternative approaches can be found in Roy Palmer's pioneering anthology *A Touch on the Times: Songs of Social Change, 1770 to 1914*.[4] The ballad, in particular, is often alert to the cost of change, to the hard conditions of labour and to the unjust divisions of class (see, for example, "The State of Great Britain, or a Touch at the Times"[5]) or to the questionable gains of increased prosperity (see "The Scenes of Manchester"[6]). Yet it can present a visit to the city as an adventure and an encounter with the new, which may sometimes turn out to be

---

[2] G. Robert Stange, "The Frightened Poets", in *The Victorian City: Images and Realities*, eds H.J. Dyos and Michael Wolff, London and Boston, 1973, 479.

[3] See, for example, the accounts in Martha Vicinus, *The Industrial Muse: A Study of Nineteenth-Century British Working-Class Literature*, London, 1974; and Judith Pascoe, "The Spectacular *Flâneuse*: Women Writers and the City", in *Romantic Theatricality: Gender, Poetry, and Spectatorship*, Ithaca and London, 1997, 130-62 (an account of Mary Robinson to which I am much indebted).

[4] *A Touch on the Times: Songs of Social Change, 1770 to 1914*, ed. Roy Ernest Palmer, Harmondsworth, 1974.

[5] *Ibid.*, 88-90.

[6] *Ibid.*, 62-64.

dangerous or morally ambivalent, but which also exhibits an energy and a vitality to which many responded. So, the ballad presentations of Bartholomew Fair find much more to celebrate than Wordsworth's account in *The Prelude*; so even "The Scenes of Manchester" provides a complicating enrichment to the descriptions provided by Engels in *The Condition of the English Working Class*.

Thirdly, and crucially, this account of urban anxiety specifically excludes the female viewpoint, although such a restricted and restrictive view is as limiting as one which confines itself to the reactions of any one social class. Women did play increasingly significant roles in the city, although for most male writers, especially poets, they were either invisible or excluded from full artistic consideration, as prostitutes or actresses; such optical tactics largely "erased the presence of more affluent urban women".[7] Traditional accounts of the "Romantic city" tend to omit or to minimize shopping, fashion and the horse-riding and carriage-riding and other regular practices of prosperity. Judith Pascoe reminds us that William Wordsworth "speaks from personal, male perspective" as does De Quincey; our received emphases on the life of the city have been influenced and directed "not by the evidence of women's active presence" but by "constructions of Romanticism" (essentially, as feminist interpreters would claim, a male phenomenon). She argues in some detail for a recognition of Wordsworth's strategic blindness: "One cannot help but be struck by the several ways in which Wordsworth mutes the presence of women on his remembered London streets."[8] Yet it is worth remembering that, in some ways, neither Wordsworth nor De Quincey was typical; many of the prose writers (notably, Hazlitt, Lamb, Hunt and the contributors to the *The London Magazine*) were much more engaged with the pleasures and excitements of city life. If we exclude such elements, we are indulging a narrow and specialized view of "the Romantic". On the other hand, what Wordsworth and De Quincey were able to register, in their different ways, was the transformation of London from a town (or even a town within a town) with its many reassuring comforts, into a

---

[7] Pascoe, *Romantic Theatricality*, 135.
[8] *Ibid.*, 136.

larger city, a *terra incognita* in which, deprived of "all the ballast of familiar life", the individual could no longer feel at home.[9]

A survey of the city poetry written by women in this period does suggest that, for the most part, women poets did not extensively engage with the phenomenon of the city, as opposed to the town. Raymond Williams once notably claimed that "perception of the new qualities of the modern city had been associated, from the beginning, with a man walking, as if alone, in its streets".[10] His influential account in *The Country and the City* (1973) supports this claim, not least by its accounts of William Wordsworth and Blake but, insofar as the claim is true, it would seem to exclude most women writers, not least of the Romantic period. The phenomenon of a woman walking, as if alone, on the streets of the city was more or less unthinkable at that time, especially for the respectable. As Janet Wolff has written "Women could not stroll alone in the city".[11] This central limitation certainly affected the relation between the woman writer and the city; not least, it posed problems of perspective and of intimacy. In many cases, it may have discouraged or prevented any creative engagement. Yet these restrictions and these limitations should not deceive us into neglecting the fact that a number of women poets also contributed to the poetic treatment of the modern city. Examples include Joanna Baillie whose "London" observed from the distance of Hampstead is "a goodly sight through the clear air" and which gradually assumes the recognizable features of an urban sublime, especially after dark when one can mark "Her luminous canopy" and hear the "roar of many wheels"; Anna Barbauld who offers an extended treatment of London in "Eighteen Hundred and Eleven" where commerce exacts its inevitable penalty ("Crime walks thy streets, Fraud earns her unblessed bread") and where the city's greatness troublingly reminds

---

[9] Wordsworth's phrase for the effects of finding himself in a crowd, in *The Prelude* VII, 603 (1805-1806 version only).

[10] Raymond Williams, *The Country and the City*, Frogmore, 1975, 280. This sentence is cited by Deborah Epstein Nord as one of the epigraphs to *Walking the Victorian Streets: Women, Representation, and the City*, Ithaca and London, 1995, and is referred to on page 1 where she offers her extended translation and apparent endorsement: "As Raymond Williams rightly remarks, the entire project of representing and understanding the exhilarating and distressing new phenomenon of urban life began, in some important sense, with this figure of the lone man who walked with impunity, aplomb, and a penetrating gaze." See also page 11.

[11] Janet Wolff, "The Invisible *Flâneuse*: Women and the Literature of Modernity", in *The Problems of Modernity*, ed. Andrew Benjamin, London, 1989, 148.

her of the fate of other great and self-confident cities of the past such as Tadmor, Carthage, Troy and Babylon; Felicia Hemans whose "The Illuminated City" uses its urban setting to explore the insensitivities and moral complexities of a public celebration of military victory; and Letitia Elizabeth Landon's two poems – "St George's Hospital, Hyde-Park Corner", which explores the contrast between the "crowded street" and the painful intensities of life on the ward, and "Scenes in London: Piccadilly", which examines the wonders of the common street with its smoke, noise and dust set against the larger structure of the day and the sobering and questioning contexts of history which should cause us to examine more critically "The pressure of our actual life". All of these poems deserve much fuller attention but the present paper will focus on some engagements with the urban by two poets who were very different both from all of these and from each other – Anna Seward and Mary Robinson.[12]

Anna Seward

The case of Anna Seward (1742-1809) is interesting and indicative. Once known as "the Swan of Lichfield" and recognized as a writer of some significance, Seward was one of the poets who acknowledged the facts of industrial growth. Specifically, she focused on Birmingham rather than London yet the difficulties that she experienced with this subject are an indication of the larger and general challenges which it posed for the writer whether female or male. Seward's two poems on the subject, the sonnet "To Colebrooke Dale" (written *c.* 1785-87, published 1799) and the more extensive "Colebrook Dale" (written *c.* 1785-90, published 1810) provide evidence of the ambivalence of her own responses, her desire to recognize the importance of the industrial in environmental terms and her attempt to evolve an appropriate poetics set against a reluctance to abandon the past and its poetic models.[13] Coalbrookdale in Shropshire

---

[12] Texts of these poems can be found as follows: Joanna Baillie, "London" and Letitia Elizabeth Landon, "Scenes in London: Piccadilly", in *Romantic Women Poets 1770-1838: An Anthology*, ed. Andrew Ashfield, Manchester, 1995, 100-101, 210-12; Anna Barbauld, "Eighteen Hundred and Eleven", Felicia Hemans, "The Illuminated City", and Letitia Elizabeth Landon, "St George's Hospital, Hyde Park Corner", in *Romantic Women Poets: an Anthology*, ed. Duncan Wu, Oxford, 1997, 10-18, 577-78, 607-609.

[13] "Colebrook" (or "Colebrooke"), it might be argued, recalls an original designation, whereas "Coalbrook" embodies in itself the very ambivalence that exercised Anna Seward.

had assumed importance in the industrial revolution because it had brought together the natural resources of coal and ironstone and Abraham Darby's revolutionary technique for smelting iron ore with coke. Darby's products were first transported by barge to Bristol and then to customers across a wider world. The initial achievements of Coalbrookdale were a source of pride to those who had created them; the iron bridge, in particular, also attracted numerous artists. Seward's two poems, one long and one short, are testament to some uncertainty in spelling which may, or may not be, merely orthographic but, much more suggestively, point to a crisis, or at least a challenge, in poetics which she articulates and engages with in ways which are suggestive for the development of English poetry.

The leading terms are set out in the sonnet, where Seward records an experience that might be compared to the more or less contemporary verses of the young Wordsworth and especially of Blake:

> Thy Genius, Coalbrooke, faithless to his charge,
> Amid thy woods and vales, thy rocks and streams,
> Formed for the Train that haunt poetic dreams,
> Naiads, and Nymphs, – now hears the toiling Barge
> And the swart Cyclops, ever-clanging forge
> Din in thy dells; – permits the dark-red gleams,
> From umbered fires on all thy hills, the beams,
> Solar and pure, to shroud with columns large
> Of black sulphureous smoke, that spread their veils
> Like funeral crape upon the sylvan robe
> Of thy romantic rocks, pollute thy gales,
> And stain thy glassy floods; – while o'er the globe
> To spread thy stores metallic, this rude yell
> Drowns the wild woodland song, and breaks the Poet's spell.[14]

Like Blake in "To the Muses", Seward here identifies a crisis for poetry but, unlike Blake in that poem, she specifically points to the challenge constituted by the emergence of the industrial in a landscape previously consecrated to the focused intensities of poetic meditation. Francis D. Klingender, who has discussed the question in knowledgeable detail, has expressed the artistic dilemma very clearly:

---

[14] My text is based on that in *Romantic Women Poets 1770-1838: An Anthology*, ed. Ashfield, 2. There is a lightly modernized version in *Eighteenth Century Women Poets: An Oxford Anthology*, ed. Roger Lonsdale, Oxford and New York, 1989, 316.

> As an industrial centre, Coalbrookdale also exercised an almost irresistible attraction over the artists of the English school of landscape drawing from its first beginnings to its culmination. This was largely due to the unique circumstance that the most modern and impressive industrial enterprise of the period was situated in an exceptionally romantic landscape. It thus became, as it were, the test place for studying the new relationship between men and nature created by large-scale industry.[15]

Klingender also quotes a passage from Arthur Young, who had visited the scene in 1776 and considered its significance in *Annals of Agriculture* (1785):

> Coalbrook Dale itself is a very romantic spot, it is a winding glen between two immense hills which break into various forms, and all thickly covered with wood, forming the most beautiful sheets of hanging wood. Indeed too beautiful to be much in unison with that variety of horrors art has spread at the bottom: the noise of the forges, mills, &c. with all their vast machinery, the flames bursting from the furnaces with the burning of the coal and the smoak of the lime kilns, are altogether sublime, and would unite well with craggy and bare rocks, like St. Vincent's at Bristol.[16]

Klingender's own account, which deliberately employs a scientific or perhaps business term in "test place", serves as a useful historical and sociological pointer as does his quotation from an astute and observant contemporary; together, these reactions help us to understand the conflicting factors which must have exercised a sensitive observer such as Seward.

The sonnet offers an early account of the evidence of the industrial: the "toiling Barge", the "ever-clanging forge", the "dark-red gleams", the polluted atmosphere of lines 6 to 12 that forms the central portion of the poem and which embraces the wider environment, the air and water. These intrusive particulars are at odds with the more pastoral mythologies which traditionally peopled the woods and vales and the "romantic rocks": Coalbrookdale has betrayed its trust in allowing

---

[15] Francis D. Klingender, *Art and the Industrial Revolution* (1947), ed. Arthur Elton, Chatham, 1968, 86-87. See especially, "Coalbrookdale and the Sublime", 86-93, and, for illustrations, *passim* but especially opposite page 110.

[16] Cited in Klingender, *Art and the Industrial Revolution*, 89. Young's use of "art" in this passage should be observed.

them access to a landscape "Formed for the Train that haunt poetic dreams, / Naiads and Nymphs". Yet even if the poem laments their loss, and implies its own anachronism in the face of such changes, it also expresses these feelings in a mode which draws upon the threatened traditions and which translates the alienating details into the picturesque or sometimes the sublime. So the coming of industrialism does not totally eliminate the force of classical mythology but shifts its emphasis: instead of watching naiads and nymphs, the reader now hears "the swart Cyclops['] ever-clanging forge" (the point is made more brutally in the longer poem where "their fresh, their fragrant, and their silent reign" is "Usurpt by Cyclops"). The poetic diction and the aesthetic perspective translate the signs of industrialism into a form which acknowledges the force of an ambivalent presence:

> – permits the dark-red gleams,
> From umbered fires on all thy hills, the beams,
> Solar and pure, to shroud with columns large
> Of black sulphureous smoke, that spread their veils
> Like funeral crape upon the sylvan robe
> Of thy romantic rocks, pollute thy gales,
> And stain thy glassy floods.

Behind these lines one can sense traces of Pope's famous description of the camp-fires of the Trojans in his translation of the *Iliad*; like Pope, who described the Homeric passage as "the most beautiful Nightpiece that can be found in Poetry", Seward is attentive to *chiaroscuro* and to the effects of the picturesque ("umbered fires" may even signal a direct influence though the example of Shakespeare was also available).[17] An emphasis on such possible debts might easily conceal what is most remarkable about the passage in "To Colebrooke Dale" – that is, Seward's attempt to find appropriate language to give expression to an experience and an effect which are both largely

---

[17] "Full fifty guards each flaming pile attend, / Whose umber'd arms, by fits, thick flashes send" (Pope, *The Iliad of Homer*, 8.706); "Fire answers fire, and through their paly flames / Each battle sees the other's umber'd face" (Shakespeare, *Henry V*, iv, Chorus, 8-9). Seward herself was partial to these and related industrial effects: "Wide o'er the waste, in noon-tide's sultry rays, / The frequent lime-kiln darts her umber'd blaze; / Her suffocating smoke incessant breathes, / And shrouds the sun in black convolving wreaths" ("As conscious Memory, with reverted glance", ll. 7-10, in *Romantic Women Poets 1770-1838*, 6).

unprecedented. Both Shakespeare and Pope had used "umber'd" to describe a night effect which was connected with battle; for Seward, it helps to capture one of the appearances of industrialism which even confounds what might have seemed traditional distinctions between night and day. The other lines protest against the polluting consequences of industrial enterprise but in expressing this protest they also achieve what might be described as "the industrial sublime". The "columns large / Of black sulphureous smoke" are new, or relatively new, to poetry although such phenomena had captured, or would soon capture, the imaginations of many artists. Anna Seward may have felt the need to register the incursions of the sublime in a style that could speak a new and appropriate language. These results she was prevented from achieving both by her own timidity and by the limited capacities of English poetry at this time, yet her sonnet deserves credit for addressing itself to a problem which represented a challenge to all her poetic contemporaries and which was recurrently avoided.

The terms of this confrontation are set out at greater length in her longer poem written in 1790 that seems to develop and build on a number of the phrases and insights which feature in more concentrated form in the sonnet.[18] Here Seward allows herself more space to imagine the nymphs and naiads who inhabited the groves in "times long vanished"; here, too, there is a description of the industrialized landscape though "dark-red gleams" are now "red ... fires", "umbered fires" are "umbered flames", the rocks are "aspiring" not "romantic", the "glassy floods" are now "glassy waters" and the sulphureous smoke is "thick" rather than "black". All these are minor adjustments but Seward seems to attempt a larger, and not wholly fortunate, act of self-translation when the shrouding effect of the columns of smoke "that spread their veils / Like funeral crape" becomes more specifically and yet more vaguely, "like palls, / That screen the dead". Now, the conflict is between the "soft, romantic, consecrated scenes" and the "tribes fuliginous" who invade them (here, as elsewhere, Seward succumbs to the temptations of Latinate poetic diction although later in the same passage she can write unaffectedly of "thick, sulphureous smoke"). There is a more explicit sense of

[18] For a text, see *Romantic Women Poets 1770-1838*, 7-9; for a modernized extract, see *The New Oxford Book of Eighteenth Century Verse*, ed. Roger Lonsdale, Oxford and New York, 1984, 754-55.

contagion and especially of invasion, expressed in terms which are unmistakeably sexual: the vanished nymphs give animation to a landscape which is itself a victim – the "soft scenes" and the "coy dales" constitute elements in the larger landscape which Seward addresses as "violated Colebrook!" The poet's resentment of this inappropriate intrusiveness is expressed with force in these lines that have no equivalent in the sonnet:

> See, in troops,
> The dusk artificers, with brazen throats,
> Swarm on thy cliffs, and clamour in thy glens,
> Steepy and wild, ill suited to such guests.

For all the modifying force of the rhetorical invitation to "See" and for all the apparent grandeur of the unfocused second line (both the artificers and the brazen throats have Miltonic precedents), the emphatic indignation is unmistakeable.

At the centre of this poem, though, there are two passages that seem to reverse its direction and celebrate the virtues and attributes of "far resounding" Birmingham with an enthusiasm and a local patriotism that qualifies the lamentations with which it begins and ends. Seward starts by imagining that "the larger stores of thy metallic veins" form part of an exchange of world-wide scope, including not only Europe but "either land", Ceylon, Peru, Brazil and India. The reach of business was a recurrent theme with eighteenth-century poets who characteristically associated it with London and the Thames and the force and influence of British imperialism. Seward provides her own variation on this celebration of the imperial stretch of trade but she links it with the regret that, in her view, these operations are essentially unpoetic and the complaint that "Britannia" might just as successfully find an alternative source for the appropriate metals ("regions better suited to such aims") rather than "Coalbrook's muse-devoted vales". This hesitation, or reservation, modulates into an account of Birmingham and its activities which is increasingly and cumulatively informed by appreciation of what is termed "the boast, / The growing London of the Mercian realm" and "our second London". Birmingham is "the mart / Of rich inventive Commerce" but, as Seward chooses to demonstrate, the successes of commerce are closely related to the progress of scientific enquiry. "Science there / Leads her enlightened sons", she tells her readers, "enlightened" suggesting that this concentration of focus should be seen as part of that process of rational consideration and exploration by which certain eighteenth-century scientists and philosophers asserted their own liberty from the claims of superstition and traditional thinking. (Although this claim is suitably, or frustratingly, generalized, it is likely that it was based, at least in part, on the activities of the Lunar Society and on Erasmus Darwin, whose poetic example influenced the work of Anna Seward and whom she knew personally.)

Seward proposes a direct link between scientific advance and the growth of commerce, notably in "the Mercian realm", by enumerating the virtues of the steam engine in a style that is at once characteristic of the practices of other eighteenth-century poets and which, especially by its Miltonic echoes, seems to aspire to the mechanical sublime:

> … and with great design
> Plan the vast engine, whose extended arms,
> Heavy and huge, on the soft-seeming breath
> Of the hot steam, rise slowly; – till, by cold
> Condensed, it leaves them soon, with clanging roar,
> Down, down, to fall precipitant.

This description, which seems to lean heavily on the example of Erasmus Darwin and especially on his account of the functioning of steam-power in Birmingham in *The Botanic Garden* (1791), includes a characteristic reversal since the "clanging" which in the sonnet is associated with the noisy presence of the forge is here listed ("with clanging roar") as one of the formidable properties of the steam engine. These lines which attempt to capture something of the mysterious force of machinery, partly by suggestions of personification much as in Darwin, are followed by the invocation of the "famed Triumvirate, in every land / Known and revered": an author's note confirms that this grand echo of Roman history points to Matthew Boulton and James Watt who had worked together in developing the steam engine, and James Keir who had managed their works at Birmingham at this time. These three were members of the Lunar Society as was Joseph Priestley, "the rapt sage" whose scientific enterprises are evoked and claimed for Birmingham in the following lines.

The connection between Birmingham and science is strongly enforced in this passage. The next verse paragraph takes the celebration to a different level and represents more clearly than any other part of this poem (finding no equivalent in the sonnet) Seward's acknowledgement of the virtues of a new city:

> While neighbouring cities waste the fleeting hours,
> Careless of art and knowledge, and the smile
> Of every Muse, expanding Birmingham,
> Illumed by intellect, as gay in wealth,
> Commands her aye-accumulating walls,
> From month to month, to climb the adjacent hills;
> Creep on the circling plains, now here, now there,
> Divergent – change the hedges, thickets, trees,
> Upturned, disrooted, into mortared piles,
> The street elongate, and the statelier square.

Readers might respond that it is not the most imaginative or the most interestingly achieved passage in the poem, nor even the most suggestively troubled, but it deserves some consideration, not least because it represents a tribute to the achievements of a new city ("expanding Birmingham") which is unusual among English poets of this time, either male or female, although one notable exception is provided by the enterprising James Bisset who included his "Ramble of the Gods through Birmingham" in *A Poetic Survey Round Birmingham ... Accompanied by a Magnificent Directory* (1799).[19]

---

[19] For an excerpt from Bisset's poem, see *The New Oxford Book of Eighteenth Century Verse*, 836-38. Here the opportunities of mythological endorsement are comically seized as a central premise of the narrative; in particular, Seward's "swart Cyclops" is happily engaged in industrial activities ("Next, at the Gun-Works, they surprised beheld / The lusty Cyclops musket-barrels wield", and again, "Whilst sturdy Cyclops, anvils ranged around, / With thund'ring hammers made the air resound"). An interesting, but critical, account can be found in Letter XXXVI of *Letters from England* (1807) which Robert Southey published under the thin disguise of a Spanish visitor, Don Espriella. Among other things, the letter notes: "I am still giddy, dizzied with the hammering of presses, the clatter of engines, and the whirling of wheels; my head aches with the multiplicity of infernal noises, and my eyes with the light of infernal fires .... Every man whom I meet stinks of train-oil and emery. Some I have seen with red eyes and green hair; the eyes affected by the fires to which they are exposed, and the hair turned green by the brass works" (Robert Southey, *Letters from England*, ed. Jack Simmons, London, 1951, 196-97). For artistic approaches, see Maxine Berg, "Representations of Early Industrial Towns: Turner and his Contemporaries", in *Prospects for the Nation: Recent Essays in British Landscape, 1750-1880*, eds Michael Rosenthal, Christiana Payne and Scott Wilcox, New Haven

Seward sets the solidity of Birmingham against the superficialities of "neighbouring cities" who "waste the fleeting hours, / Careless of art and knowledge" and who fall beyond artistic consideration. The eighteenth-century balance of "Illumed by intellect, as gay in wealth" represents an extension of the claims for the city's intellectual supremacy explored in the previous paragraph.

Most surprisingly, perhaps, at this point the poem seems to present growth and expansion in a positive light. Commentators on eighteenth-century London, for example, were recurrently exercised by the size and scale of its growth: Smollett's Matt Bramble, who envisioned it as "an immense wilderness", exclaimed testily: "Pimlico and Knightsbridge are now almost joined to Chelsea and Kensington; and if this infatuation continues for half a century, I suppose the whole county of Middlesex will be covered with brick".[20] Seward might be expected to present her own version of such anxieties yet her local patriotism seems, if only briefly, to transcend them. The "aye-accumulating walls" are a sign of the power of the centre that "Commands" such operations with a personified urban authority. Disturbances to the landscape, which trouble the sonnet and which are lamented at length elsewhere in this poem itself, here seem to represent the irresistible (and admirable) force of the expanding city. If this means that hedges, thickets and trees must be changed, even "Upturned, disrooted", such transformations may, or even must, be accepted since they are part of a process contributing finally to an impressive urban architecture that is a sign of achieved prosperity. The whole campaign that is directed by the supervisory force of Birmingham itself, a commanding centre controlling the syntax as powerfully as the building operations, ultimately results in satisfactory and highly visible evidence which proves its point as tangibly as it concludes the verse paragraph: "The street elongate, and the statelier square." It was precisely such metamorphic powers which later caused Dickens to write with almost surreal imaginative force about the disruptive and intrusive influence of industrialism in general and of the railway in particular; here, almost against the implications of words such as "Upturned, disrooted", and certainly against the

---

and London, 1997, 115-31, and Louis Hawes, *Presences of Nature: British Landscape 1780-1830*, New Haven, 1982, 77-80.

[20] Tobias Smollett, *The Expedition of Humphry Clinker*, eds Thomas R. Preston and O.M. Brack Jr., Athens and London, 1990, 86 (Letter of 29 May).

intimations of the poem as a whole, Seward seems to make an exception for Birmingham whose capacity to rewrite the landscape is an index not so much of thoughtless commercial and industrial rapacity as of a new social force which must be recognized and celebrated.

Francis Klingender was right to claim that "Anna Seward's attitude here is essentially ambivalent". Thinking of "Colebrook Dale" he notes her resistance to industrial transformation:

> Yet the engines and forges installed in the Dale served also to rouse in Anna Seward a sense of vastness and power. The gloomy halls and smoking furnaces produced that state which Burke praised in Milton's description of Death where "all is dark, uncertain, confused, terrible, and sublime to the last degree". Even the sulphurous fumes of which Anna Seward complained could be supposed to contribute to the sublimity of the scene. Does not Burke enumerate among the cause[s] of that emotion excessive bitters and intolerable stenches?[21]

This ambivalence marks the poem as a whole that only briefly succeeds in abstracting Birmingham from guilt for the brutal changes which it has caused, directly or indirectly. Like the sonnet, "Colebrook Dale" is conscious of the cost but, with an explicitness that does not feature in the sonnet, it makes a special case for Birmingham and for Coalbrookdale. Wolverhampton and Sheffield have a different relationship to the local landscape since their prosperity does not involve the destruction of anything picturesque:

> … see
> Grim Wolverhampton lights her smouldering fires,
> And Sheffield, smoke-involved; dim where she stands
> Circled by lofty mountains, which condense
> Her dark and spiral wreaths to drizzling rains,
> Frequent and sullied; as the neighbouring hills
> Ope their deep veins, and feed her caverned flames;
> While, to her dusky sister, Ketley yields,
> From her long-desolate, and livid breast,
> The ponderous metal.

---

[21] Klingender, *Art and the Industrial Revolution*, 92-93.

The poem goes on to refer to "Sheffield's arid moor" and "Ketley's heath". Two of Anna Seward's notes,[22] reprinted by Andrew Ashfield and Roger Lonsdale, read in partial explanation: "Wolverhampton has the greatest part of her iron from Ketley, a dreary and barren wold in her vicinity", and "The East-moor, near Sheffield, which is dreary, though the rest of the country surrounding that town, is very fine".

Even more crucially, perhaps, Seward is prepared to draw a distinction between Birmingham and its environs and the worlds (or perhaps wolds) of Wolverhampton and Sheffield, whose "visionary dreariness" does not suit the main direction of her poetics, and which she regards as fundamentally unsuited to mythology and the specially animated apprehensions of poetry:

> No aerial forms
> On Sheffield's arid moor, or Ketley's heath,
> E'er wove the floral crowns, or smiling stretched
> The shelly sceptre; – there no Poet roved
> To catch bright inspirations.

At stake here is the survival of poetry itself or rather of a kind of poetry which insists on its own definitions of appropriate subject matter. Seward even allows herself to imagine the possibility of its privileged status and become an uncontaminated or perhaps decontaminated poetic subject:

> Warned by the Muse, if Birmingham should draw
> In future years, from more congenial climes
> Her massy ore, her labouring sons recall,
> And sylvan Colebrook's winding vales restore
> To beauty and to song ...

Poetic ore, it would seem, is strictly segregated from the other kinds. Seward's reactions are influenced by her firm sense of what is suitable "To beauty and to song"; the conjunction is both indicative and limiting and reminds us how in the opening invocation she had lamented the unfortunate concessions of a time "To beauty unpropitious and to song". But Seward draws a clear distinction between these requirements and what she classifies as "unpoetic

---

[22] *Romantic Women Poets; 1770-1838*, 294; *New Oxford Book of Eighteenth Century Verse*, 754.

scenes" from which Birmingham can draw "her rattling stores, / Massy and dun" but which the true poet may safely ignore.

The conflict is perhaps generic: it involves a confrontation between the pastoral (whether in art or literature or perhaps literature informed by the example of art) and a new realistic poetics demanded by industrial developments but rejected by Seward as "unpoetic". Many years earlier, similar generic difficulties had already been recognized by Gay and by Swift whose city descriptions amuse themselves and their readers by demonstrating knowledge of prevailing classical traditions while attending to the urgencies, the emergencies and the pressing facts of daily life in the streets of the city:

> Sweepings from Butchers Stalls, Dung, Guts, and Blood,
> Drown'd Puppies, stinking Sprats, all drench'd in Mud,
> Dead Cats, and Turnip-Tops come tumbling down the Flood.[23]

For Anna Seward this struggle is enacted partly through the evocation of an imaginary poet and a poetic condition. In the sonnet we are told that Coalbrookdale is "Formed for the Train that haunt poetic dreams" while the poem ends by observing, with the enforcement of its final rhyme, how "this rude yell [the sounds of industrial encroachment] / Drowns the wild woodland song, and breaks the Poet's spell". Much the same polarities are introduced into "Colebrook Dale" where we are reminded of the privileged view of the poet: "What, though to vulgar eye, / Invisible, yet oft the lucid gaze / Of the rapt Bard, in every dell and glade / Beheld them wander." (The adjective "rapt" here used to describe the concentration of the poet is employed forty-six lines later to describe Priestley, "the rapt sage", in a formulation which briefly and suggestively implies a connection between poetic inspiration and the creative attitudes of science).

At the conclusion, the poem again insists on the displacing force of industrial practices and presences and their effect on poetic imaginings: the "Genius" of the place

> hast allowed
> Their rattling forges, and their hammer's din,

---

[23] "The Description of a City Shower", first published in *The Tatler* 238 (17 October, 1710), in *Selections from The Tatler and The Spectator of Steele and Addison*, ed. Angus Ross, Hamordsworth, 1982, 182.

And hoarse, rude throats, to fright the gentle train,
Dryads, and fair haired Naiades; – the song,
Once loud as sweet, of the wild woodland choir
To silence; – disenchant the poet's spell,
And to a gloomy Erebus transform
The destined rival of Tempean vales.

The frame of reference is, of course, familiar: in some ways, it can be linked to laments in Keats for "the beautiful mythology of Greece" which sometimes enabled one to "catch a glimpse of Fauns, and Draydes / Coming with softest rustle through the trees", and to Shelley's complaint in the unfinished "The Woodman and the Nightingale" against those brutal and insensitive presences who 'expel / Love's gentle Dryads from the haunts of life, / And vex the nightingales in every dell".[24] The setting is specifically Coalbrookdale but the points of reference are Greek – Dryads, Naiades, Erebus and the Vale of Tempe. The figure of the poet who can profit from these proximities draws its strength from his ability to exclude the noises and distractions of an outside world and to practise a specialized concentration. In this construction, "poetic dreams" are not an escapist indulgence but an enabling dimension.

The sonnet ends by reminding its readers, and perhaps those who were responsible for introducing the traces of industry to Coalbrookdale, that the noisy evidences of the industrial world were inimical to the potential and privileged world of the poet: "this rude yell / Drowns the wild woodland song, and breaks the Poet's spell." This visionary faculty is introduced into the longer poem where "the lucid gaze / Of the rapt Bard, in every dell and glade / Beheld them wander", but it reaches its climax at the conclusion which extends and rewrites the ending of the sonnet. In both cases, the sustaining powers of the poet are directly affronted and undermined by the disturbing sounds of a new order.

On the evidence of these poems, Seward's main recourse was to plead that Birmingham should find an alternative source for its supplies; poetically, and generically, she can only cope by acknowledging a crisis which her own poetics cannot transcend. The

[24] John Keats, *Endymion*, Preface and "I stood tiptoe upon a little hill", ll.153-54, in *Complete Poems*, ed. Jack Stillinger, Cambridge, 1982, 51; Percy Bysshe Shelley, "The Woodman and The Nightingale", ll. 68-70, in *Poetical Works*, ed. Thomas Hutchinson, London, 1967, 564.

main interest of her two poems bears some similarity to Wordsworth's more intense and imaginative engagement with Bartholomew Fair in *The Prelude*; both poets write against the grain and provide strong testimony to the force of those very tendencies which they would like to resist and whose noisy multiplicities seem to challenge or subvert their own system of poetic and moral values.

Mary Robinson

It might seem too easy to choose another woman poet to represent the limitations of Anna Seward's approach and to credit her with a rival set of poetic virtues apparently produced by the simplifying forces of contrast and generalization. Yet the case of Mary Robinson does seem to offer an instructive alternative, and perhaps an indication of poetic possibilities, provided one concentrates largely on the example in question and remains sceptically cautious about its larger significance. Mary Robinson was sixteen-years younger than Anna Seward and her career as an actress had necessarily exposed her to the pressures and challenges of a more direct encounter with the realities of city life than the seemingly more privileged daughter of the Canon of Lichfield.[25] Unlike the well-known male Romantics, Mary Robinson does not tend to present a persona which is obviously related to her biographical self nor to write poetry which can be easily interpreted as autobiographical or confessional; but even if she occludes herself, her best poetry seems to have a vigour, a liveliness, and a sense of detail which is informed by her own personal experience. For her, the predominant city is not Birmingham but London as in "London's Summer Morning" which was written in 1794, only four years after "Colebrook Dale". Unlike Seward she has no recourse to mythology but, unlike many city writers, her London does not relate to a map or help one to be created: place names are scrupulously avoided.

Her account of London begins by enumerating some of the sounds that characterize a London morning in summer. The poem which gives ear to these "busy sounds" is itself busy in registering them and recording them in verse. The descriptive capacities of the writing are marked by an adjectival series of definitions: the pavement is "hot", the chimney-boy is "sooty", his face "dingy" and his covering "tatty",

---

[25] For a detailed account of Robinson's career, see *Mary Robinson: Selected Poems*, ed. Judith Pascoe, Toronto, 2000; for a discussion of the relation between her personal experience and her poetry, see Pascoe, *Romantic Theatricality*, 130-62.

while the housemaid is still "sleepy"; in the previous sentence the sounds are "busy", the smoke is "sultry" and London is "noisy". Such adjectival definition does not display unusual originality or intensity of observation but it does achieve a cumulative descriptive force. In particular, Mary Robinson's version of London includes a number of details which insinuate the idea that the city expresses its character and existence through the very diversity of its sounds and their resistance to any controlling structure of harmony. So the chimney-boy "shrilly bawls his trade", the "milk-pail rattles" and the dustman announces his cleansing function by means of a "tinkling bell".

This cacophony reaches an inharmonious climax in lines 9-14:

> Now begins
> The din of hackney-coaches, waggons, carts;
> While tinmen's shops, and noisy trunk-makers,
> Knife-grinders, coopers, squeaking cork-cutters,
> Fruit-barrows, and the hunger-giving cries
> Of vegetable-venders, fill the air.

Here the poem achieves a new dimension of plurality that reminds us of the suggestive ambiguity of the opening. "Who", it asks, "has not wak'd to list the busy sounds / Of summer's morning … ?" Now, the density and crowdedness of the text suggests that although the primary meaning of "list" is to listen (a usage which is poetic and perhaps slightly archaizing), the secondary meaning is to make a list, which is entirely appropriate to the multiple phenomena that it records with attentive exactness. These lines make themselves open both to the multiplicity of city experience and particularly to the wide range of its "busy sounds".[26] Where many of her male poetic contemporaries and near contemporaries characteristically avoided the uncomfortable plurals that delighted the unashamedly urban imagination of a prose-writer such as Charles Lamb; where female contemporaries such as Joanna Baillie resorted to the picturesque securities of the panorama (not unlike William Wordsworth "On Westminster Bridge"); where Anna Seward preferred the untroubled reveries of poetic dreams and

[26] Pascoe notes: "The poem is preoccupied with business, and in fact the word 'busy' repeatedly appears" (*Romantic Theatricality*, 144). It is worth noting, though, that even if Robinson's picture of city life concentrates on trades or ways or life, it is also fascinated by activity: there is "busyness" here (as detected in London by Ben Jonson among others) as well as "business".

the songs of nymphs in "gentle train[s]", a protected species in the magically exempt woodlands; Mary Robinson accords her full attention to the crowded and cacophonous plurality of city life. These five lines alone find room for twelve plurals following each other in a close proximity which exactly fulfils the undifferentiated sequencing of a "list" and which presents, or represents, the inescapable variety of city sound.

This is the expression of an urban vitality that is characterized not least by its unfashionable range and by the ways in which it does not conform to any traditional concept of harmony. Just as Lamb's London gives voice to its joyously unthinking and unconventional liveliness because it "rattles" (precisely the sound which distressed Anna Seward who detected it in "rattling stores" and "rattling forges"), Mary Robinson's summer London expresses its existence by the uncompromising diversity of its noisiness. Judith Pascoe is right to observe that "the separate noises serve as advertisements or announcements of trade" (street cries had long been a feature of life in the metropolis and had been notably transformed into music by Orlando Gibbons). But Robinson's London also manifests the wider range of urban noise noticed by Robert Southey through his Spanish traveller who notes "a succession of cries, each in a different tune, so numerous, that I could no longer follow them in my inquiries" but who also records "The clatter of the night coaches had scarcely ceased, before that of the morning carts began".[27]

This noisy identity is captured not only by the way in which the poem incorporates a catalogue of urban phenomena but also by the way in which it absorbs these potentially disruptive forces within the larger patterns of its generally regular and fairly comfortable blank verse. The strain involved and the pressure required to contain the inharmonious within the traditional boundaries of harmony is finely suggested by the curious behaviour of lines 11 and 12:

> While tinmen's shops, and noisy trunk-makers,
> Knife-grinders, coopers, squeaking cork-cutters ...

---

[27] Pascoe, *Romantic Theatricality*, 144; Southey, *Letters from England*, 47. Interesting testimony to the noisiness of London is provided by Joseph Haydn, who, very shortly after his arrival, complained on 8 January 1791 that he wished for the quiet of Vienna because "the noise that the common people make as they sell their wares in the street is intolerable" (*The Collected Correspondence and London Journals of Joseph Haydn*, ed. H.C. Robbins Landon, London, 1959, 112).

Up to this point, every line in the poem has concluded with a monosyllable (technically, a "masculine rhyme") with the exception of the line which indicates this sequence starting "Now begins". Yet even this marginally deviant example conforms to the requirements of a verse-form where lines do not exceed the standard measure of ten syllables. Clearly, lines 11 and 12 go considerably further than this since both end with words ("trunk-makers" and "cork-cutters") that conspicuously break the pattern which the poem now seems to have established and that noticeably (and noisily) conflict with the reader's expectation. By their position at the end of succeeding lines, and by their unregenerate awkwardness, both words (and the subject-matter which they introduce) indicate their inappropriateness for the verse into which they are, so uncomfortably, incorporated.

One might have wished for a more exactly specific adjective than the general "noisy" to characterize the particular sound created by trunk-makers, not least in a passage which is sparing in its attribution of adjectives, preferring to concentrate on the accumulation of suggestive nouns, both non-human and human, – "waggons carts ... / Knife-grinders, coopers". Yet the combination embodied in "squeaking cork-cutters" is effectively and precisely suggestive and succeeds in introducing to the poem a particular kind of noisiness which mimetically enacts a specific contribution to the overall effect of the city's disharmonies and dissonance. Anna Seward had insisted on a contradiction between the sounds of industrial activity and the activities of poetry: as she put it, "this rude yell / Drowns the wild woodland song," (this wildness belongs to the woodland rather than to any Bacchic revelry) "and breaks the Poet's spell". In place of a woodland choir, one can hear the distracting and inharmonious "clang" of "ponderous engines" or the sound of "rattling forges" (elsewhere "rattling stores"), the "hammer's din", "hoarse, rude throats" or the "brazen throats" of the "dusk artificers". In contrast, Mary Robinson presents attentively but without comment the soundscape of a summer morning in London which, in its turn, is part of a greater heterogeneous multiplicity. Where Anna Seward imagined the poet's spell as broken by rude yells, Mary Robinson notices that "the pot-boy yells discordant" and emphasizes the effect by finishing her sentence and her observation with an exclamation mark.

This poem has already identified its own limited targets by alerting its readers to the fact that it is a "Description". Yet such apparent innocence should not suggest that what is involved is merely descriptive, a passive and undifferentiated recording of surface appearances. The poem's use of sound might already suggest that it is intended, among other things, to contest any received association between the urban and the harmonious. It is particularly concerned to create an impression of impressions, especially of immediacy. In particular, Mary Robinson reminds us both of the freshness of the appearances which she registers and that they belong to a particular moment in time. So in lines 9 and 10, "Now begins / The din of hackney-coaches"; in line 15 we are told "Now ev'ry shop displays its varied trade"; in lines 20-21, "Now the sun / Darts burning splendour"; in lines 23-25, "Now ... / Sits the sweet damsel"; in lines 27-28, "Now pastry dainties catch the eye minute / Of humming insects"; in lines 29-30, "Now the lamp-lighter / Mounts the tall ladder"; in lines 35-36, "now the bag/ Is slyly open'd" (in the pawnbroker's shop); and finally in lines 39-40, "The porter now / Bears his huge load". In most cases the "now" and its associated action leads the reader over the line ending so helping to keep the poem in motion. This pattern of repetition is also worth noticing because it has a cumulative force and it helps to structure a poem which might easily dissolve into a collection of impotent particulars. But here, as so often, the very details which might seem to suggest an immediate engagement with the details of everyday life are themselves literary or traditional or, one might even say, generic.

"London's Summer Morning" creates an effect of discordant and insistent vitality but it is also a poem that draws on a tradition of art and of literature. In this mode, emphasis on the individual or specific moment is modified by a larger sense of how it fits into a pattern whether of the progress of the day or the sequence of the four seasons. The tradition of art is perhaps best exemplified by Hogarth's *The Four Times of the Day* (four pictures first painted in 1736 and later engraved) that introduce a rich context of artistic illusion which makes them a great deal more than documentary.[28] An obvious literary ancestor is Swift's "A Description of the Morning" (1709) which

[28] See Jenny Uglow, *Hogarth: A Life and A World*, London, 1997, 39-40, 302-11: "The four paintings ... have often been celebrated, from the late eighteenth century onwards, as illustrating Hogarth's originality, translating the tropes of pastoral poetry into city life. In fact they are yet another instance of his buoyant adaptation of artistic, rather than literary conventions" (302). See Sean Shesgreen, *Hogarth and the Times-of-Day Tradition*, Ithaca and London, 1983; and also Ronald Paulson, *Literary Landscape: Turner and Constable*, New Haven and London, 1982, 22-26, 35-36.

begins with the word "Now" which is repeated on three other occasions in the course of its eighteen lines.[29] A similar emphasis can be found in "A Description of the Spring in London" (dated to 1754) which also begins with "Now" which is repeated on three other occasions in the course of its eighteen lines. This example indicates very clearly how its "nowness" is related to a sense of development within a larger scheme: for example, "'Large stewing oysters!', in a deepn'ing groan, / No more resounds, nor 'Mussel!' shriller tone", or again, "Now, in the suburb window, Christmas green, / The bays and holly are no longer seen" (ll. 13-14; 19-20). The details in this city description may come from direct observation but the figures who feature in them are also characteristically traditional or generic (the spruce apprentice, the barrow-trader, "Moll", the truant schoolboy, beaux and belles).

This structure was to be adopted much later and with great success by Dickens in *Sketches by Boz*; even more relevantly perhaps it was put to use by Leigh Hunt in "A Now, Descriptive of a Hot Day" (a piece especially admired by Keats) which he published in *The Indicator* on 28 June 1820. Writing more or less twenty-five years after Mary Robinson, Hunt devotes the main part of his descriptive essay to exploring the possibilities of a cumulation of details all introduced by what he defines as "this very useful and ready monosyllable". For example:

> Now jockies, walking in great coats to lose flesh, curse inwardly. Now five fat people in a stage coach, hate the sixth fat one who is coming in, and think he has no right to be so large. Now clerks in offices do nothing, but drink soda-water and spruce beer, and read the newspaper. Now the old clothes-man drops his solitary cry more deeply into the areas on the hot and forsaken side of the street; and bakers look vicious; and cooks are aggravated: and the steam of a tavern kitchen catches hold of one like the breath of Tartarus. Now delicate skins are beset with gnats ....

The closeness to Dickens of this kind of urban attentiveness and its inclusion of the comic should not be ignored. In all, Hunt begins thirty-one sentences, some long and some short, with the word "Now" and allows himself to exploit the paratactic possibilities of such a perspective by joining together many of the details through a

[29] *New Oxford Book of Eighteenth Century English Verse*, 15.

connective chain of ands. As he himself expresses it, not perhaps entirely seriously yet with point, the word can be more than merely functional since it has the power to effect its own structural alignments: "that masterly conjunction ... possesses the very essence of wit, for it has the talent of bringing the most remote things together."[30] The title of his essay suggests that his exploitation of this rhetorical device is designed in part to transform a convenient adverb into the dignity of a substantive ("Now" becomes "A Now").

Hunt's amusing and suggestive excursion could not have influenced Mary Robinson; if anything the influence must have worked the other way. However, it serves to show that her presentation in "London's Summer Morning" is, in some ways at least, part of a tradition that extends generously on both sides of her poem. Her own contribution, then, indicates that her work places her in a line which was predominantly masculine but which does not seem to allow for gender distinctions. What certainly distinguishes her from Anna Seward is that she is able to record such urban phenomena, including the discordant and the "unpoetic", with energetic attentiveness and apparently without distaste or intrusive moral judgement. Unlike Seward's two attempts to engage with Colebrook Dale, her "Description" is mainly not impeded by a poetic diction that holds the subject at a safe distance through the use of periphrasis or Latinate phrasing. The listing of city noises provides a vivid and unpretentious example; one might add, almost at random, "Now ev'ry shop displays its varied trade, / And the fresh-sprinkled pavement cools the feet / Of early walkers", or "the sun / Darts burning splendour on the glittering pane / Save where the canvas awning throws a shade", or "All along / The sultry pavement, the old-clothes man cries / In tone monotonous". What these quotations show is that, in spite of some inversions, Mary Robinson's presentation in this poem is characteristically only marginally "literary" in its word order and choice of language. This kind of poetry is not concerned to present a vision which is uniquely personal or related to an identifiable perceiving presence with the consequence that the words are usually unobtrusive and functional.

This apparently easy allocation of poetic authority is slightly complicated by the ending of the poem:

---

[30] *The Indicator*, June 1820, 301-302.

> The porter now
> Bears his huge load along the burning way;
> And the poor poet wakes from busy dreams,
> To paint the summer morning.

The first effect of these lines is to introduce "the poor poet" as the last in a sequence of urban characters beginning with the "sooty chimney-boy", most of whom are mentioned specifically (for instance, the "sleepy housemaid", the "dustman", the "smart damsel", the "lamp-lighter" and the "pot-boy"). If "poor" here means "impoverished", there is a close connection to another poem by Mary Robinson called "The Poet's Garret" which she wrote in 1800, the year of her death, and which was first published in 1804.[31] In this self-consciously literary poem Mary Robinson signals a borrowing from Shakespeare's description of the melancholy Hamlet in line 20 and is probably indebted also to a well-established eighteenth-century tradition which features in Hogarth's *The Distrest Poet* and in the desperate and unrecognized London bard in *The Dunciad*.[32] So, in some ways, her poor poet like her description of the summer morning in London is itself traditional and argues a knowledge of city archetypes. Like his predecessors, Robinson's poet (who is grammatically and unmistakeably male) lives in an attic home which gives evidence of his poverty (the inflated style gently exploits the contrast between grand poetic aspirations and sordid domestic circumstances which include a broken window and "a shelf / Yclept a mantelpiece").

Robinson concludes by addressing him:

> Poor poet! Happy art thou, thus remov'd
> From pride and folly! for in thy domain
> Thou can'st command thy subjects; fill thy lines;
> Wield the all-conqu'ring weapon heav'n bestows
> On the grey goose's wing! which, tow'ring high,
> Bears thy sick fancy to immortal fame![33]

This conjunction at least suggests that the poet at the end of "London's Summer Morning" may be similarly impoverished by his inappropriate ambitions though it might be argued that the choice of

---

[31] Text from *Mary Robinson: Selected Poems*, 354-56.

[32] For an illustration, see Uglow, *Hogarth*, 29; Alexander Pope, *The Dunciad*, London, 1742, I, 29-78.

[33] Text from *Mary Robinson: Selected Poems*, 356.

the adjective "poor" is routinely characterized like other adjectives in this urban description. Yet, even if this is the most obvious meaning, a reading which can be supported from other sources, the poem itself at least allows the possibility that the poet may be poor, in the sense of unfortunate, because he wakes from the world of dreams to accept the responsibilities involved in a realistic engagement with the facts of a summer morning. However the word "poor" is interpreted, it is evident that these final lines are reflexive and that "the summer morning" which the poet paints must represent the account we have just read. The "busy dreams" from which he has woken contrast suggestively with the opening lines: "who has not waked to list the busy sounds / Of summer's morning in the sultry smoke / Of noisy London?" In this equation, "busy sounds" are necessarily substituted for "busy dreams", pressing realities for imaginative fantasy.

On one level, Mary Robinson has experienced some difficulty, as is often the case with "descriptive" texts, in the allocation of perceptive responsibility. The poem, which begins in this embracingly general fashion, ends by introducing a more specific authority when it tells us that it is in fact the work of the "poor poet". This may also suggest some uncertainty on the part of Mary Robinson and it may relate to the anxiety of authority created by this kind of poetry which presents itself with the seeming objectivity of a sketch or a description.[34] Judith Pascoe has written tellingly about her "disguises" and her "theatrical personas" and has claimed that "her multiple poetic voices represent a form of truth concerning a fragmented self";[35] she indicates some of the ways in which Robinson exploited these possibilities. Sometimes she published her poems under the names of "Oberon" or "Portia" (interesting pseudonyms for a Shakespearean actress who was widely known as "Perdita"). She was also "Laura Maria", "Sappho", "Julia", "Lesbia" and "Bridget". On a number of occasions, she was "T.B." or, more explicitly, "Tabitha Bramble" who also featured in several titles. Tabitha was the sister of Smollett's London-hating Matt in *Humphry Clinker* who, according to one critic, is played "almost entirely for laughs ... [since Smollet] consistently emphasizes more than anything else her greed, self-absorption, and

[34] For an account of the relation between poetry and artistic practice, and especially of the feminine pursuit of sketching, see Richard C. Sha, *The Visual and Verbal Sketch in British Romanticism*, Philadelphia, 1998.
[35] Pascoe, *Romantic Theatricality*, 173-78.

general crudity of feeling – her nearly total inability, until the end, to relate to the rest of the world".[36] However Mary Robinson read this novel, her choice of name suggests both a capacity to laugh at herself, and some authorial flexibility and dexterity with personae: one ode, which appeared in the *The Morning Post* on 8 December 1797, is called "Tabitha Bramble Visits the Metropolis By Command of her Departed Brother". As Pascoe suggests, the role of this "brusque, sexually undesirable female" provided her with the opportunity to write the "sharply critical poetry" which could not be attributed to Laura Maria or Oberon (or to Sappho).[37]

For whatever reason, "London's Summer Morning" is overtly engaged in an act of displacement that transparently allocates responsibility for its own existence not to Mary Robinson herself but to a "poor poet", not specifically gendered but (one might reasonably assume) male. This strategy compares interestingly to the two Coalbrookdale poems that associate superior poetic creation with the figure of a "Bard" or a "Poet" or a "poet" whose creative imaginings are damaged or impeded by the ugly facts of industrial development. Another example is provided by Joanna Baillie's "London" (written *c.* 1800) which distances and generalizes the whole experience of absorbing the impact of this "grand imperial town" and centres its final section around a "distant traveller" whose reactions are presented in a sequence of moving from "He wondering looks" to effects on his ear, soul, breast and mind. Parallels can be found in Mary Robinson who introduces a "wilder'd traveller" and a "pensive traveller". Although such examples might seem to confirm that women poets tended to transpose the urban experience to a supposed male observer, it should also be remembered that, especially around the turn of the century, male poets themselves sometimes showed some diffidence in claiming experiences as uniquely their own. The thoughtful traveller was perhaps as much a poetic fixture as the self-portrait of the artist with an easel. It is no surprise that the travellers of Baillie and of Robinson find their parallels in William Wordsworth's "pensive traveller" in "A Night-Piece" (probably first written in 1798).

There is no such uncertainty or any apparent need for evasive

---

[36] Jerry C. Beasley, *Tobias Smollett: Novelist*, Athens and London, 1998, 198-99. For full details of Robinson's pen-names, see the full list of her publications printed by Pascoe in *Mary Robinson: Selected Poems*, 394-429.

[37] Pascoe, *Romantic Theatricality*, 174.

rhetorical strategy in Mary Robinson's other notable poem on the subject which is entitled "January, 1795" and which was originally published on 29 January of that year under the name "Portia".[38] This poem is composed of eleven stanzas, each of which is a quatrain, rhyming aabb. The overall effect, which is quite different from that of "London's Summer Morning", is panoramic and is more concerned with assessing the conflicting energies and the contradictory dispositions of the city than with providing a painting. The description is generalized and moral rather than precisely descriptive and the perceiving poet is absorbed into the accounts and its judgements, though in this case there is no reflexive reference nor any attempt to distance or discipline the representation.

The poem begins with four stanzas that quickly modulate from anything which might seem merely descriptive to a listing of details with larger implications for an urban conscience:

> Pavement slip'ry; People sneezing;
> Lords in ermine, beggars freezing;
> Nobles, scarce the Wretched heeding;
> Gallant Soldiers – fighting! – bleeding!
> Lofty Mansions, warm and spacious;
> Courtiers, cringing and voracious;
> Titled Gluttons, dainties carving;
> Genius, in a garret, starving!
> Wives, who laugh at passive Spouses;
> Theatres, and Meeting-houses;
> Balls, where simpring Misses languish;
> Hospitals, and groans of anguish.
> Arts and Sciences bewailing;
> Commerce drooping, Credit failing!
> Placemen, mocking subjects loyal;
> Separations; Weddings Royal!

As these lines show, the focus is energetic and critical and the effect is cumulative. Through all its forty-four lines the poem sustains the rhetorical strategies established here at the outset. The moral structure is immediately clear and is based on a sequence in which contrasts are made either within the individual line or by juxtaposition between

---

[38] *Mary Robinson: Selected Poems*, 356-58 (in 1806, among other changes, the "Nobles" of l. 3 become "Misers"); a rather different version is printed in *Eighteenth Century Women Poets*, 474-75.

lines which are expressively placed next to each other (for example, the clash between "Balls" and "Hospitals" at the beginning of lines 11 and 12 and between the affected "languish" at the end of the first of these lines and the "groans of anguish" which conclude the following line).

Two features are particularly noticeable. First, the poem allows itself no complete sentences. Like "London's Summer Morning" it is a collection of particulars but, unlike the earlier poem, it does not need the support of traditional syntactic structures but presents itself as a list, not innocent or random, but deliberately pointed. In these ways, it admits the plurality and heterogeneity of the city and its strange juxtapositions, while allowing itself the wider perspective of sceptical observation or moral judgement. Here, once again, there seems to be precedent in the tradition for Mary Robinson's practice whether she was consciously aware of predecessors or not. Consider the opening of "A Description of London" (1738):

> Houses, churches, mixed together,
> Streets unpleasant in all weather;
> Prisons, palaces contiguous,
> Gates, a bridge, the Thames irriguous.
> Gaudy things enough to tempt ye,
> Showy outsides, insides empty;
> Bubbles, trades, mechanic arts,
> Coaches, wheelbarrows and carts.
> Warrants, bailiffs, bills unpaid,
> Lords of laundresses afraid;
> Rogues that nightly rob and shoot men,
> Hangmen, aldermen and footmen.[39]

This poem by John Bancks is more obviously driven by the need to list the features of London and to react to its bewildering plurality but from the start it also anticipates Mary Robinson's interest in juxtapositions: houses and churches are "mixed together" and prisons and palaces are puzzlingly, or thought-provokingly, "contiguous". Bancks ends his "Description" by asking: "This is London. How d'ye like it?" Robinson does not pose so explicit a question; nor does she need to since "January, 1795" is calculated to suggest to its readers similarly troubling problems. Its seemingly passive, merely notational,

---

[39] Text from *New Oxford Book of Eighteenth Century English Verse*, 275.

perspective is jaunty and animated, though informed by a moral vision that is not satisfied by the striking contrasts which it records.

Secondly, and suggestively, there is the matter of poetic form. Like Anna Seward's poems, "London's Summer Morning" makes use of blank verse even if its own discomfort with the limitations of the verse produces some notably expressive effects at its centre. "January, 1795" is set out in a completely different form: of its forty-four lines only six do not end in a feminine rhyme, that is, a rhyme of more than one syllable. This is much more comprehensive than the practice of Bancks' poem where there seems to be a general pattern of feminine rhyme, an impression established by the first stanza, but where in fact half the lines end in monosyllables (even if in a few cases, such as "shootmen" and "footmen" the predominant effect is of the feminine). In the case of Robinson's poem, the effect is sustained, with the result that her presentation of London is inverted with a movement and an instability which is quite foreign to the less flexible traditions of blank verse.

What underlines and confirms this sense of movement is Robinson's characteristic use of the present participle. The pattern is established in the first quatrain where each of the first four lines ends in a participle ("sneezing" "freezing" "carving" "starving"). Altogether the poem includes sixteen lines which end in "ing" so that the overall effect allows for much variation but is still recurrently defined by this grammatical form: by way of comparison, Robinson's own "Winkfield Plain" of 1800 has ten lines out of thirty-four which end in this way, but Bancks' "A Description of London" includes only one participial line-ending in its twenty-four. This suggests that, while Robinson may be generally indebted to the conventions of the "description" and especially to its use of feminine rhyme, her predilection for the combined effect of the feminine rhyme and the present participle may also have answered some personal need. Her catalogue of city activities based on an accumulation of participles certainly finds ancestors in prose. Consider, for example, Matt Bramble's indignant and negative reaction in Smollett's *Humphry Clinker* to the excessive and aggressive energies of London: "they are seen every where rambling, riding, rolling, rushing, justling, mixing, bouncing, cracking, and crashing in one vile ferment of stupidity and corruption – "[40]

[40] Smollett, *The Expedition of Humphry Clinker*, 88 (letter of 29 May).

Yet for all its forcefulness, Smollett's listing still operates within the limits of prose. Closer to the point, similar effects can be found in the verse of Joanna Baillie, in Southey and later in Wordsworth; but Mary Robinson exploits these possibilities with a particularly concentrated and repetitive force which suggests a spirit, or an atmosphere, which is both energetic and restless. So, for example, we are reminded of "Nobles, scarce the Wretched heeding; / Gallant Soldiers – fighting – bleeding!", of "Arts and Sciences bewailing; / Commerce drooping, Credit failing!", and of "Some in luxury delighting; / More in talking than in fighting". The overall impression is of activities which have not been completed but which are still going on: the participle achieves a present tense which has much in common with the device of "Now" but which creates a distinct sense of incompletion. This also corresponds, but with some difference of effect, to the implications of continuing action which mark some of the details in the second half of "London's Summer Morning". There, "the limy snare / Waits to enthral" the humming insects; the lamplighter mounts the ladder "To trim the half-filled lamp"; the poet wakes "To paint the summer morning". These formulations lightly suggest the purposive but they also indicate small chains of consequence and future movement under the apparently static surface of the poem's "painting". The participle expresses more effectively patterns of activity, which can be local and specific ("sneezing") or which can carry wider moral implications ("Merit, silently deploring!").

Robinson's use of this device seems to look forward to her own achievement in "The Camp" (revised and reprinted in 1804 as "Winkfield Plain; or, A Description of a Camp in the Year 1800") which was written and published in the last year of her life under the name of "Oberon".[41] (It is worth recording, perhaps, that on 16 October 1778 Robinson had appeared as Lady Plume in the first performance of "The Camp", widely attributed to Sheridan, with scenery by Philippe de Loutherbourg whom Robinson had celebrated in "Lines", partially published in 1791). Here she employs to full effect both feminine rhyme and the present participle so that the heterogeneity and the restless energy of this temporary city are strongly suggested. Here she identifies "Noise that ev'ry noise surpasses! / All confusion, din, and riot – / NOTHING CLEAN, and

[41] *Mary Robinson: Selected Poems*, 294-95.

NOTHING QUIET." What helps to enforce these impressions of noisy confusion is the recurrent use of the participle and the cumulative effect of the first sentence which is constituted of one sentence made up, almost entirely, of self-enclosed one-line units. Of course, Robinson's camp is not a city, but her ability to articulate its unfocused energies and her responsiveness to the vitalities of its multiple existence derive from the kind of responsiveness and the technical invention which also marks some of her city poems.

Mary Robinson could not have known it but her presentation of the city finds a parallel, briefly though very suggestively, in Shelley's *Peter Bell the Third* which was written in late 1819 but did not appear till 1839; Canto the Third of Shelley's poem seems to owe a debt to the panoramic traditions of the city description which Robinson also seems to have drawn on. During his account of the desperate plurality of Hell (which is "a city much like London"), Shelley includes a phenomenon which is characterized by a collection of participles: "Thrusting, toiling, wailing, moiling, / Frowning, preaching – such a riot!"[42] Stuart Curran has acutely observed the effect of this crowded succession of verb-forms, this syntax of Hell which is so uncharacteristic of Shelley:

> In this world, there is no rational order, no harmony of purpose and pursuit. Society is not an incorporated body, but a concatenation of individuals each clawing to get ahead of his competitors. Goals are short lived, perhaps even undefined, but no less assiduously pursued in the scramble.[43]

And again: "Present participles dangling without specific reference, mirror the inchoate strivings of this society."[44] Much later still, a development of such techniques was used by Christina Rossetti in "Goblin Market" (1862) where, as Angela Leighton comments, she "defies her heritage of metrical correctness and womanly propriety".[45] In particular, she employs both feminine rhymes and participles to suggest "irresponsible, pleasure-loving energy":

---

[42] Percy Bysshe Shelley, *Peter Bell the Third*, ll. 197-98, in *Shelley's Poetry and Prose*, ed. Donald H. Reiman and Neil Fraistat, New York and London, 2002, 348.

[43] Stuart Curran, *Shelley's Annus Mirabilis: The Maturing of an Epic Vision*, San Marino: CA, 1975, 143.

[44] *Ibid.*, 144.

[45] Angela Leighton, *Victorian Women Poets: Writing Against the Heart*, London, 1992, 139.

Laughed every goblin
When they spied her peeping:
Came towards her hobbling,
Flying, running, leaping,
Puffing and blowing,
Chuckling, clapping, crowing,
Clucking and gobbling,
Mopping and mowing,
Full of airs and graces,
Pulling wry faces ....[46]

Such parallels must be approached with caution yet they seem suggestive. It is one of the many little-noticed merits of Mary Robinson that she had anticipated this expressive possibility and exploited it centrally in some of her own presentations of the city.

[46] Christina Rossetti, "Goblin Market", ll. 329-38, in *The Complete Poems*, Text by R.W. Crump, Notes and Introduction by Betty S. Flowers, Penguin, 2001, 13-14.

Joanna Baillie's Embarrassment

Dorothy McMillan

Introducing Mrs Hemans' prize-winning poem, "Wallace's Invocation to Bruce", in *Blackwood's Edinburgh Magazine* in September 1819, John Wilson wrote: "Scotland has her Baillie – Ireland her Tighe – England her Hemans."[1] The £50 prize had been offered by a philanthropic Scotsman who gave it as part of a package which included £1000 towards the erection of a monument to Sir William Wallace. Honouring Hemans in this way, Wilson was taking part in the debates and discussions about national characteristics in and out of writing which had gone through various stages of intensity for more than a hundred years, and which, for the Scots, had peculiarly mattered since the Union of 1707. Debates about Scottishness often proceeded, of course, in tandem with the related pressure and desire to feel British. It is a commonplace since Linda Colley's *Britons* that British national identity and the notion of Great Britain "was an invention forged above all by war".[2] There were also, as will emerge, more positive reasons for being British but it was certainly an anti-radical stance, proclaiming commitment to an idea that transcended factional and class interests.

In 1819 then, four years after the end of the Napoleonic Wars, Wilson was comfortable in claiming Hemans as an English national writer at the same moment as celebrating her "Scottish" poem. Hemans is permitted to appropriate Scottish history just as Joanna Baillie had appropriated English history in her two part, ten Act tragedy, *Ethwald*. But the story of Ethwald in 1802 was little known

[1] *Blackwood's Edinburgh Magazine*, V (September 1819), 686.
[2] Linda Colley, *Britons: Forging the Nation, 1707-1837*, New York and London, 1992, 5.

whereas Wallace was repeatedly celebrated as the exemplary national hero by English and Scots alike: Jane Porter's *The Scottish Chiefs* was published in 1809, Joanna Baillie's *Metrical Legend of Wallace* which draws on Porter's novel, appeared in 1821, although it was written before Baillie was able to read Hemans' poem. Baillie refers to Hemans' poem and to David Anderson's rather weak play which nevertheless had sixteen performances at Covent Garden, probably a tribute to the popularity of the subject rather than the quality of the theatrical piece.[3] It does seem as though, at least in the years following the end of the French wars, it was possible for an English writer to celebrate a Scottish subject, and to win a Scottish prize without being felt to have stepped out of line, a point tellingly made by the *Edinburgh Monthly Review*:

> On this animating theme (the meeting of Wallace and Bruce), several of the competitors, we understand, were of the other side of the Tweed ... Mrs Hemans's was the first prize, against fifty-seven competitors. That a Scottish prize for a poem on a subject, purely, proudly Scottish, has been adjudged to an English candidate, is a proof at once of the perfect fairness of the award, and of the merit of the poem. It further demonstrates the disappearance of those jealousies which, not a hundred years ago, would have denied to such a candidate anything like a fair chance with a native – if we can suppose any poet in the south then dreaming of making the trial, or viewing Wallace in any other light than that of an enemy, and rebel against the paramount supremacy of England. We delight in every gleam of high feeling which warms the two nations alike; and ripens yet more that confidence and sympathy which bind them together in one great family.[4]

The *Edinburgh Monthly* might additionally have pointed out that Mrs Hemans was born in Liverpool, had a father who was a native of Ireland and a mother of mingled Italian and German descent and had spent her early life in Wales. In 1819 social, political and literary miscegenation seemed "a good thing". But, of course, literary, social and political relationships among the countries of Britain had been before, and would again become, much more edgy than this. Certainly

[3] John Genest, *Some Account of the English Stage from the Restoration in 1660 to 1830*, 10 vols, Bath, 1832, IX, 49.
[4] *Edinburgh Monthly Review*, II (November 1819), 575.

national relationships were widely discussed. Reading the letters, memoirs and diaries of the period leaves one with the impression that national differences and the relative merits of the intellectuals of Scotland and England particularly, were persistent subjects of conversation; and it is common to find reflections in essays and reviews about what constitutes national character in lives and works.

Nationality and national differences, shortcomings or superiorities seem to have been often on the agenda in the Hampstead literary circles in which Joanna Baillie moved, in the correspondence of the various groups to which she was attached and in her public writings, and, of course, those of her close friend, Walter Scott. The interest in the matter of nation was naturally stimulated by the interaction of visitors from Scotland to Scottish expatriates. As early as 21 April 1791, Samuel Rogers reports a conversation at the house of Miss Williams in Hampstead occasioned by a visit from Henry Mackenzie, author of *The Man of Feeling*: it may be taken as exemplary. The conversation unsurprisingly turned to Scotland and Mackenzie held forth:

> I believe, said he, conversation is more cultivated there [Edinburgh] than here. In London the ardour of pursuit is greater. The merchant, the lawyer, and the physician are enveloped in their different professional engagements, but the Scotchman will retire early from the counter or the counting-house to lecture on metaphysics, or make the grand tour of the arts and sciences. I believe we have a more contemplative turn than you, and it arises partly from a defect – the little commerce and agriculture we have among us. We are also more national, and there is not a labourer among us that is not versed in the history of his country.

Mackenzie then tells an anecdote about "an innocent trick that was once played on an Englishman" who was induced to believe that Wilkie, "the celebrated author of the 'Epigoniad'" and an eccentric who dressed like a labourer, was indeed an ordinary peasant:

> "But after all," said Mr Mackenzie, returning to his subject, "Dr Johnson was perhaps right when he said of us that every man had a taste, and no man a bellyful."
>
> "And yet you will allow that there are many exceptions to the last rule, sir?" said Miss Baillie, a very pretty woman with a very broad Scotch accent. "Mr Adam Smith" –

> "Yes, ma'am," Mr Mackenzie interrupted with a warmth he seldom discovered, "Mr Smith was an exception. He had twice Dr Johnson's learning – who only knew one language well, the Latin – though he had none of his affectation of it."[5]

Adam Smith, was a friend of Joanna Baillie's uncle, the anatomist and surgeon, William Hunter, and Smith's *Theory of Moral Sentiments* almost certainly informs her Preface to her *Plays on the Passions*. But the whole exchange exemplifies the way in which such conversations were conducted, with generalizations being made and specific counter-instances being adduced. The interest in accent is also a feature of all these discussions of national characteristics.

I shall return to the retention of a Scottish accent by Joanna Baillie and her sister, Agnes, but they were not the only Scottish expatriates to continue to sound like Scots throughout a long life spent outside the native country. The mathematician, Mary Somerville, eighteen years younger than Joanna Baillie, seems also to have sustained her Scotticisms throughout her life. Mary Somerville was intimate with the Baillies after she moved to London in 1816. Her reminiscences display the kind of problematic relationship with Scottishness that was typical of expatriate Scots. In her *Recollections* she speaks of one of the games at her boarding school, kept by Miss Primrose at Musselburgh:

> In our play-hours we amused ourselves with playing at ball, marbles, and especially at "Scotch and English", a game which represented a raid on the debatable land, or Border between Scotland and England, in which each party tried to rob the other of their playthings. The little ones were always compelled to be English, for the bigger girls thought it too degrading.[6]

But Mary Somerville seems to have made more effort than the Baillies to smooth out her Scotticisms. Maria Edgeworth reports in a letter to her mother, in 1822, that Mary Somerville had a "remarkably soft voice though speaking with a strong Scottish pronunciation – yet

---

[5] P.W. Clayden, *The Early Life of Samuel Rogers*, London, 1887, 165-67.

[6] Mary Somerville, *Personal Recollections from Early Life to Old Age. With Selections from Her Correspondence, by Her Daughter, Martha Somerville*, London, 1873, 22-23.

it is a well bred Scotch not like the Baillies".[7] Mary Somerville, again with that obsessive attention to the national, remarks in turn that Maria Edgeworth had "all the liveliness and originality of an Irishwoman".[8] Mary Somerville's daughter reports that she was self-conscious about her lack of formal education on which she blamed her possible "lapses" into vernacular:

> She herself was always diffident about her writings, saying she was only a self-taught, uneducated Scotchwoman, and feared to use Scotch idioms inadvertently. In speaking she had a very decided but pleasant Scotch accent, and when aroused and excited, would often unconsciously use not only native idioms, but quaint old Scotch words.[9]

But mathematics was certainly not then felt to be a peculiarly national discipline and Joanna Baillie inevitably had a more fraught relationship with the meaning and significance of Scotland than her friend. And so just as Baillie, like other Scots living in England, made actual journeys back to her native land, so she made literary trips throughout her writing life.

Apart from her lyrics, her Scotch songs in particular, Joanna Baillie turned to Scottish subjects on three significant occasions at roughly ten year intervals. In 1810 her *Family Legend* was produced at the Theatre Royal in Edinburgh; in 1821 her *Metrical Legends* included the exemplary domestic heroine, Lady Griseld Baillie, and the national martial hero, William Wallace; and in 1836 her three volume *Dramas* included the musical play, *The Phantom*, and more importantly, the prose drama, *Witchcraft*: – both plays had been written previously, *Witchcraft* having, Baillie says, been prompted by her reading of Scott's *Bride of Lammermoor* (1819) and she had given the manuscript of the play to Scott in April 1828.[10] Baillie's relationship to Scotland and her sense of that country's relationship to Britishness inevitably underwent a series of shifts during her writing life just as there were over these years a series of Scotlands and a variety of ways of being Scottish.

---

[7] Maria Edgeworth, *Letters from England, 1813-1844*, ed. Christina Colvin, Oxford, 1971, 321.

[8] Somerville, *Personal Recollections from Early Life to Old Age*, 155-56.

[9] *Ibid.*, 120.

[10] Sir Walter Scott, *Journal*, Edinburgh, 1950, 524.

One of the most enduring ways of understanding and representing Scotland, and the one that underpinned Baillie's first major Scottish work, *The Family Legend*, was, of course, the Ossianic. Remarking on Lady Jane Wilde's explanation of her son's name, "He is to be called Oscar Fingal Wilde. Is not that grand, misty and Ossianic?", Fiona Stafford points out that what is sometimes regarded as "a curious phenomenon of the later eighteenth century" had an "enduring appeal" as is clear "from the steady stream of reprints, selections and new editions that continued to appear for the next hundred-and-fifty years".[11] It is, of course, true that a Scotland with a misty, heroic past, presented in a fashionably melancholy manner, was a much less threatening Scotland than one sending the wild descendants of these heroes across the border to rout the English, or assertively claiming its political rights. Scotland (and Ireland and Wales) could be encouraged to enjoy their romantic pasts, provided that their people increasingly committed themselves to a British present and future.

While the Ossian poems had a European currency it was often the Scots themselves who were fervently committed to the whole Ossian package – Mary Somerville remembers enthusiastically reading Ossian and enjoying the Highland scenery the more for her experience of the poems[12] – but enthusiasm was not confined to those lowland Scots who had little actual experience of Highland traditions. For a number of commentators Highland society was becoming a paradigm for values that had been insufficiently understood before they were destroyed or undermined. Some kind of appreciation of Highland culture can be said to inform much of the understanding of other more distant cultures during the early nineteenth century. Probably no one writing in Scotland in the Romantic period worked harder to make Highland culture valued and understood before it was swept away or corrupted than Anne Grant, Mrs Grant of Laggan, and she was to some extent an insider to that culture as well as a commentator on it.

Anne Macvicar [Grant] was born in Glasgow of parents with Highland connections, but from the age of three she spent ten years in America in and around Albany on the River Hudson, her father having a commission in the regiment of the Earl of Eglinton. After the end of the war in Canada the Grants returned to Scotland where at twenty-

[11] James Macpherson, *The Poems of Ossian and Related Works*, ed. Howard Gaskill with an Introduction by Fiona Stafford, Edinburgh, 1996, v.
[12] Somerville, *Personal Recollections from Early Life to Old Age*, 66.

four Anne Grant married the Rev. James Grant, a former army chaplain who had been settled for some years in the parish of Laggan in Invernesshire. Anne Grant became the loving, although not uncritical, interpreter to the wider world of the culture she found in Laggan: she herself learned Gaelic to promote cultural understanding. She subsequently published both on Highland culture and on the societies she remembered in America. She generally praises Highland society at the expense of Southern sophistication on both sides of the border. She writes from Fort William to her Glasgow friend, Harriet Reid:

> I know nothing so silly as the disgust and wonder your cockney misses show at any custom or dress they are not used to. I now think plaids and faltans (fillets) just as becoming as I once did the furs and wampum of the Mohawks, whom I always remember with kindness.[13]

In her first volume, *Poems on Various Subjects*, Anne Grant includes translations from the Gaelic and publishes a defence of the authenticity of Macpherson's Ossian.[14] Her *Essays on the Superstitions of the Highlanders* is committed to a view of Highland culture and society that supports and is supported by the Ossianic. If anyone in the period might have been trusted on Gaelic culture it was Anne Grant: the contemporary attractiveness of Macpherson's Ossian is made clear by her commitment to it.

The Ossianic view of Scotland's heroic past may seem now like the kind of reductive packaging of the country that we deplore when we encounter the clichés of the tourist shops or the heritage industry, and it is certain that the appeal of this version of Scottishness was generally conservative. But there is no doubt that the relationship with their native places of the Scottish Romantic writers, especially those who had elected or been obliged to live out of them, was a much more serious matter than can be covered by any notion of incipient kitsch. There is considerable evidence that even among those Scots that had become most English or at least most British, and who would have been horrified by any notion that they were disloyal to the country

---

[13] Anne Grant, *Letters from the Mountains; being the Correspondence with Her Intimate Friends between the Years 1773 and 1803*, 3 vols, London, 1806, I, 48.

[14] A contemporary remarked that had Anne Grant been obliged to relinquish belief in either Ossian or the Lord, it would have been a near run thing, which given her well-known piety, is a strong comment.

south of the border, there developed a moral and emotional tie to Scotland which gives the land and its landscapes something of the status in moral and emotional terms that the Lakes had for Wordsworth, with a significance perhaps beyond that since Scottish landscapes and the life associated with them could be more readily enlisted in support of larger than local values. Similarly Edinburgh was not simply the focus of the intellectual life of North Britain but, it could be argued, rivalled London itself as the great British centre of the life of the mind.

Even Scots who stayed in Scotland usually made some kind of tour of the Highlands and a visit to Edinburgh was obligatory for anyone claiming intellectual status. Elizabeth Hamilton (1758-1816), born in Ireland, brought up by her aunt in Stirlingshire, began her prolific and various writing career with a journal of a highland tour. The novelist, Mary Brunton, remarks a little ruefully in a letter to her brother that her own special relationship with the Highlands is disappearing into fashion, "As for the Highlands, you know they are quite the rage. All the novel-reading Misses have seen and admired them in the verdure and sunshine of July."[15] Scott himself made a number of excursions to the north while providing, of course, the fodder for the "novel-reading misses". Scott's friend and collaborator, Lady Louisa Stuart, a Scot who was obliged to live in London, records how restorative an early journey to Scotland was for her; she stresses places and people, Scotland's tourist attractions: "The journey and every other novelty delighted me – Dalkeith and it's [*sic*] environs, Rosline castle, Hawthornden, Leith races, Edinburgh, Holyrood, Dr Robertson, Dr Blair, all the places and all the people I had been many a day longing to behold."[16]

These are only a few examples of the way in which tourism by native and non-native helped shape Scotland as Scotland helped to shape the tourists. But there remained problems about the Ossianic version of Scotland's heroic past which Anne Grant's treatment of Highland culture highlights: Lowlanders could only feel themselves part of it by adoption; they were in some senses as much outsiders to the places and meanings of the North of Scotland as were the English,

---

[15] Mary Brunton, *Emmeline with Some Other Pieces*, ed. Caroline Franklin, London, 1992, lxvii.

[16] Lady Louisa Stuart, *Memoire of Frances, Lady Douglas*, ed. Jill Rubenstein, Edinburgh, 1985, 65.

and the simplicity of the culture of one half of Scotland could be used, as Anne Grant uses it, to reprove the affected manners of the other. And so one of the problems that confront any writer looking for a national subject is that it may be difficult to compliment one section of the Scots without alienating another.

Joanna Baillie made the obligatory visit to Scotland before she wrote *The Family Legend*. In the spring of 1808 she visited the West Highlands and Glasgow, her native area; from there she "proceeded to Edinburgh, and took up her abode for a week or two under Scott's roof". While she was still in Glasgow Scott wrote that he hoped her Scottish trip would spur her writing: "Nothing will give me more pleasure than to hear that you have found the northern breezes fraught with inspiration."[17] Apparently they were, since Scott writes to Joanna Baillie in August 1809, that Henry Siddons, the manager of the Theatre Royal in Edinburgh "is delighted with the piece, determined to bring it out with as much force as he can possibly muster".[18] *The Family Legend*, unlike Baillie's earlier plays, was performed before it was printed.

The Family Legend was a co-operative Scottish effort: Lockhart confirms that Scott: "exerted himself most indefatigably in its behalf. He was consulted about all the Minutiae of costume, attended every rehearsal, and supplied the prologue."[19] From Scott's letters we derive most of the detail about performances and audience reaction. The *Dublin University Magazine*, confirming the success of the play, marks it as a national event: "The Edinburgh public were pleased and flattered by a national story, given to them by a countrywoman; it was received with warm applause for fourteen consecutive nights, frequently repeated afterwards, and remained long on the stock list of the theatre."[20] But this rather glosses over some of the problems of the production.

The play was published in 1810. In her prefatory "Address to the Reader" Joanna Baillie unreservedly identified herself with Scotland, her "native land", which so affectionately received her play. Her pleasure at the kindness of the audience "who willingly and cordially felt that I belonged to them" seems as unaffected as it is gracious: "I

---

[17] J.G. Lockhart, *Memoirs of the Life of Sir Walter Scott*, Edinburgh, 1842, 161-62.
[18] Sir Walter Scott, *Familiar Letters*, 2 vols, Edinburgh, 1894, I, 143.
[19] Lockhart, *Memoirs of the Life of Sir Walter Scott*, 186.
[20] *Dublin University Magazine*, XXXVII, (April 1851), 531.

have truly felt, upon this occasion, the kindliness of kin to kin, and I would exchange it for no other feeling."[21] Walter Scott's Prologue concludes by asking "Caledon" to "approve / the filial token of a daughter's love" and the Prologue is also addressed to Scottish exiles, expatriates on "India's burning coasts" or "Acadia's winter-fetter'd soil".

Both Prologue and Address admit something of the anxiety of exiles who still feel their deepest ties with the country they have elected to leave, and by Scott on one side of the border and Joanna Baillie on the other, Scotland is claimed for the Scots wherever they live. Scott's Prologue turns Scotland into "romantic Caledon" providing a vision of Scotland that will make the "wanderer" a "denizen of Scotland once again", but Joanna Baillie's Address a little ruefully admits some of the problems that have to be overcome to achieve a suitably romantic and heroic vision of the country for present denizen and exile alike. For it has proved, she admits, very difficult to provide a version of the character of the chieftain of the Macleans that would be at all acceptable, and although she defends her dramatic practice, she feels that the character may not have been "very skilfully executed". Scott's Prologue speaks of those physical features of the Scottish landscape that were, as I have suggested, crystallizing into a marketable version of the land:

> … his native dell,
> The woods wild-waving, and the water's swell;
> Tradition's theme, the tower that threats the plain,
> The mossy cairn that hides the hero slain;
> The cot, beneath whose simple porch was told
> By grey-hair'd patriarch, the tales of old.[22]

But as Baillie's Address makes clear, the story upon which the play is based shows a coward rather than a hero in hiding and reveals the untellable within "the tales of old". Baillie's explanations of her shaping of Maclean into something not heroic but at least representable betrays the awkwardness of accommodating "family legends" to contemporary tastes. Offering Caledon to India and Canada and Edinburgh was, after all, a delicate packaging job; and it

[21] Joanna Baillie, *The Dramatic and Poetical Works*, London, 1853, 480.
[22] *Ibid.*, 481.

is because *The Family Legend* was conceived of as a wholly Scottish play that it caused these embarrassments.

The Family Legend is a simple enough tale: Helen, the daughter of the Earl of Argyll has married the chief of the clan Maclean: the marriage is intended to heal the ancient enmity between the two clans and Helen refuses the love of an English gentleman, Sir Hubert De Grey, to make it. But the followers of the Maclean do not wish amity and eventually by threatening to withdraw their loyalty wear down the resistance of the pusillanimous chief and persuade him to get rid of his wife by exposing her upon a rock which is submerged at high tide. The plan fails because Helen's brother, John of Lorne, and Sir Hubert, who have been making a clandestine but innocent visit to Helen, pass the rock and rescue her. Maclean is tricked into coming to the stronghold of the Argylls in mourning for his wife, who has allegedly died naturally. He is killed in single combat by John of Lorne (Helen, of course, begs for his life); his followers are led off to punishment after Sir Hubert enters with Helen's baby whom he has rescued from being held hostage by the Macleans.

Joanna Baillie got the story, she says, from Mrs Damer, and it presumably came to her with the inevitable biases of its origin, for the Campbells of Argyll are certainly the injured. Anne Damer was the daughter of Field-Marshall Henry Seymour Conway, soldier and politician, and Caroline Campbell, daughter of Lieutenant-General John Campbell, later 4th Duke of Argyll. The Third Duke, Archibald, John Campbell's cousin, was famously one of the architects of the Union of 1707. You could not say that the Campbells were not Scottish and you could not say that they were not British.

The Macleans, who are the villains of the story, could not so comfortably make these claims. The Macleans of Duart fought on the Jacobite side at Culloden and their property was confiscated after 1745. If any family had to be offended by Joanna Baillie's Scottish play, then obviously it would be better to offend the Macleans than the Campbells, but more desirable not to offend anyone at all. Therefore in two ways Joanna Baillie plays down the guilt of the Macleans: in the first place the chief is represented placed under peculiar pressure by his followers and the special relationship of clan and chief is stressed to make this plausible; secondly the names were changed in performance to protect the guilty. Macleans becomes Clangillian and its head becomes Duart, from the seat of the chief, although since that had been confiscated after Culloden, there must have been raw wounds there too.[23] As much as possible was done to enable Scottish audiences at home and abroad to identify with the virtues of Helen and the dashing courage of her brother, John of Lorne, without their being too upset by the behaviour of the dastard, Duart. Whether it was a wise move to make the gentle Sir Hubert De Grey an Englishman I cannot say.[24]

In spite of name changes and the sheer spectacle of the be-tartaned clans, which seems to have been generally approved, Lucy Aikin reports from Edinburgh in a letter to Mrs Barbauld on November 1811 that a Highland minister had told her "that the clan McLeod [presumably a mistake for McLean] are offended with Miss Baillie's representation of their ancestor, and that Their Poet has written a long Erse ballad giving himself well acquainted with the traditions about it".[25] But Joanna Baillie's play proved more powerful than Maclean ripostes. An account of the clan Maclean "by a Seneachie", a Highland transmitter of family lore, in 1838 accepts that *The Family Legend* had made Lachlan Cattanach Maclean notorious and admits that his character "both private and public is not such as to admit of a single palliative".[26] But the author succeeds in making his admission a validation of the integrity and heroism of all other Maclean chiefs: thus the black sheep enables a whitewash and everyone is presumably happy.

---

[23] Henry Siddons wrote to Joanna Baillie on 19 December 1809: "A great deal will depend on the Actor who performs McLean of Duart …. By the way I think the fear of giving offence to that Clan by the character of the Chief was a false fear; but this notwithstanding, if the lines be accommodated to the pronunciation of Duart, the name more heroic and poetical that the everyday surname of McLean, the actor may infuse a dignity into the yielding which may in good measure remove any objection" (in Royal College of Surgeons, London, Hunter-Baillie papers, IX, 50).

[24] The fuss about potential offence is highlighted by the fact that Thomas Holcroft had already, apparently unknown to Baillie or Scott, had a version of the story performed as *The Lady of the Rock* in Drury Lane in 1805 without any withers being wrung. Holcroft's version of the story which he takes, he says, from the Honourable Mrs Murray's *Guide to the Western Isles of Scotland*, gives Maclean the excuse of his wife's barrenness: Holcroft feels he has to add jealousy, not to protect the Macleans, of course, but to convince a modern audience.

[25] Lucy Aikin, *Memoirs, Miscellanies and Letters*, ed. Philip Hemery Le Breton, London, 1864, 84-85.

[26] *Historical and Genealogical Account of the Clan Maclean, from its first settlement at Castle Duart, in the Isle of Mull to the present period, by a Seneachie*, London and Edinburgh, 1838, 28.

There is no doubt that *The Family Legend* was intended to be, and was on the whole received as, a distinctively Scottish production. It consolidated Joanna Baillie's claim to be the Scottish female writer of the period. Even at this high point in the celebration of a national subject on the Edinburgh stage, there was much that was uncomfortable, but on the whole Joanna Baillie's feelings "not of triumph, but of something much better"[27] seem fully justified. But I suspect that Joanna Baillie still felt from time to time that her Scottishness was under attack.

A letter in 1813 from the novelist Mary Brunton suggests ways in which Joanna Baillie's friends might still be able to make her feel guilty about settling out of her native land. That value that I have proposed the Scots found in the scenery of their native land is invoked by Mary Brunton against her friend Joanna Baillie, the length of whose stay in England is likely to have been to the detriment of her commitment to her own place:

> I suppose you are now returned from your Devonshire excursion and I trust you have brought with you a stock of health and strength for the winter .... However I hope you will be so national as to let me say that a pretty little English knowle is not half so exhilarating as the top of a Scotch hill. Perhaps my feeling on this subject is partly prejudice but it is not quite so; therefore, though you should not join in it do not hold it in utter derision! I have jumped with joy when from the top of one of our own mountains I have unexpecting seen as it were just at my feet some well known object which I thought far beyond my sight – but in the middle of a wide prospect where all is new and strange; one feels emphatically a stranger with all a stranger's cheerless unconcern in the objects round him. However England is no strange land to you, so some winding avenue or some smoke curling above its woods may carry your imagination as pleasantly away as mine follows a burn dancing in the sun or a glen that shelters the house of a friend.

Mary Brunton follows this friendly dig at the corruption of her friend's taste with lengthy descriptions of Highland scenery and a story in which a pawky Highlander gets the better of a snooty and impercipient Englishman but ends at least by saluting Joanna Baillie as a "true-hearted Scotchwoman".[28]

---

[27] Baillie, *The Dramatic and Poetical Works*, 481.
[28] Brunton, *Emmeline with Some Other Pieces*, lx, lxi-iv.

Autumn 1820, unsurprisingly then, found Joanna Baillie back in Edinburgh and Abbotsford for her last restorative draught of Scotland and, if we are to believe Lucy Aikin's memoir of Joanna Baillie, the Baillies might have felt themselves to be among the last Scots, their nationality in a sense preserved in aspic during their life in England:

> It appeared practicable in her to love Scotch things and persons more, without loving the English less. Yet in many respects she never Anglicised in the least degree. Whether she and her sister actually took pains to keep up their native dialect, I know not, but it is certain that on their revisiting Glasgow twenty or thirty years after they first quitted it, their friends were surprised to find them speaking with a broader accent then themselves, by whom the English pronunciation had long been anxiously cultivated as a genteel accomplishment.[29]

The problem, of course, is that to be more Scottish than the Scots is perhaps not to be really Scottish at all, and Joanna Baillie may have begun to think herself not quite of either country.

At this stage, however, Joanna Baillie seems to have decided to play safe in her latest literary raid into Scotland, for her metrical legends on Lady Griseld Baillie and William Wallace are among her most cautious and conservative works, the former, indeed, seemingly attacking her own craft. The pressure of Scott's poems on these legends scarcely needs to be proved, although more than Scott she privileges character over incident and atmosphere. But the Scottish characters that Baillie chooses are unproblematic in terms of the nature of their heroism and its appropriateness to gender. Wallace had recently been the subject of Jane Porter's novel, *The Scottish Chiefs* and of a poem by Miss Holford. Joanna Baillie is quite clear about the nature of his qualifications for national heroism: "The hero of my first legend is one, at the sound of whose name some sensation of pride and of gratitude passes over every Scottish heart." Wallace is incontrovertibly a Scottish hero, but he is equally, Baillie goes on to claim, a universal one. Nor is there any inconsistency in celebrating his instrumentality in securing Scotland's independent freedoms, while at the same supporting the Union of the northern and southern kingdoms. Scotland is fortunate, unlike Ireland, to have joined with England as an equal nation. Indeed, Wallace may be said to have

[29] Aikin, *Memoirs, Miscellanies and Letters*, 9.

protected Scotland from subordination and England from becoming a despotic power. There seems little likelihood, then, that Baillie's historical hero will be a threat to Scottish, English or British feeling. Nor does she feel the need to soften Wallace into the "man of feeling" that he becomes in Jane Porter's version. Baillie offers a quite sophisticated justification for writing narrative history and she supports all her legends by copious quotations from her sources; but she does not have to combat likely dissenting voices from her general sense of Wallace as a true, disinterested patriot, fighting for country only, unlike Bruce who fought also for the crown.[30]

Lady Griseld Baillie is, if anything, an even more conservative choice and can easily be invoked to enlist Baillie on the Hannah Moreish side of gender relations: Griseld Baillie operates within her proper sphere, and is the perfect national, domestic heroine. The crucial events of Griseld Baillie's life are derived by her remote descendant, Joanna, from the manuscript version of her life by her daughter, Lady Murray. The salient characteristic of that life is loving devotion to duty, to her father and his associates, to her siblings and then to her husband and children: her heroism is wholly private, yet it is not without its adventurous touches. Joanna Baillie follows Lady Murray's narrative of her mother's childhood heroism during the troubles of Charles II's time when she visited her grandfather in prison and later, twelve years old, ministered to her father who was in hiding in a vault of Polwarth church. Baillie does not comment, except in the historical footnotes, on the wider political scene that necessitated Griseld's heroism: this is a wholly personal narrative.

Yet the social and political pressures on Lady Griseld and her unfailing subordination of self to country and family do emerge in a manner that makes her peculiarly unself-pitying. Lady Griseld Baillie's commitment to the family from her earliest days is largely the reason why her most substantial literary monument is her Household Book and not her songs. Lady Murray describes the interruption of her compositions during the family's exile in Utrecht: "I have now a book of songs of her writing when there; many of them interrupted, half writ, some broke off in the middle of a sentence."[31]

---

[30] Baillie, *The Dramatic and Poetical Works*, 707-708.

[31] Lady Murray (of Stanhope), *Memoirs of the Lives and Characters of the Right Honourable George Baillie of Jerviswood and of Lady Grisell Baillie*, Edinburgh, 1824, 49.

Joanna Baillie quotes Lady Griseld's claim that these days were "the happiest and most delightful of her life" but slips over the abortive attempts at composition. Indeed, in the moralistic conclusion to her poem Joanna Baillie stamps on the literary ambitions of her heroine more firmly than either family or duty had done: Lady Griseld's dutifulness is used to reprove recalcitrant female scribblers, "Whose finger, white and small, with ink-stain tipt, / Still scorns with vulgar thimble to be clipt."[32]

Joanna Baillie writes to Miss Berry in 1821 that she is told that the *Metrical Legends* "are pretty well received in Scotland, but I don't think they are much liked in this Southern part of the Kingdom".[33] The *Monthly Review* is particularly severe on the quality of Baillie's poetry.[34] The conservatism of her poems had not really, it seems, paid off. And the approval which the poems were given in Scotland is actually rather damaging since it now so clearly rests on national feeling rather than poetic merit. The *Edinburgh (Scots) Magazine* gushes, "With great pleasure, exalted by a degree of national pride, we again recognise Miss Baillie in her last and not least meritorious production." The whole spirit of the review is distressingly different from the generous reception of Mrs Hemans in 1809. English writers are told that they should have kept their hands off Scottish heroes:

> We would beseech those ladies besouth the Tweed to content themselves with celebrating King Arthur and all the numerous train of English warriors who well deserve celebration; and we, in return, can assure them, that our Scottish muses will never sing the praises of the first Edward or the eighth Henry. What horrible pleasure can these fair and ingenious Saxons find in singing the crimes, the perfidy, and cruelty, of their own countrymen?[35]

After this Baillie went back to Scotland twice in her drama: in the musical drama, *The Phantom*, which was usually at least mentioned in reviews of the published volumes in 1836 and which has some lightweight virtues; and in *Witchcraft* which is a much more serious piece of work. It was, Baillie explains in her Preface, suggested by a scene in Scott's *The Bride of Lammermoor*.

---

[32] Baillie, *The Dramatic and Poetical Works*, 758.
[33] Royal College of Surgeons, Hunter-Baillie papers, IX, 17.
[34] "Joanna Baillie's Metrical Legends", *Monthly Review*, 96 (1821), 74.
[35] *Edinburgh (Scots) Magazine*, VIII (January-June 1821), 260, 261.

I am inclined to agree with Lockhart that *The Bride of Lammermoor* is perhaps the most intense tragedy that Scott wrote. It is, I think, written in a spirit of depression about the subordination of human values to self-interest and greed. It is also, in the view of a number of its critics, written in a spirit of profound antipathy to Whiggism, and the narrator displays some dissatisfaction with the current state and status of Scotland. Certainly Scott by this stage did not have an uncomplicated love affair with his own country nor with its Union with England. By 1822, to be sure, Scott was enthusiastically acting as stage manager for the visit of George IV to Scotland and the "tartan frenzy" that transformed Highland dress into Scottish national dress was at its height and unquestionably formed largely by Scott, but Scott's confidence in Britain deteriorated again shortly afterwards. In 1826 Scott published first in the *Edinburgh Weekly Journal* and then as a pamphlet his equivalent of Swift's *Drapier's Letters*, *The Letters of Malachi Magrowther*. The ostensible subject of the letters is the currency question – the Government was proposing to stop the Scottish banks from issuing their own banknotes – but the tone of the letters is aggressively and proudly nationalist. Scott makes it clear through Malachi that he resents the erosion of Scottish traditions and the way in which the Government seems prepared to ride roughshod over Scottish sensibilities:

> I am old, sir, poor, and peevish, and, therefore, I may be wrong; but when I look back on the last fifteen or twenty years, and more especially on the last ten, I think I see my native country of Scotland, if it is yet to be called by a title so discriminative, falling, so far as its national, or rather, perhaps, I ought to say its provincial, interests are concerned, daily into more absolute contempt.[36]

Assuming that Baillie was writing *Witchcraft* round about 1827-28, then she was doing so after an awkward episode in the relationship between Scotland and central government and one in which Scott had been intensely involved. It seems an odd time, then, to invoke Scotland's bad witchcraft record. Interest in the black arts and the

---

[36] Sir Walter Scott, *Letters of Malachi Malagrowther*, Preface and essay by P.H. Scott, Edinburgh, 1981, 4. It can be argued that Scott's is an anti-radical stance and that he is afraid that a Scotland deprived of dignity and pride in its own traditions will become a dangerously radical place (see J.G. Lockhart, *Memoirs of the Life of Sir Walter Scott*, 614).

supernatural in general was still, of course, running high, but Joanna Baillie might well have thought that this was not the best time to let those south of the border think that the sooner the relics of darker days in Scotland were smoothed away in the interests of British uniformity the better. Is this just a case of Joanna Baillie being naive about the possible readings of a play about Scottish witchcraft, or is it that her undoubted fascination with the psychological implications of a genuine belief in the possibility of consorting with the Devil overbore any sense she might have had of the social and political implications of what she was writing? I believe there are signs that Baillie, now in her late sixties, was far from naive about the political implications of her play and that she was also involved in a tense examination of class and gender structures.

In the first place Baillie had given the play a lot of thought.[37] She was determined that some work focusing on witchcraft should get written, and, since she unsurprisingly could not persuade Scott to write it, she decided to take it on board herself. This, of course, merely reinforces the second of my options that she found the subject compelling. But she could have taken the course of most of her other dramas and situated the play in another time and a place far from Scotland: there is no scarcity of European witch-burning. Baillie makes then a quite conscious decision to locate the play in Scotland and in a Scotland not all that far removed from the present: the abrogation of the laws against witchcraft happens in the course of the play which places it in 1734. The actual events of the play are based not on Scott's story but on the last major Scottish witchcraft trial in Renfrewshire in 1697, five years after Salem. Joanna Baillie had certainly read about the trials, although she is vague in her note to the play about where she found her account.

The accuser in the Renfrewshire trials was an eleven-year-old girl, Christian Shaw, daughter of the laird of Bargarron in the parish of Erskine: the similarity of the name to Dungarron, the setting of the play in Renfrewshire and the business which surrounds a piece of cloth torn from the gown of the alleged witch, which was an issue in

[37] Lucy Aikin writing to the Rev. Dr Channing in Boston in 1836, speaks of Joanna Baillie's own preference for *Witchcraft* among the three volumes of dramas she published that year: "She tells me that her own favourite is 'Witchcraft', and I think it perhaps goes deeper into human nature than any of the rest" (*Memoirs, Miscellanies and Letters*, 337).

the Renfrewshire trials, makes it clear, as the *Athenaeum* reviewer suggests, that it was these late seventeenth-century trials that provided the material for the play.

If the unacceptable aspects of *The Family Legend* can be swathed in tartan, no similarly spectacular distractions aid the presentation of evil in *Witchcraft*. Joanna Baillie seems to have decided in this last Scottish play to take a full look at the worst, and when we see what values she plucks out of this courageous and clear-sighted presentation of superstition and evil, we shall surely feel her experiment justified: the Scotland that emerges from *Witchcraft* lacks the misty heroism and colourful pageantry of Baillie's previous versions but it faces up to the problem and power of evil and, in admitting the oppressions of class and gender, goes some way to aiding their removal. If *The Family Legend* was Baillie's "Highland play" which contributed to the packaging of Scotland into a manageable idea, then *Witchcraft* is her Lowland nightmare. Indeed, to set a play at all in Paisley in the late 1820s and publish it in the 1830s might in itself seem a political statement. For Paisley was no misty glen but a rapidly expanding textile town which was developing a serious problem with the urban poor. It is twice remarked in *Witchcraft*, once indeed by the villainess and "real" witch, that witches are always old and miserable and poor (Act I, scene i; Act III, scene ii): to remark this kind of demonization of the poor and the dispossessed in the history of a town which was lurching towards its actual bankruptcy in the 1840s might well seem dangerously radical.[38]

And the poor witches are not the real villains of the play. The plot of *Witchcraft* is complicated, although coherent: Violet Murrey, the daughter of a man condemned as a murderer and believed dead, loves and is loved by Robert Kennedy of Dungarren. His mother, Lady Dungarren, is superstitious and has been induced to believe that her sick daughter is being cursed by three old witches. The old women are led by Griseld Bane, an enigmatic figure of unknown origins, who does believe that she has congress with Satan, but who wishes the child no harm.[39] A rich and class-conscious relative of Lady

[38] See Michael Lynch, *Scotland: A New History*, London, 1991, 391, for a discussion of this phase of Paisley's life.

[39] Lady Murray's *Memoirs* of her mother were printed in 1824. I have not seen the manuscript version Baillie uses, but in the printed version Lady Murray gives the commonly accepted version of her mother's name i.e. "Grisell". What is important,

Dungarren, Lady Annabella, loves Dungarron and resents his attachment to Violet. She contrives to have Violet accused as a witch and arranges for a piece torn from Violet's gown to be planted in the child's bedroom. This would probably not in itself work but Violet's father is not dead: the body believed to be his was that of a servant dressed in his clothes after Murrey had escaped from prison. Murrey is not guilty of murder since he struck in self-defence but the only witness who can clear him has disappeared. Violet is meeting her father in secret in the wood at the same time as the witches are consorting. The local minister, going to comfort Lady Dungarren and the sick child, sees Violet talking to a "dead" man and this overcomes his previous scepticism. Violet is unable to answer the charge of witchcraft without betraying her father and she and one of the poor, distracted witches, Mary McMurren, are condemned to burn at the stake. At the eleventh hour an Officer of the Crown arrives to proclaim the repeal of the laws against witchcraft. With the Officer is Fatheringham, Murrey's needed witness who had been captured by pirates, and had in any case believed Murrey to be dead. Meanwhile Annabella, who had procured a view of the execution from the upper storey of a nearby house, has been strangled by Griseld Bane. Fatheringham identifies Griseld Bane as an Inverness woman who went mad after the execution of her husband for murder. Griseld is led off and Violet and Dungarren, who had throughout believed in her innocence, are reunited.

The play is written entirely in prose, except for a few verse incantations made by Griseld, and Joanna Baillie makes it clear in her prefatory note that she intends the language to be a realistic version of the contemporary speech of high and low at the time. The *Athenaeum* reviewer is unhappy with Baillie's choice of prose throughout, feeling that "the beauty and the innocence, and the distress of Violet Murrey and the pure affections of Dungarren, would, we apprehend, be more effective in verse. We are willing to permit the conversations of the Westland hags, and the murderous envy of Annabella, to remain in humble prose."[40]

But it is Baillie's refusal to make Violet Murrey linguistically different not just from the villainous Annabella but from the strange,

---

however, is not whether the Lady was Grisell or Griseld but that Joanna Baillie names the chief witch in *Witchcraft* "Griseld Bane".

[40] *Athenaeum*, (January-December 1836), 5.

seemingly mad Griseld Bane that makes *Witchcraft* such an interesting play. Drama is full of Violet Murreys, loyal, loving and lovely; it is equally full of vengeful Annabellas, but Griseld Bane is a most unusual witch and it is she in the end who is the agent of justice. Violet Murrey, who is like Griseld Baillie in her succouring of her father, finally needs Griseld Bane to achieve the domestic bliss to which she aspires; the flower garden round Violet Murrey's cottage is actually preserved rather than threatened by the dark other that Griseld Bane seems to represent. It cannot be an accident that Joanna Baillie chose the name Griseld for her principal witch, nor that the second name is so darkly reminiscent of Lady Griseld's and, indeed, her own. Joanna Baillie seems to be recognizing in Griseld Bane the demonic other that she has in her *Metrical Legends* cast out of her picture of Scottish ideal womanhood: Griseld Bane may actually be one of the first of these persistent nineteenth-century "madwomen in the attic".[41]

There is no doubt, too, that Griseld Bane is given a number of most impressive speeches during her delusive congress with the Devil. Anne Grant makes superstition the underpinning of real belief in her explanations of Highland customs.[42] Joanna Baillie, belonging as she does both north and south of the border, allows us to cross with her between them in *Witchcraft*. We are permitted the perspective of English rationality, which diminishes Griseld at the end of the play into a mad old wife from Inverness, but we have also been allowed to glimpse Griseld's power, to feel ourselves in the grip of something other, certainly dark but paradoxically a force for good.

With unperformed theatre, that is also not much commented upon by author or reviewer or readers, there is relatively little that we can speak of securely. By the time that Joanna Baillie was writing *Witchcraft* she was probably too well known a phenomenon for the difference of *Witchcraft* to be noticed: after all it appeared in print with many other plays. The sad result is that an unusual play has slipped away from us and can never really have the variety of meanings that it might have had, had Joanna Baillie written it as a younger woman; yet ironically, it is perhaps more astonishing as the production of an ageing woman. It is probably unfortunate that the

---

[41] See Sandra M. Gilbert and Susan Gubar, *The Madwoman in the Attic: The Woman Writer and the Nineteenth-Century Literary Imagination*, New Haven, 1979.

[42] Anne Grant, *Essays on the Superstitions of the Highlanders of Scotland, with Translations from the Gaelic*, 2 vols, London, 1811.

National Drama of Scotland subsequently went the way of *The Family Legend* rather than that of *Witchcraft*: the marketability of mist and tartan and ladies clinging to rocks is obviously greater than the appeal of a mad old agent of justice from Inverness; nor is Griseld Bane convertible into a quaint peasant even though her charisma is reduced at the end of the play.[43] But when Joanna Baillie is proffered, as she still sometimes is, as charmingly conservative and inoffensive, it is as well to have *Witchcraft* up one's sleeve as proof that her affinities are as much with the demonic as the dutiful.

---

[43]Adrienne Scullion discusses these features of *The Family Legend* that are expected in the developing Scottish National Drama: Scullion also briefly discusses *Witchcraft* and is the only modern critic I have encountered who recognizes the difference and power of the play (Adrienne Scullion, "Women of the Nineteenth Century Theatre", in *A History of Scottish Women's Writing*, eds Douglas Gifford and Dorothy McMillan, Edinburgh, 1997, 156-78).

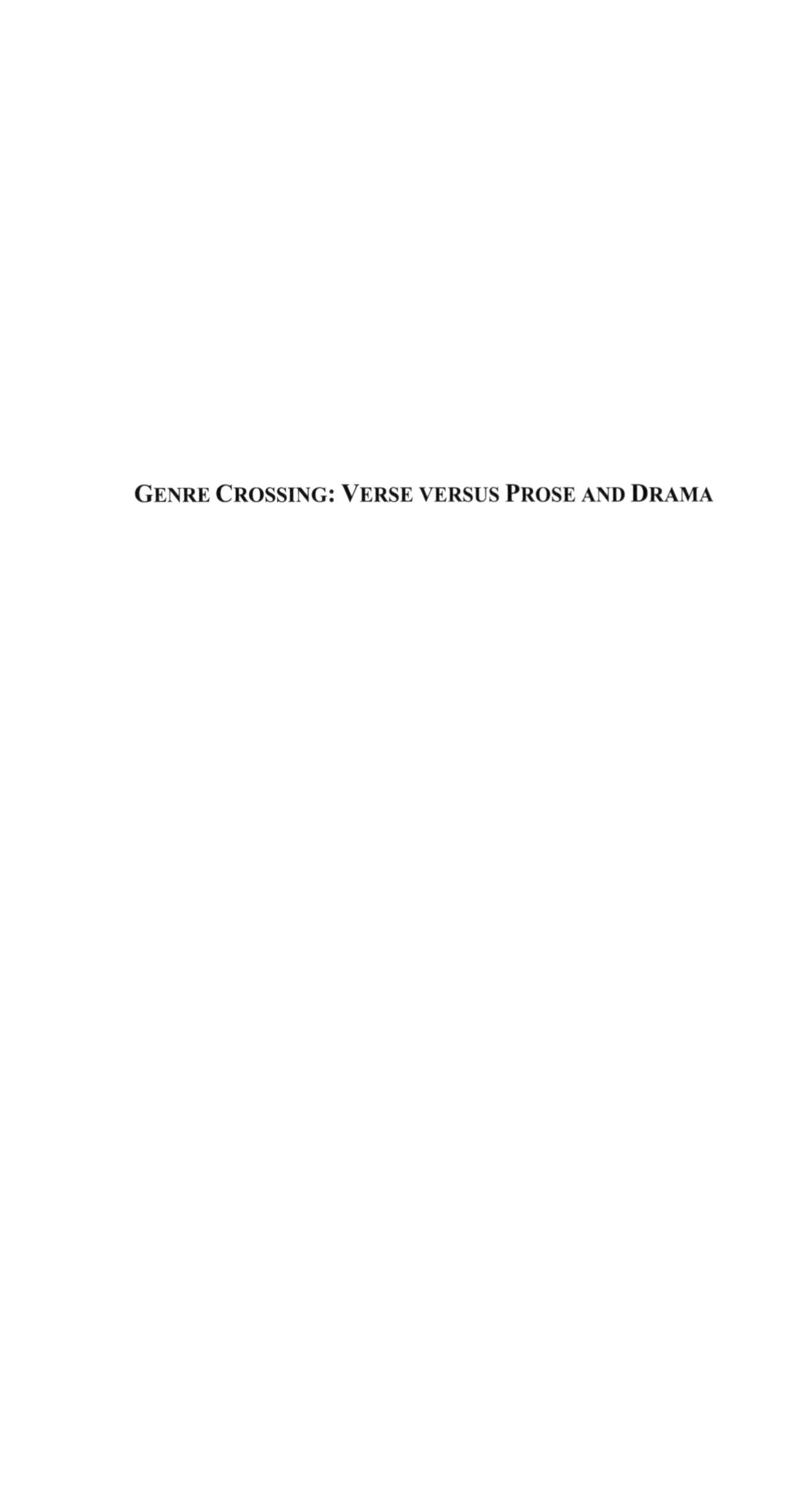

Genre Crossing: Verse versus Prose and Drama

THE "PIECES OF POETRY" IN ANN RADCLIFFE'S *THE MYSTERIES OF UDOLPHO*

BEATRICE BATTAGLIA

They might be sung by Shakespear's Ariel.[1]

Though over the last few decades numerous critical efforts have been made to restore Ann Radcliffe to her rightful place as the mother of Romantic sensibility, it is still necessary to reassess her verse,[2] in order to look at her work from a wider and more adequate perspective. Conventional stereotypes die hard and can only be buried under serious cultural historical work such as Deborah Rogers' and Rictor Norton's critical biographies.

By collecting a large number of contemporary and nineteenth-century opinions, Deborah Rogers shows the huge popularity Radcliffe enjoyed at her time, thereby explaining why she could not be ignored by the poets of her generation and, even less, by those of

---

[1] Mrs Barbauld, Introductory Preface to "Mrs Radcliffe", in *The British Novelists; with an Essay; and Prefaces Biographical and Critical*, 50 vols, London, 1810, VIII, vi.

[2] Ann Radcliffe's verse includes the poems contained in *The Castles of Athlin and Dunbayne* (1789), A *Sicilian Romance* (1790), *The Romance of the Forest* (1791), *The Mysteries of Udolpho* (1794), in addition to others published posthumously together in *Gaston de Blondevill*e (1826), and some that appeared in her husband's paper. Two editions with anonymous editors were issued in London in 1815 and 1816 (*The Poems of Mrs Ann Radcliffe*, which includes poems whose authorship is still uncertain), while 1834 saw the publication of *The Poetical Works of Ann Radcliffe*, London. Similarly anonymous was the editor of the 1834 edition of *The Poetical Works of Ann Radcliffe*, 2 vols, London. (see Michael Sadleir, "Poems by Ann Radcliffe", *TLS*, XXVII/1365 [March 29, 1928], 242).

the following generations.[3] In his cultural biography, Rictor Norton[4] leads us to understand that if a writer who was considered ignorant and "wanting education"[5] could in fact write one of the most successful best-sellers of all times, it was not merely by chance or by lucky intuition. Both scholars follow the lines pointed out by Virginia Woolf, who suggested looking for an explanation for Radcliffe's enormous success in the taste that had made it possible.[6]

In analysing the response of Radcliffe's contemporaries to the art of the "great enchantress", "sorceress" or "magician" (as they called her),[7] two prevailing reactions can be traced: fear and anxiety, when faced with the suspense of her Gothic atmospheres, and enthusiasm and enjoyment, when faced with her descriptions of nature. Accordingly, if Gothic romance is considered from Maurice Lévy's critical perspective (with its focus on the Renaissance theme of usurpation in a social-historical context), and if natural landscape and its transformations in eighteenth-century Britain are viewed through the cultural lenses of Ann Bermingham, Nigel Everett, John Barrell, W.J.T. Mitchell, and others,[8] it becomes evident how these approaches combine to substantiate a picture of the eighteenth-century inner mind in which the circuitous journey, so convincingly documented by M.H. Abrams's in *Natural Supernaturalism*,[9] is the dominant pervading theme. This, I believe, is a vital starting point in the endeavour to

---

[3] *The Critical Response to Ann Radcliffe*, ed. Deborah D. Rogers, London and Westport: CT, 1994.

[4] Rictor Norton, *Mistress of Udolpho: The Life of Ann Radcliffe*, London, 1998.

[5] See Julia Kavanagh, *English Women of Letters: Biographical Sketches*, London, 1862, 235-331, and B.G. MacCarthy, *The Later Women Novelists 1744-1818*, New York, 1948, 168.

[6] Virginia Woolf, "Gothic Romance" (review of Edith Birkhead's *The Tale of Terror: A Study of the Gothic Romance*), *TLS*, XX/1007 (May 5, 1921), 288.

[7] The descriptions are respectively by Walter Scott ("Prefatory Memoir to Mrs Ann Radcliffe", in *The Novels of Mrs Anne Radcliffe*, Edinburgh, 1824, X, xx); T.J. Mathias (*The Pursuit of Literature: A Satirical Poem in Four Dialogues*, London, 1794, 20n.); and "Estimate of the Literary Character of Mrs Ann Radcliffe", *Monthly Magazine*, XLVII (1819), 125, reprinted in *The Critical Response to Ann Radcliffe,* 114, 105 and 93.

[8] Ann Bermingham, *Landscape and Ideology: The English Rustic Tradition 1740-1860*, London, 1987; Nigel Everett, *The Tory View of Landscape*, New Haven and London, 1994; and *Landscape and Power*, ed. W.J.T. Mitchell, Chicago and London, 1994.

[9] M.H. Abrams, *Natural Supernaturalism: Tradition and Revolution in Romantic Literature*, New York, 1971.

understand the constitutive features of the Romantic "interior landscape" that are responsible for the peculiar atmosphere Radcliffe captured so successfully.

Indeed, as Abrams explains, though incorporating aspects of the Plotinian odyssey and Christian *peregrinatio*, the Romantic journey differs from these from various respects, primarily in the definition of its destination, in which Nature has come to stand for Eden and the harmonious unity of the origin. Despite the consolatory pre-Hegelian notion of a return to a higher level, or the Wordsworthian faith in the possibility of a conjugal intercourse between Man and Nature, such going back to Nature is felt as uncertain, if not unreachable or lost forever. This was the world that, in the wake of the machinations of Milton's Satan, had lost Paradise; and then, together with the knowledge of the loss, the fear grew that it was unrecoverable and that the wandering and exile were endless. Satan's farewell to Paradise – "Farewell happy Fields / Where Joy for ever dwells" – is the great original of a long series of farewells to the parental home, native village, maternal island – "Nè più mai toccherò le sacre sponde … "[10] – and countless invocations to melancholy flooding the popular literature of the time, while the new word *nostalgia* – a scientific term indicating *Heimweh* or homesickness[11] – was coming into common use.

Therefore the exceptional success of *The Mysteries of Udolpho* can be explained by its being a "romance" in Northrop Frye's sense of the word[12] – a secular epic in prose and partly in verse, based on what in the eighteenth century had become the emotional fulcrum of the Western conscious and unconscious collective mind: that is, Nature[13] (or more specifically Man's relation to Nature). It was not by chance that Radcliffe's contemporaries compared her to great epic poets such as Spenser, Ariosto, Milton and Shakespeare rather than other novelists. Nature is in fact the protagonist of *The Mysteries of Udolpho* – a character eclectically portrayed from all angles according to the contemporary taste that Radcliffe was able to delight, since, she

[10] First line of a well-known sonnet (also under the title "A Zacinto", 1801) by Ugo Foscolo: "Never more will I touch the sacred shores …."

[11] Jean Starobinski, "The Idea of Nostalgia", *Diogenes*, 54 (1966), 81-103.

[12] Northrop Frye, *The Secular Scripture: A Study of the Structure of Romance*, 1976, 15.

[13] Christopher Hussey, *The Picturesque Studies in a Point of View*, London, 1927 (reprinted 1967), 5-12.

possessed, as Scott remarked, “the eye of a painter with the spirit of a poet”,[14] and also, as her own poems testify, the ear of a minstrel. It is because “her landscape is the centre of her plot”, and “with her the landscape acquires a personality and suggests the plot”[15] that Radcliffe developed her famous word-painting, by drawing on the pictorial techniques of Salvator Rosa’s sublime, of Claude’s beauty and, particularly, of Richard Wilson’s picturesque. Thus she deserved recognition as “the most illustrious of the picturesque writers”.[16] By adapting Gilpin’s teaching to literature and by developing it along the same lines as Cozens and Constable – that is, by allowing more freedom to imagination – Radcliffe paved the way for Turner: first, her style looks forward to Turner’s pre-impressionist use of light, and second, by means of her art she achieves a new balance between the verbal and the visual by replacing the visual hegemony by a greater reliance upon the verbal.[17]

Radcliffe’s word-painting technique is picturesque in its essence, since it fits the criteria established by Gilpin in *Three Essays*. Emily’s journey through France and Italy is also picturesque in its continuous alternation between the sublime and the beautiful, light and shade.[18] The dominant picturesque dimension of *The Mysteries of Udolpho* becomes particularly relevant when the work is read, in accordance with Frye’s notion of romance, as “secular scripture” or epic. In fact, as recent criticism has argued, the picturesque is to be seen not simply as an eighteenth-century aesthetic category and popular fashion, but also as the very mode or set of principles informing the expressive logic of western culture, and, consequently, a “life style” and a “transformational psychic process”.[19]

---

[14] Scott, “Prefatory Memoir to Mrs Ann Radcliffe”, vi.

[15] J.M.S. Tompkins, *Ann Radcliffe and Her Influence on Later Writers* (Diss, 1921), New York, 1980, 74-75.

[16] C.B. Brown, “On a Taste for Picturesque”, *Literary Magazine and American Register*, II (1804), 163-65.

[17] *Reading Landscape: Country, City, Capital*, ed. Simon Pugh, Manchester and New York, 1990, 3.

[18] Elizabeth Wheeler Manwaring, *Italian Landscape in Eighteenth Century England*, London, 1925, 117.

[19] See Bermingham, “The Picturesque and Ready-to-Wear Femininity”, 88, and David Punter, “The Picturesque and the Sublime: Two Worldscapes”, in *The Politics of the Picturesque: Literature, Landscape and Aesthetics since 1770*, eds Stephen Copley and Peter Garside, Cambridge, 1994, 225.

As one of Radcliffe's disciples, Robert Louis Stevenson, would say, the romance is an invitation to the reader to get on board the same boat as the narrator and share a choral adventure appealing to what all men have in common. The adventure in *The Mysteries of Udolpho* is indeed choral, cathartic and consolatory: all the fears and anxieties of the romantic journey far from home are dealt with and resolved in the end.

The romance opens with the picture of an Arcadian life in harmony with a mythical Nature. However, the intervention of the acquisitive spirit – bourgeois and urbane – of economic prestige (represented by St Aubert's relatives and by Montoni himself)[20] upsets the natural order of things. The characters are taken far from home and dragged into a long series of mishaps and frightening adventures that will come to an end with the re-establishment of the old order and the return to the initial Arcadia. Clearly this situation differs from true Gothic, as Coleridge noticed when he observed that it was above all a romance of suspense.[21] So once the suspense is resolved, *The Mysteries of Udolpho* ends up being consolatory. Garber rightly notices that melancholy appears "woven less deeply" in the texture of the narrative than sensibility.[22] The absence of the hopeless bleak prospect that is proper to true melancholy prevents her famous natural descriptions from being sublime in Burke's sense of the word. In this romance the Romantic sublime appears rather mannered because Radcliffe was never really afraid of Nature. Indeed, despite its eclectic variety of aspects,[23] her sublime is fundamentally neo-classical.[24] Nature is the mirror of its great author where one can come in contact with the "Deity" (in Radcliffe's word) and abandon oneself to its laws. This may explain the reassuring power of *The Mysteries of Udolpho* for such a large audience: the most authentic relationship between the self and Nature is one of complete oneness, and this is mostly evident in some of her most beautiful lyrics ("The Glow-Worm", "The

---

[20] See Mary Poovey, "Ideology and *The Mysteries of Udolpho*", *Criticism*, XXI, (1979), 323.

[21] S.T. Coleridge, "The Mysteries of Udolpho, a Romance", *The Critical Review*, 2nd series, XI (August 1794), 362.

[22] Ann Radcliffe, *The Mysteries of Udolpho: A Romance Interspersed with Some Pieces of Poetry* (1794), ed. with an Introduction by Bonamy Dobrée and Explanatory Notes by .Frederick Garber, Oxford, 1970, 675.

[23] Ann K. Mellor, *Romanticism and Gender*, New York and London, 1993, 85-102.

[24] Robert Kiely, *The Romantic Novel in England*, Cambridge: MA, 1972, 68.

Butterfly to His Love", "The Sea-Nymph" and even "Song of the Evening Hour") where the poetic self, far from attempting to absorb Nature, dissolves and becomes part of it. In "The Butterfly to His Love", considered one of Radcliffe's best lyrics, the poetic voice is embodied by an element of Nature expressing its pleasure and joy of living as part of "questa bella d'erbe famiglia e d'animali".[25] The same thing happens in "The Sea-Nymph", which Coleridge, not by chance, chose to quote unabridged in his 1794 review.

The fact that this immersion, or rather dispersion, in Nature takes place in a fantastic and dream-like dimension[26] – and imagination and dreams are the vehicles of myth – explains the cathartic power of *The Mysteries of Udolpho*. In Radcliffe's Nature all the anxieties and fears of the painful journey of self-assertion seem to have disappeared, as if we were brought back in time to a state before the separation from the great maternal organism and by miracle reattached to its vital flow. It is significant that three of the poems in *Udolpho* deal with a return journey ending in tragedy ("The Mariner", "Storied Sonnet", "The Pilgrim"); two poems, "The Traveller" and "The Piedmontese", deal with the happy journey back home after having escaped respectively from a life-threatening danger, and the pernicious lure of wealthy Venice. Most of the remaining twenty are devoted to a hedonistic and sensual immersion into the animate world of Nature.

The "pieces of poetry" considered here are an integral part of the peculiar type of romance characterizing *The Mysteries of Udolpho*. This work indeed belongs to a new species of romance narrative essentially marked by interspersed passages in verse, such as – among others – Charlotte Smith's fiction, which, as Coleridge's review suggests, many contemporaries appreciated. The emergence and spread of the Romantic novel was very likely furthered by the need to please the reading public or to elevate the tone of a female genre, with the aim of securing the reviewers' interest and approval. However, such considerations do not entitle us to deduce that the poems were "inserted" in *Udolpho* by "random intrusions", without "any explained logic", with the "immediate effect of freezing the narrative", in a

[25] A quotation from the Italian poet Ugo Foscolo's *I Sepolchri* (1807), l. 5: "this beautiful family of grass and animals."
[26] Radcliffe never saw her celebrated foreign landscapes, but only imagined them.

"superfluous", "ephemeral", "parenthetical" fashion.[27] Nor can we conclude that to evaluate the poems favourably, as Gary Kelly does,[28] means being subjected to Romantic ideology, while culpably neglecting the point of view of a novel-centred criticism gratuitously exhumed (after Scholes and Kellog had buried it in the 1960s). Favret's critical approach, in fact, is totally inadequate to *The Mysteries of Udolpho*, since the latter is explicitly a romance and not a realistic novel. In Radcliffe's fiction, as Kelly writes, "verse, as the literary or the expressive, marks the outer and innermost borders of the narrative".[29]

The verses, or (as they are called in the title-page) "pieces of poetry" – interspersed throughout *The Mysteries of Udolpho* more abundantly than in any other romance – consist of quotations, mainly used as epigraphs to the chapters, and original poems. Though having different functions, they all contribute to evoking the musical dimension that is so essential in a romance. It is from this dimension that the atmosphere derives its suggestive power and the depth of its overtones evoking the irrational and linking up to the unconscious.

The epigraphs (fifty-seven in all) are much more than decorative additions. Taken individually they fulfil the function of introductory keys both to the events described in the chapter and to the psychological atmosphere of the main episode. Taken together and sequentially, they acquire the evocative force of the chorus in a play: in this case a powerful chorus made up of the voices of Thomson, Shakespeare, Beattie, Collins, Mason, Goldsmith, Milton, Sayers, Gray, Hannah More, Pope and Samuel Rogers, each in its turn accompanying the drama of the circuitous journey.

The first voice belongs to her favourite poet, the author of *The Seasons*. It extols the place the journey starts, and it is by no chance that the temporal perspective is that of *Autumn*:

> .... home is the resort
> Of love, of joy, of peace and plenty, where,
> Supporting and supported, polish'd friends
> And dear relations mingle into bliss.[30]

---

[27] Mary A. Favret, "Telling Tales about Genre: Poetry in the Romantic Novel", *Studies in the Novel*, XXVI/2 (Summer 1994), 162 and 165.

[28] Gary Kelly, *English Fiction of the Romantic Period, 1789-1830*, London, 1989.

[29] *Ibid.*, 55.

[30] Radcliffe, *The Mysteries of Udolpho*, 1 (Vol. I, Chapter 1).

Immediately afterwards, in the ghostly words of Hamlet's father, Shakespeare warns that it will be a terrible story, "a tale …. whose lightest word / Would harrow up thy soul" (Vol. I, Ch. 2), as terrible as Macbeth's "unnatural deed" (Vol. IV, Ch. 16),[31] or the "nameless deed" mentioned earlier in the title-page. It is again Shakespeare's voice – from *King John*, *Richard II*, *Julius Caesar*, but above all *Macbeth* – which repeatedly rises to evoke the "wicked, heinous fault" (Vol. II, Ch. 9) and the consequent "unnatural troubles" (Vol. IV, Ch. 16), and to indicate the primal cause in the will to power: "Such men as he be never at heart's ease, / While they behold a greater than themselves" (Vol. II, Ch. 3), and to remind the readers that "Bloody instructions … return./ To plague the inventor" (Vol. IV, Ch. 17).[32]

The third voice – another warning – belongs to her beloved Beattie, who alternates with Thomson in exalting Nature and regretting the sin of abandonment:

> Oh how canst thou renounce the boundless store
> Of charms which nature to her votary yields!
> The warbling woodland, the resounding shore,
> The pomp of groves, and garniture of fields;
> All that the genial ray of morning gilds,
> And all that echoes the song of even;
> All that the mountain's shelt'ring bosom shields,
> And all the dread magnificence of heaven;
> O how canst thou renounce, and hope to be forgiven!
> ….
> These charms shall work thy soul's eternal health,
> And love, and gentleness, and joy, impart.[33]

If the Chorus, with its variety of poetic voices, enunciates interpretative keys endowed with prophetic resonance, the poems, by illustrating these anticipations, reinforce their oracular power while extending the involvement of the reader to the emotional and irrational field, and, more precisely, to the field of poetry, music and song. A necessary respondence and formal economy, therefore, link the epigraphs and the poems: the latter develop the prophetic hints of the

---

[31] *Ibid.*, 19 and 641.
[32] *Ibid.*, 295, 641, 182 and 654.
[33] *Ibid.*, 27 (Vol. I, Ch. 3).

epigraphs and, like them, may be distinguished into narrative, elegiac and lyrical.

Compared to the epigraphs and the prose narrative, however, the language of the poems appears much simpler. This difference can be significantly seen when we compare the verse and prose descriptions of Nature: in the latter the language appears much more layered and richer in quotations and well as in literary and pictorial allusions. Indeed, from a technical and stylistic point of view, Radcliffe's narrative language is anything but simple. In spite of the apparent simplicity characteristic of the popular writing of romance, Radcliffe's prose narrative is rich in metaphors that give the events, characters and scenes symbolical haloes and allegorical echoes capable of reaching deep into the sensibility of the period. As Walter Scott wrote, if "actual rhythm shall not be deemed essential to poetry", then we are verily dealing with poetry, with the difference, it must be added, that whilst Radcliffe's "poetry in prose" is more concerned with the eye, thereby invading the visual and pictorial field, her "poetry in verse" prefers to trespass and merge into sound and music.[34] In the poems, which are often called "song", "carol", "lay", "air", and "rondeau", the simple language and rather conventional images have the effect of releasing and accentuating the musicality of the verses which, already musicalized by rhyme, can touch the chord of sensibility, and therefore, as Coleridge wrote, their evaluation is a matter of "taste".

In Radcliffe's romance, the aural dimension proves no less important than the visual. However strong and subtle the evocations may be, no real terror can be created because the prosody – mostly alternating rhyming iambic pentameters and tetrameters – constantly suggests the reassuring presence of a fixed pattern, recurring as in a minuet and harmonious as in a concerto of her beloved Paisiello, where even the strongest and most tormenting emotions cannot affect the stability of the underlying structure. From this point of view, then, the poems in *Udolpho,* taken as a whole, can be truly described as the musical equivalent of the translation of the picturesque into literature.

Indeed the poems enable us to understand the relationship between the elegiac tone, predominating throughout the romance, and the tone that may be more properly defined as lyrical. The latter is in fact merely a development of the elegiac feeling at the moment when the

---

[34] Scott, "Prefatory Memoir to Mrs Ann Radcliffe", iv.

nostalgic vision reaches such intensity that all awareness dissolves into the panic emotion. And it is precisely the triumphant authenticity of the panic moment that throws a shadow of mannerism onto the other poetical tones, including the elegiac and the nostalgic. It was not simply by chance, nor out of mere chivalry,[35] that Coleridge chose to quote "The Sea-Nymph", one of the best manifestations of the panic moment. He quoted it entirely (all 100 lines), justifying his choice by saying he could not resist its fascination and "poetical beauty". Indeed, as Jacques Blondel claims,[36] in these lyrics Radcliffe's vision is confirmed as being certainly one of light rather than of gloom.[37]

The notion of poetry in *Udolpho* as music and song – these being the privileged means of expressing myth and the past, or Eden and Nature – may be exemplified and summarized in a comparison with a contemporary sonnet, "Nè più mai toccherò le sacre sponde" by Ugo Foscolo (1801). In the sonnet, better known as "A Zacinto", the poetic "I", before being able to vent his nostalgic yearning, is lost in an oneiric vision of his native island. This vision fills the whole poem with its light, colours, and sounds: in a word, with its physical beauty which finally materializes in the image of Venus, the Goddess of Fecundity, whose smile inspires poetry, the only dimension in which myth is able to live and to which it always returns.

The Mysteries of Udolpho allows an oneiric return to Nature, just as Foscolo's sonnet allows an analogous return to his maternal island. This was why, despite the many faults Radcliffe's contemporaries found in her romance, they were irresistibly fascinated by it. In this fascination the "pieces of poetry" played a substantial part, if not for their conventional poetic value, at least for their mere presence and function both in the texture and structure of the narrative.

As the Zakynthos poet reiterates and the Orpheus myth testifies, it is only poetry that can bring the past back to life, and thereby allowing the present to rejoin it to share and propagate the vitality of myth. Without its poems, *The Mysteries of Udolpho* would be a Gothic romance more or less similar to many others. This is the case with *The*

---

[35] Favret, "Telling Tales about Genre: Poetry in the Romantic Novel", 156.

[36] Jacques Blondel, "On Metaphysical Prisons", *The Durham University Journal*, LXIII (1971), 136.

[37] Significantly one of her favourite painters was Claude Lorrain who excelled precisely, according to Constable, in "brightness … serene beauty … sweetness and amenity, uniting splendour and repose, warmth and freshness" (see Manwaring, *Italian Landscape in Eighteenth Century England*, 43).

Italian that is devoid of "pieces of poetry", though containing poetical descriptions in prose that many critics consider superior to those of *The Mysteries of Udolpho*. It is absolutely true that "One is led to believe that poetry is an entirely common occurrence in the world of the novel, practised by nearly everyone upon nearly every premise". But, far from being a defect of *Udolpho* as a novel, as Favret appears to claim,[38] this is one of its merits as a romance and certainly its most authentic interpretative key. Indeed, as far as *Udolpho* is concerned, Scott's praise attributing to the author of *The Romance of the Forest* (1791) "the eye of a painter, with the spirit of a poet",[39] should be completed with the addition "and the ear of a minstrel".

Any attempt to measure the originality of her poems by a comparison with her beloved Thomson and Beattie would be misleading. Since Radcliffe's poems are an integral part of romance, and are essentially characterized by choral writing, they must reflect common and collective feelings. But they are doubtless original in the effect that, like words for music, they produce on readers. This effect depends on the way they appear to be interspersed throughout the narrative: in other words, it depends on the narrative form. *The Mysteries of Udolpho* may be defined as a melodramatic narrative or, rather, a prose melodrama. Only a critical perspective taking into account the vogue of the melodrama at the end of the eighteenth century can allow an adequate interpretation and convincing explanation, in Frye's words,[40] of the "mediumistic" quality, of Radcliffe's writing and its relationship with the world of the unconscious.

If the interspersed poems are an extension of the poetry within the prose, turning it, through their rhythm and rhyme, into music, they also provide, through their themes and their position in the plot, the focal points for outlining the emotional map of the romance's interior landscape. Through a few examples I will briefly illustrate, first, that these poems are organically bound to the rest of the narrative, contributing to its development by playing a precise function (as is the case with "Storied Sonnet"); and second, the profound and lasting

[38] Favret, "Telling Tales about Genre: Poetry in the Romantic Novel", 162.
[39] Scott, "Prefatory Memoir to Mrs Ann Radcliffe", vi.
[40] Northrop Frye, *A Study of English Romanticism*, New York, 1968, 29.

influence they exercised on later artists (as was the case with "The Sea-Nymph").

"Storied Sonnet" is set at the centre of the Alpine scenes, immediately after a prose passage describing "precipices … still more tremendous and … prospects still more wild and majestic … the rough pine bridge thrown across the torrent …. with cataract foaming beneath". This "piece of poetry" depicts the very same images: "The weary traveller … / … tremendous steeps, / Skirting the pathless precipice /… / … hideous chasm … / … the cleft pine a doubtful bridge displays … / … / … Far, far below, the torrent's rising surge, / And … wild impetuous roar …."[41]

The lyrical version of the scene simplifies the various pictures and further accentuates the conventionality of the images, making them more clearly emblematic and effective in the building-up of the atmosphere. At the same time, both rhyme and rhythm (like choral music accompanying a dramatic scene) enlarge and amplify the allegorical resonance of the entire scene, thus recalling the echoes of many other, different voices. One voice, for instance, might be Shaftesbury's apocalyptic voice:

> See! With what trembling Steps poor Mankind treads the narrow Brink of the deep Precipice! From Whence with giddy Horror they look down, mistrusting even the Ground which bears'em; whilst they hear the hollow Sound of Torrents underneath …. [42]

The version in verse aims to transform the heroine's personal experience into a choral one. However, the reader's involvement is not confined to the narrative and musical dimensions, but is further developed on a level we may properly term pictorial, through clear visual images that, as T.S. Eliot maintained in his Dante essay, are the very substance of allegorical language.[43] The subsequent scene presents, in fact, a subject – Hannibal's passage over the Alps – which had been described by Thomas Gray as one fit for Salvator Rosa's painting. Indeed it proved more than fit for the acknowledged "sister

[41] Radcliffe, *The Mysteries of Udolpho*, 164-65 (Vol. II, Ch. 1).

[42] Shaftesbury, *The Moralists,* in Manwaring, *Italian Landscape in Eighteenth Century England*, 18.

[43] See T.S. Eliot, *Dante* (1929), London, 1965, 15.

of Salvator Rosa",[44] or "the Salvator Rosa of English novelists".[45] By a deft handling of narrative perspectives, Radcliffe in fact produced so splendid a version (though in her style of the picturesque sublime) that in the end the reader finds him or herself, along with the heroine, on the edge of the precipice, in the very place as Hannibal's fighting soldiers.

Since I have no intention of entering into a discussion of possible influences, I limit myself to the suggestion that in 1776 John Cozens exhibited a "Landscape with Hannibal crossing the Alps".[46] In 1812 Turner painted another "Hannibal and His Army Crossing the Alps" (which was to be repeatedly engraved), while in his *Etchings and Engravings for the Liber Studiorum* there are some copies of an Alpine bridge, "The Devil's Bridge. Mt St Gothard" (dating from about 1806-1807), which were probably studies of Richard Wilson's impressive pencil drawing called "Ponte Alpino, built by Hannibal". The Rosean bridge perilously hanging over the abyss[47] evidently became a powerful symbol in the collective unconscious, and particularly poignant in the second half of the eighteenth century. At the same time, I will not touch upon the reasons why Radcliffe's "cleft pine" should at best be overlooked as trivial and manneristic, but will only mention Rictor Norton's suggestions about the difficulty of neutralizing Radcliffe's subversive voice.

"The Sea-Nymph" is a better example of a poem whose great influence on later writers has been completely overlooked.[48] In the Venetian scenes, "The Sea-Nymph" occupies the same position as that held by "Storied Sonnet" in the Alpine scenes, and, like the other poem, it is preceded by a faithful version in prose. However, while "Storied Sonnet" describes the "wild forms of danger" and the tragic end of the journey, this poem represents the pleasure deriving from a

---

[44] Charles Bucke, *Beauties, Harmonies, and Sublimities of Nature*, London, 1837, 122-23.

[45] Robert Chambers, "Ann Radcliffe", in *Cyclopaedia of English Literature*, Edinburgh, 1844, 554.

[46] Samuel Holt Monk, *The Sublime: A Study of Critical Theories in Eighteenth-Century England* (1935), Ann Arbor: MI, 1960, 235.

[47] According to Lynne Epstein Heller (*Ann Radcliffe's Gothic Landscape of Fiction and the Various Influences upon It*, New York, 1980, 225) perilous bridges with the cataract foaming beneath it are first to be seen in Salvator Rosa's "Landscape" and "Landscape with a waterfall".

[48] Radcliffe, *The Mysteries of Udolpho*, 179-81 (Vol. II, Ch. 2).

panic immersion in Nature through the heroine's (and the reader's) fantastic metamorphosis into a sea creature incarnating the spirit of the watery city.

If in the nineteenth century the Venetian scenes were considered unsurpassed, and Byron only able to imitate them,[49] it is because at their heart lies the lay of the sea-nymph. In this poem Radcliffe crowned her fantastic transformation of the Venice she had inherited from artistic and literary tradition, by producing a picturesque and Romantic version whose poetical beauty would deeply influence writers and artists after her.[50] It is from this lay, which "might be sung by Shakespeare's Ariel",[51] that many images and metaphors were drawn by "greater and more serious writers"[52] in order to express their relationship with the mythical watery city.

This lay gave rise to an authentically and radically feminine Venice, which, from then on, would elicit in male visitors and writers a typically double reaction of desire and repugnance, love and hate. Therefore the city has at times appeared as an "exquisite sea-thing" benevolent and saving,[53] while at other times Protean and unreliable, potentially dangerous "like a woman" with "depths of possible disorder in her light-coloured eyes".[54]

I cannot mention the other poem, "To a Sea-Nymph", without wondering how the young Romantic poets, including Byron and Shelley, could come to Italy without remembering the mythical rite celebrated on the seashore, the "invocation delivered in the pure and elegant tongue of Tuscany, and accompanied by few pastoral instruments", and the singing of a chorus and semi-chorus.[55] Of course, the nymphs and mythical marine creatures descend from

---

[49] Chambers, "Ann Radcliffe", 558.

[50] See my "Ann Radcliffe in the Representational History of Venice: The Influence of *Udolpho*'s Venetian Scenes", in www.lingue.unibo.it/acume/agenda/cyprus/ papers/b battaglia.htm.

[51] Anna Laetitia Barbauld, "Mrs Radcliffe", in *The British Novelists*, 50 vols, London, 1810, XLIII, vi.

[52] Tony Tanner, *Venice Desired*, Oxford, 1992, 5. "Coral bower's", "crystal court", "sparry columns", "glassy halls", "pale pearl", "sapphire blue", "moonlight waves", "warbling shells", "dolphins" etc., will inspire images of the sea world that recur in the works by Ruskin, Melville, Proust, James, Rilke and the other authors mentioned in Tony Tanner's book.

[53] *Ibid.*, 12-14: Robert Browning (see "The Sea-Nymph", quatrains 16-22).

[54] *Ibid.*, 27: Henry James (see "The Sea-Nymph", quatrains 6-10).

[55] Radcliffe, *The Mysteries of Udolpho*, 420 (Vol. III, Ch. 7).

Botticelli's Venus and works by other painters of the same subject, but there is no denying the fact that their Romantic descendants would reach a far wider public than their more illustrious predecessors. And it was this larger and popular reading-public, possibly somewhat unrefined and uneducated, that Coleridge and Mrs Barbauld had in mind when they expressed their fear that these elegant "pieces of poetry" would be neglected as something unessential or superfluous. The present essay is an attempt to recover the unrecognized power of Radcliffe's "pieces of poetry" both in relation to the question of women's poetic self-inscription and as regards their crucial role within the narrative of the romance and the aesthetic and philosophic debates of the time.

ENDING THE ROMANCE: WOMEN POETS AND THE ROMANTIC VERSE TALE

DIEGO SAGLIA

Originating at the unstable intersection between the romance, the epic and the ballad, verse narratives were one of the most popular and lucrative forms of poetry in the period between the early 1800s and 1825-26, when the publishing industry was hit by a severe financial crisis. Already present in late eighteenth-century literature, the verse narrative flourished first with Scott and Southey and then with Byron, and, curiously, the crisis in the 1820s that brought about its rapid decline was the same chain of events that caused the bankruptcy of Scott, the very writer who had given this genre a new lease of life in the early 1800s.[1] This complex and significant literary form has long been overlooked, or relegated to non-canonical status within conceptions of Romanticism dominated by forms of lyrical effusion and self-revelation. Nonetheless, the verse narrative is a crucial component of British Romantic writing, not only because almost every poet experimented with it, but especially because the revival of romance (one of its major elements) is genealogically keyed to the roots of Romanticism itself. In Stuart Curran's words, "The etymological root of Romanticism, it is easy to forget, is romance"; however, in acting as a concentration of the cultural, aesthetic and ideological preoccupations of Romantic culture, the verse romance superimposes different epochal fault lines through an inexhaustible

[1] On the crisis in the publishing industry that brought about the demise of poetry and the metrical tale as dominant genres, see Lee Erickson, *The Economy of Literary Form: English Literature and the Industrialization of Publishing, 1800-1850*, Baltimore and London, 1996, 26-48.

discursive proliferation that Curran has defined as its "constant imaginative inventiveness".[2]

The inter-generic conditions of the verse narrative, as well as its actual generic status, have been carefully researched and partly laid to rest by Hermann Fischer, who, on the basis of Francis Jeffrey's review of Byron's *The Corsair* and *The Bride of Abydos* (*The Edinburgh Review*, April 1814), with its groundbreaking examination of the contemporary metrical tale, defines it as "a separate branch of poetry".[3] The attempt to establish the generic delimitations of verse narratives, however, seems to be a way of avoiding the most productive and disconcerting aspect of this intergeneric complex, namely its liminality or "inbetweeness", its creation of a cultural admixture in which fact and fiction coalesce, magic and superstition are embedded in Enlightenment rationalism, and the past becomes inextricably linked to the present. In Curran's words, "The romance of British Romanticism tests limits, and it is no coincidence, but rather the inevitable carry-over from this defining genre of the period, that this is a fundamental aspect of all its poetry"[4] – Romanticism as a cultural threshold and as a culture of thresholds, therefore, and the verse romance or metrical tale as its discursive embodiment.

Among the countless intersections at play in the Romantic verse tale, one of its outstanding transitional dimensions is produced by the contact between the masculine and feminine contents of these narratives, a gendered confrontation tellingly located in an inter-generic (inter-modal and inter-formal) nexus. Jacqueline Labbe's *The Romantic Paradox* (2000) examines the interconnections between gender and genre, discussing the romance (but not the verse narrative at large) as being predicated on gendered sites of behaviour fictionally transformed into the generic roles of villain, hero and heroine, which in turn act and react within the confines of the Romantic reinventions and inversions of the genre. Drawing upon conventional connections between gendered and generic roles, the Romantics "manipulate these

---

[2] Stuart Curran, *Poetic Form and British Romanticism*, Oxford, 1986, 129, 132.
[3] Hermann Fischer, *Romantic Verse Narrative: The History of a Genre*, trans. Sue Bollans, Cambridge, 1991, 52.
[4] Curran, *Poetic Form and British Romanticism*, 145.

certainties, even as they exploit their familiar appeal",[5] ultimately producing a sometimes drastic defamiliarization of the romance.

Accordingly, the romance and the more inclusive verse romance contain elaborations of masculinity and femininity that variously support and contest prescriptive cultural discourses between the eighteenth and nineteenth centuries, while, at the same time, opening up a written space of confrontation between principles of male and female authorship and authority. Indeed, literary history seems to have consigned the verse narrative to a male literary tradition in which Scott, Southey and Byron are usually followed by Keats, Shelley, Leigh Hunt and Wordsworth.[6] Of course, despite the various re-evaluations from Bishop Hurd's onwards, the verse romance remained a less muscular genre than the epic and a fundamentally vernacular form of verse without any classical ancestry; yet, by contrast, as shown by Caroline Franklin, male authors such as Scott, Southey, Rogers and Hunt actively re-masculinized the romance in the 1800s and 1810s through a variety of strategies such as the use of annotation (not unknown to women writers such as, for instance, Charlotte Smith and Lady Morgan) and, more decisively, by immolating the female heroines of their popular verse narratives on the altar of a beleaguered patriarchal structure centred on the father figure.[7]

Notwithstanding the feminine features of the romance – such as its insistence on chivalry and the love ethic, its lack of direct relevance and its escapist themes – the metrical tale appears to be a male-authored genre in which the Romantic re-masculinization of literature is especially relevant and, seemingly, successful.[8] Still, what seems to have disappeared from literary-historical reconstructions until very recently is that women poets also actively rewrote the romance, by reorganizing its structure and reworking its themes. And in the period between the 1800s and the 1830s Romantic women poets published an imposing number of verse narratives, a genre that was also an important part of their legacy to Victorian women's verse. Although the career of Letitia Elizabeth Landon started with the publication of

---

[5] Jacqueline M. Labbe, *The Romantic Paradox: Love, Violence and the Uses of Romance, 1760-1830*, Basingstoke, 2000, 140.

[6] See Fischer, *Romantic Verse Narrative: The History of a Genre.*

[7] Caroline Franklin, *Byron's Heroines*, Oxford, 1992, 12-37.

[8] Alan Richardson, "Romanticism and the Colonization of the Feminine", in *Romanticism and Feminism*, ed. Anne K. Mellor, Bloomington: IN, 1988, 13-25.

lyrics and songs in William Jerdan's *Literary Gazette*, it effectively took off thanks to her best-selling verse romances of the 1820s, especially *The Improvisatrice* and *The Troubadour*, written in an expansive narrative format which later fed into her successful novels of the 1830s from *Romance and Reality* (1831) to *Ethel Churchill* (1837). Mary Russell Mitford also began her successful career as a writer in the 1810s by composing long verse narratives (*Christina, the Maid of the South Seas*, 1811, and *Narratives Poems on the Female Character*, 1813). Felicia Hemans published *The Abencerrage* in 1819 and *The Forest Sanctuary* in 1825, a long poem combining action and meditation which she considered to be her best achievement. Matilda Betham with her *The Lay of Marie* (1816) and Mary Tighe with *Psyche; or, the Legend of Love* (1805, 1811) figured prominently among the authors of medievalizing verse narratives. At thirteen Elizabeth Barrett published her epic *The Battle of Marathon* (1820), whereas in her old age Joanna Baillie produced a poetic narrative about the historic Indian female ruler *Ahalia Baee* (1849).

Any such excursus will necessarily fail to convey an adequate idea of the overwhelming number of verse narratives published in the early nineteenth century by women as well as men. What matters, however, is the combined presence of male- and female-authored verse romances and, especially, the ensuing confrontation between different uses of the genre, as Byron and Scott remained hugely influential models for women authors. Indeed, apart from mere repetitions of well-established and successful formulas, female-authored verse narratives present departures, changes and innovations that turn them into interesting textual sites for an examination of gendered modification of the literary in Romantic-period culture.

Indeed, verse romances by women poets often show minor variations of widely shared characteristics foreshadowing more significant transformations from a generic and an ideological point of view and specifically located in the various areas of contention between male and female writing addressed in current critical discourse. For instance, Jacqueline Labbe's recent study of the fragmentation of the romance focuses on the specific ways in which women poets – especially Mary Robinson, Hemans and Barbauld – interrupt the traditional romance plot through the intervention of violence, more often than not directed at men. This is a far cry from the idyllic resolutions ascribed to a transhistorically conceived romance by Gillian Beer on the grounds of Harold Bloom's idea of Romantic poetics as the "internalization of quest-romance". In Romantic literature the verse romance, according to Beer, "expresses the lost or repressed emotional forces of the imagination", while

> For the poets of the high Romantic period romance was essentially an introspective mode: its pleasure domes and faerie lands were within the mind. The extensive landscapes of medieval and renaissance romance have become *paysages intérieurs*".[9]

Yet, harmonization conceals tensions, and the homogenizing generic category of "introspection" has failed to account for the variety of modes and forms adopted by the verse narrative in Romantic-period literature. Above all, this category hides the distinctively unfinished dialogue between male and female versions, an exchange that is inscribed in the textual expressions of the metrical tale itself, as is revealed by the frequent narrative re-elaborations of the ending with their attendant ideological consequences.

Conclusions may seem an odd textual feature to focus on, since endings are usually very conventional moments in these poems, textual *loci* where authors reproduce rather trite ways of bringing their often upsetting tales to a close. Yet, interestingly, in many verse narratives the end of the romance is not the actual end. One frequent, and intriguingly irregular, feature in many of these tales is a final coda in which the story is over, the plot and its temporal structure are suspended, and tale, narrator and reader find themselves outside the main narrative but not yet free from it, for its events still linger and bear on the present:

> There late was laid a marble stone;
> Eve saw it placed – the Morrow gone!
> It was no mortal arm that bore
> That deep-fix'd pillar to the shore;
> For there, as Helle's legends tell,
> Next morn 'twas found where Selim fell;
> Lash'd by the tumbling tide, whose wave
> Denied his bones a holier grave:
> And there by night, reclin'd, 'tis said,
> Is seen a ghastly turban'd head:

[9] Gillian Beer, *The Romance*, London, 1970, 59-60.

> And hence extended by the billow,
> 'Tis named the 'Pirate-phantom's pillow!'
> Where first it lay that mourning flower
> Hath flourish'd; flourisheth this hour,
> Alone and dewy, coldly pure and pale;
> As weeping Beauty's cheek at Sorrow's tale!

These lines from the conclusion of Byron's *The Bride of Abydos* of 1813 (II, 717-32),[10] one of his most influential verse romances, illustrate the type of coda found in Romantic verse narratives and its forms of suspension. Here the revolutionary Selim and the beautiful Zuleika, daughter of the Ottoman tyrant against whom Selim is fighting, are both dead after the defeat of the hero's unsuccessful rebellion. The tumultuous events of Byron's plot have come to an end, and by line 725 ("And there by night") the reader is transported onto a different diegetic level, having left the plot but still remaining within the story. Time shifts quickly from the narrative past (ll. 717-24) to the present expressions of "'tis said" (l. 725) and "this hour" (l. 730) that correspond to posterity, the "ever after" formula of the romance projecting the tale into futurity and eternity. The conclusion therefore amounts to a narrative fragment, a relic of the tale that survives the end of the romance and occupies a time that both is and is not that of the tale to which it is juxtaposed. Temporally this relic is a fragment of the past projected into a future that is the reader's present. Moreover, this interweaving of temporal planes is embedded in the generic features of this kind of conclusion, not only because it is one possible ending of this narrative form but also because it is intimately connected with the originative landscape of the genre, which has its presumed origins in oral and narrative popular literature, as Byron's "'tis said" implies.

Objects such as the stone pillar, the "ghastly turban'd head" and the flower serve to memorialize the narrative, functioning as its material residue. Romantic-period verse tales abound with such relics. Walter Scott's *Lay of Last Minstrel* (1805), *Marmion* (1808) and *Rokeby* (1813) close with similar, albeit extremely compressed, conclusions, which are in practice mere assertions to the effect that the successfully resolved tales have remained in everyone's memory

---

[10] Byron, *Poetical Works*, ed. Frederick Page, revised edition ed. John Jump, Oxford, 1989, 276.

through the centuries. Further, Wordsworth's *White Doe of Rylstone* (1815) provides perhaps the most conspicuous instance of the narrative relic, as the white doe herself is the material testimony embodying the tale of the Norton family, and Emily in particular, whilst providing the occasion from which the narration starts. Most importantly, the inter-generic status of this type of unfinished ending is further illustrated by its emergence in a variety of narrative genres – verse romances, ballads and shorter narrative poems – such as Robert Southey's "The Lovers' Rock" (1798), Mary Robinson's "The Savage of Aveyron" (1800), most of Anne Bannermann's *Tales of Superstition and Chivalry* (1802),[11] Byron's *The Giaour* (1813) and *The Island* (1823), Leigh Hunt's *The Story of Rimini* (1816), John Keats' *Isabella* (1820), Letitia Elizabeth Landon's *The Improvisatrice* (1825), *The Golden Violet* (1827),[12] *The Venetian Bracelet* (1828), and some of her shorter poems such as "The Guerrilla Chief", "Gladesmuir", "The Minstrel of Portugal" and "The Coniston Curse".

The fascination exerted by this irregularly recurrent textual characteristic seems to lie in its predication of the permanence of the tale and the events it narrates, the dramatic disruption of order (one fundamental hallmark of the romance), and a violent return to an initial condition that never constitutes a real or lasting solution. The relic identified in this kind of conclusion may be described as a "trace" of the narrative itself, a fragment or a splinter of it which subsists outside the frame of the tale (as if in a Genettian paratextual dimension)[13] and declares the endurance of the narrative, its value and its relevance to the present. Therefore the "trace" is also a textual phantasm, in keeping with the sense of popular superstition pervading these conclusions: it is the ghost or revenant of a narrative which reaches out to its readers across time, even as it makes plain the metanarrative potential of the genre, its ability to reflect on its

---

[11] See "The Perjured Nun", "The Penitent's Confession", "The Festival of St Magnus the Martyr", "Basil", "The Fisherman of Lapland", "The Murcian Cavalier", "The Black Knight of the Water" and "The Prophecy of Merlin".

[12] In this long poem, made up of a frame and numerous inset narratives and lyrics, not only is the violet itself a "trace" but also the inset tales repropose the same type of ending without closure as in "The Lay of the Norman Knight", "The German Minnesinger's Tale", "Tale of the Moorish Bard" and "The English Knight's Ballad".

[13] See Gérard Genette, *Palimpsestes: la littérature au second degré*, Paris, 1982.

textuality (its own treatment of time, for instance), and its position at the nexus of the romance, the ballad and the legend.

Evidence of the originative status of the "trace" is offered by one of the most popular selections of ancient romances of the period, George Ellis' three-volume *Specimens of Early English Metrical Romances* (1805), the one collection largely responsible for transferring these texts from the selected circles of learned antiquarians to a wider public through its paraphrases, interspersed with selected quotations, of twenty medieval romances. Additionally, in his lengthy introduction, Ellis offers a summary of the Lays of Marie de France, some of which present the same type of unfinished conclusion and "trace" seen in the Romantic verse narrative. Thus the endings of "Eliduc" and "Milun" express the idea that the lays have been composed for the benefit of future ages. In "Les deux Amants" ("Les Dous Amanz") the two lovers are buried in the same coffin and "the mountain [where it is placed] still retains the name of 'the two lovers'"; whereas "Around their tomb the earth exhibits an unceasing verdure; and hither the whole country resort for the most valuable herbs employed in medicine, which owe their origin to the contents of the marvellous vial".[14] Similar in tone is the conclusion to "Laustic", the lay of the nightingale: "[The lady's] gallant paramour caused his mistress's present [the bird] to be inclosed in a golden box, richly studded with gems, which he constantly carried about his person".[15]

Here, as in the later Romantic versions, the plot has seemingly reached its conclusion, and order is eventually re-established. Yet story and characters do not want to fade away and are encapsulated in an object, a place, or a tale that grants them eternal life and eternal recurrence within the sphere of the narrative. They are the text's revenants, as in Selim's "ghastly turban'd head" in *The Bride of Abydos* or as in the conclusion to Mary Leman Grimstone's *Zayda: A Spanish Tale in Three Cantos* (1820), a tale of clear Byronic descent where the death of the unhappy lovers is memorialized, and left suspended, through the trace or phantasm. The poem's closing lines duly record that, after the death of the protagonists, boatmen and fishermen have seen the heroine's ghost haunting the rocky shore where she and her lover expired, whereas a flower peculiar to that spot

---

[14] George Ellis, *Specimens of Early English Metrical Romances*, rev. edn ed. J.O. Halliwell, London, 1848, 53.

[15] *Ibid.*, 59.

grows on the rocks as the undying symbol of the lovers' unhappy tale.[16] A less literal ghostliness emerges in the conclusion to Felicia Hemans' *The Abencerrage*, a narrative set on the eve of the fall of Granada to the Christians in 1492 and based on interlocked confrontations between the values of the public sphere and private affections, the clash of imperial histories and personal stories, and the tensions between masculine and feminine views of history. Hemans' text illuminates these contrasts through conflicts of gender in a prelude to her drama *The Siege of Valencia* of 1823 where such confrontations achieve tragic clarity and intensity. In the poetic narrative of *The Abencerrage* the poet stages these interrelated conflicts through an opposition between domestic and public femininity embodied in the protagonist Zayda, who rejects her lover's offer to defect to the Christian side and, instead, takes up an active role in the Moors' resistance against the encroaching Spanish armies. So again the romance is developed as a faultline genre, testing limits and working towards a conclusion that conventionally consigns both lovers, and the conflict they personify, to death but not to oblivion:

> A few short years, and in the lonely cave
> Where sleeps the Zegri maid, is Hamet's grave.
> Sever'd in life, united in the tomb –
> Such, of the hearts that loved so well, the doom!
> Their dirge, of woods and waves the eternal moan;
> Their sepulchre, the pine-clad rocks alone.
> And oft beside the midnight watch-fire's blaze,
> Amidst those rocks in long departed days
> (When freedom fled, to hold, sequester'd there,
> The stern and lofty councils of despair,)
> Some exiled Moor, a warrior of the wild,
> Who the lone hours with mournful strains beguiled,
> Hath taught his mountain-home the tale of those
> Who thus have suffer'd, and who thus repose.[17]

The final lines feature an unmistakable instance of the "trace", as the lovers' narrative is transformed into a folk-tale, the material of

---

[16] See Diego Saglia, *Poetic Castles in Spain: British Romanticism and Figurations of Iberia*, Amsterdam and Atlanta, 2000, 182-91.

[17] *The Abencerrage*, III, ll. 607-20, in *Felicia Hemans: Selected Poems, Letters, Reception Materials*, ed. Susan J. Wolfson, Princeton and Oxford, 2000, 131-32.

traditional lore, with a shift that recalls similar developments in *Zayda* or *The Bride of Abydos*. By adapting the conclusions to oral tales or popular ballads, Hemans endows her narrative with the primitive (and primary) status of an oral account. Yet, apart from such originative and generic considerations, the poem's ending without closure acquires particular significance in the context of the reconsideration of male and female heroism permeating *The Abencerrage*. The text indeed defines its confrontational politics by redistributing the separate spheres of action and the relations between masculine and feminine codes of behaviour. The valorous Hamet is a traitor to his country and an ineffectual lover constantly bent on enclosing his beloved in the flowery prison of her domestic bower. Zayda, by contrast, is the representative of an undaunted, embattled heroism, stoically tragic in its defense of the values of home, country and the affections. Thus Hemans' tale of love in times of war both confirms and critiques the values praised by the conservative *Gentleman's Magazine* in her collection of narrative poetry of 1819: "bravery, meekness under pain, delicacy, taste, and sentiment."[18] In fact, public heroism and the cult of the affections are interwoven in Hemans' excavation of the links between devotion to home and an active experience of the public sphere that ultimately rewards Zayda's domestically based heroism. As Jacqueline Labbe observes, the poet often interrupts her romances through acts of violence against a male figure whose dead body becomes an icon of female desire and of its invariably doomed outcome. And if male heroism fails in text after text, so, in *The Abencerrage*, does female resistance to adverse destiny. Closure in Hemans' tales is always banal and frustrating, depending on a "romantic love [that] promises union but enacts disintegration".[19]

That the tragic contrast between masculine and feminine codes is now the stuff of ever-repeatable oral tales reveals that the narrative and its issues, unlike the characters, cannot find peace. Hamet and Zayda "repose", their personal sufferings resolved in death, but their story survives as the only ghostly trace of their unhappy lives. A tragedy of unbridgeable divides, Hemans' verse romance indirectly

---

[18] *The Gentleman's Magazine*, XC (March 1820), 239.

[19] Labbe, *The Romantic Paradox: Love, Violence and the Uses of Romance, 1760-1830*, 100.

asks to be narrated over and over as a haunting tale which may not be forgotten and is eternally true.

Another narrative of thwarted cross-cultural love set in Spain is Eliza Norton's *Alcon Malanzore*, published four years before Hemans' successful collection of verse tales and featuring a conclusion equally haunted by the romantic "trace":

> Ages have rolled away – yet still the stone,
> Where that stern Spirit breathed its latest groan,
> The Peasants mark and shun – and on that hill,
> Where once the wild flower, and the wandering rill,
> Enamoured bloomed and wept – is now a heath,
> Unchanged by winter's snow, or summer's breath,
> Bare as its craggy crest: – and legends tell
>
> .... that on one night
> Of every passing year, an awful sight
> Is seen by such, as with adventurous tread,
> Dare steal upon the orgies of the Dead: –
> For in that cell, with dire unearthly laugh,
> And yelling shriek, Sprites meet to dance and quaff –
> The moon gleams red – and o'er the mountain-brow,
> Gliding to solemn strains, wild, soft, and slow,
> Wreathed in a chill embrace – is seen the shade
> Of a dark Warrior, and a bright fair Maid.[20]

The conclusion to this darkly pessimistic poem of interracial love and hatred does not foresee any immediate or even distant triumph for an alternative, cross-cultural ideal of tolerance. Making an integration into either Moorish or Spanish society impossible, the Christian Rosaline's union with the Muslim commander Alcon Malanzore has relegated them to a cultural and national no man's land. The poem's tensions remain unsolved, culminating in a final scene where the lovers' ghosts join other restless spirits in a demonic sabbath, a version of the trace that does not amount to an elegiac "happy everafter" and does not merely state, in ballad-like fashion, that the intercultural sentimental ideal lives on despite the unrelenting persecution to which the lovers have been subjected. By contrast, in

[20] *Alcon Malanzore: A Moorish Tale by the Hon. Mrs Esme Steuart Erskine*, ed. E. B. Norton, Brussels, 1815, 192-93.

the open-ended conclusion to Norton's text, Alcon and Rosaline are un-dead because the tensions undermining their unhappy existences have not disappeared. "Wreathed in a chill embrace", the two lovers are still caught up in their fatal passion, their sorrowful story reduced to a "shade", and their earthly love transmuted into a terrifying "orgy of the Dead". In this fashion the narrative appurtenances of Gothic and traditional folk-stories encase a tale in which miscegenation and interracial or intercultural fusion are in constant conflict, with an un-dead and undying potential for destruction that is eternally ready to wreak havoc in the readers' present.[21]

Similarly, and in a way that appears quite removed from the male poets' treatment of the trace, death provides a conclusion but no resolution to Letitia Landon's *The Improvisatrice* of 1824. This bestselling narrative about an Italian poetess incapable of securing the love of Lorenzo, who deserts her to marry another, is a well-known re-elaboration of the foundational myths of Corinne and Sappho focusing on conflictive binaries such as woman and fame, art and love, public and private, both in the main plot and in the various lyrics sung by the improvisatrice. At length the poetess dies forsaken and Lorenzo, left a widower, mourns her loss. In this final elegiac pacification, a picture of the improvisatrice functions as the visible trace of the (still inextricable) web of issues woven by the preceding cantos. In a coda written in the third person, instead of the usual first person of the poetess's voice, the narrator visits Lorenzo's palace:

> … pictures shone around the dome.
> But there was one – a loveliest one! –
> One picture brightest of all there!
> Oh! never did the painter's dream
> Shape things so gloriously fair!
> ……………………………………
> She looked a form of light and life, –
> All soul, all passion, and all fire;
> A priestess of Apollo's, when

[21] For a different approach to *Alcon Malanzore*, see Anne Mellor's brief suggestion that "the possible end of generations of religious wars and masculine violence, here mounted in the names of Christianity and Islam, lies in the interracial love-affair of the virginal Catholic maid Rosaline with the Moorish chieftain Alcon Malanzore", in "Romanticism, Gender and the Anxieties of Empire: An Introduction", *European Romantic Review*, VIII (1997), 152.

The morning beams fall on her lyre;
A Sappho, or ere love had turned
The heart to stone where once it burned.
But by the picture's side was placed
A funeral urn on which was traced
The heart's recorded wretchedness; –
And on a tablet, hung above,
Was 'graved one tribute of sad words –
"LORENZO TO HIS MINSTREL LOVE."[22]

As in Hemans' *The Abencerrage*, man survives woman and the tragic events of the plot; and, perhaps not unexpectedly after Hemans' frequent use of the male corpse, in Landon's tale *man* is the "trace", although a less durable one than the work of art recording the improvisatrice's and Lorenzo's tale of woe. Indeed, the painting is a fit trace to inscribe the incongruity between female creativity and fulfilment through love since, much as in Hemans' "Properzia Rossi" (1828), the woman's artistic skills are finally defeated as well as indicted for bringing about the artist's unhappiness and death. And yet in Landon, as in Hemans, art is what remains. It is the enduring trace of a conflict which is only apparently resolved. Moreover, the picture is an emblem of life (as in the references to "passion" and "fire") placed next to a second trace – the urn – symbolic of death and explicitly charged with the task of "tracing" and "recording". Finally in this scene, the third, most haunting and haunted "trace" is Lorenzo himself, who exists as a living funeral monument visited by a narrator embodying posterity, and whose name is inscribed, together with that of his "Minstrel Love", on the tablet which is the key to this multiplication and superimposition of traces.

Where *The Improvisatrice* and the other tales seen here should reach closure through their carefully wrought melodramatic finales, readers are faced with further narrative developments, as if the verse romance had not quite reached its conclusion. And these developments project the text into a cycle of unending narration which falls short of Northrop Frye's authoritative definition of the romance as, in Fredric Jameson's words, "wish fulfillment or utopian fantasy" aimed at the re-establishment and celebration of order.[23] Even

[22] L.E.L., *The Improvisatrice: and Other Poems*, London, 1825, 103-105.
[23] Fredric Jameson, "Magical Narratives: Romance as Genre", *New Literary History*, VII (1975), 138.

Jameson's own attempt at historicizing this definition becomes enmeshed in a concept of textuality based on harmonization and fails to capture the unresolved disruptions and tensions in the verse romances by male and, especially, female Romantic poets. He locates at the centre of the romance a verifiable socio-cultural tension between opposite codes transfigured through the icons of good and evil, and accordingly suggests that this genre "expresses a transitional moment, yet one of a very special type: its contemporaries must feel their society torn between past and future in such a way that the alternatives are grasped as hostile but somehow unrelated worlds". For Jameson, "the great art romances of the Romantic period are only too obviously symbolic attempts to come to terms with the triumph of the bourgeoisie and the new unglamorous social forms developing out of the market system".[24] As a result, this narrative form in its Romantic incarnation is once more and quite obviously "an imaginary 'solution'"[25] to very real and pressing issues.

Nonetheless, *pace* Frye, Jameson and Beer, verse romances appear more frayed where they should achieve conclusion and deliver a final image of pacification, a structural and thematic irregularity that is common to both male- and female-authored texts. Even more specifically, as this exemplary excursus should have made plain, texts by women poets greatly emphasize the tragedy implicit in this absence of closure. The traces in Byron's, Scott's or Wordsworth's poems tend to appropriate folk-tale narrative modes to highlight the constant renovation of the narrative impulse or locate the poem in a popular context of traditions, superstitions and oral story-telling; while female-authored conclusions present more contentious and less easily effaced traces. Instead of simply insisting on the endurance of the tales and the act of narration, the women's versions focus on the protagonists and the opposing (gendered, behavioural, moral) codes they represent, avoiding conciliatory gestures and heightening conflict as is most dramatically evident in Norton's *Alcon Malanzore*.

Even if no satisfactory literary-theoretical formula may be found for such an elusive and irregular feature as the romantic trace, it may be suggested that – in texts such as Norton's, Hemans' and Landon's – this trace encapsulates the characters' gendered conflict and, by the

---

[24] *Ibid.*, 158.
[25] *Ibid.*, 161.

same token, the paramount confrontations permeating Romantic women poets' reappropriations and adaptations of the verse narrative. Their romantic traces confirm that textual tensions are not dissolved in the conclusion to their verse tales, but rather remain unharmonized at the narratives' margins. Throwing into relief the impossibility of a reconciliation, the traces haunting female-authored verse tales reveal that their fundamental issues are still tragically unresolved within the textual environment of a conclusion which is not the end of the romance.

LETITIA ELIZABETH LANDON'S *THE IMPROVISATRICE*: THE FATAL COMBINATION OF GENDER AND GENRE

SERENA BAIESI

It lies not in our power to love and hate;
For will in us is overruled by Fate.
(Marlowe)[1]

Letitia Elizabeth Landon's long poem *The Improvisatrice* was written and published in London in 1824. Landon was already a famous poet at that time, since she started at an early age publishing poems and reviews for the *Literary Gazette* edited by William Jerdan, signing her contributions with the enigmatic and intriguing initials of L.E.L. *The Improvisatrice*, her second volume, was immediately a great success and thereafter sold extremely well, increasing her fame. In the Advertisement to the poem she describes it as "an attempt to illustrate that species of inspiration common in Italy, where the mind is warmed from earliest childhood by all that is beautiful in Nature and glorious in Art". The narrator is a young artist who finds self-expression through both pencil and lute, and is "entirely Italian – a young female with all the loveliness, vivid feeling, and genius of her own impassioned land".[2] This description adumbrates the leading themes of this poem: female artistic genius set against a well-defined Italian background. My aim in this essay is to explore the representation in *The Improvisatrice* of the intersections and reciprocal influences between gender – female genius both of the author and of several characters in this poem – and genre, in particular how the oral

[1] Quotation from the title page of L.E.L., *The Improvisatrice*, London, 1825. The lines are from Christopher Marlowe's *Hero and Leander*, ll. 173-174.
[2] *Ibid.*, Advertisement.

improvisation becomes long poem in Landon's hands. The discussion will focus – with special reference to Letitia Elizabeth Landon – on how the traditional Italian culture in which the art of improvisation originated gave birth to a well-exploited literary style in Romantic literature, and how this oral art was exploited and transformed by female writers.

Landon's work contains strong echoes of Mme de Staël's *Corinne*, whose poems she translated for the English public in 1833.[3] And if *Corinne* was "*the* book of the woman of genius", *The Improvisatrice* is the poem of this female icon, because Mme de Staël's novel enormously influenced contemporary and later women writers, and for them "the myth of Corinne persisted as both inspiration and warning: it is the fantasy of the performing heroine".[4] The protagonist of this long poem, a famous Italian woman painter and poet, performs her lyrics, songs and tales in public spaces, usually on subjects requested by the audience: hence "Improvisatrice" is the only name she is known by. One day in Florence, her place of birth, she meets an English gentleman, Lorenzo, and falls desperately in love with him. It seems that this love is requited, as they meet again during a ball, at which they exchange a kiss. Lorenzo, however, is already engaged to Ianthe, whom he marries in obeisance to his family's will, despite the fact that he is not in love with her. By chance the wedding takes place in the dismayed presence of the Improvisatrice, who falls ill from the shock.

She never recovers from the disappointment, even when Lorenzo comes back to Florence, to explain his story and propose to her. She dies soon after and leaves her self-portrait to Lorenzo, as a tangible memoir of her lasting love. This main plot is interleaved by many other stories about women, love and despair, narrated by the Improvisatrice alone as monologues or as public performances before a worshipping audience.

Each of these tales has a female protagonist. The first character to be introduced is the Improvisatrice herself, who is both the heroine of the central story and the narrator of all the others. These are more or less legendary women, from both past and present time, such as

---

[3] Letitia Elizabeth Landon knew Mme De Staël's *Corinne, ou l'Italie* very well since its first publication in French in 1807. She then published the English translation for the British edition together with Isabel Hill in 1833.

[4] Ellen Moers, *Literary Women*, New York, 1972, 173-74.

Sappho, Petrarch's Laura, Corinne and many Oriental figures: Moorish, Turkish or Indian girls. These literary women of fame, who gained fortune and success during their lives, were subjects beloved of Romantic women writers: one only has to think of Felicia Hemans' poem "Properzia Rossi" (dedicated to the famous female sculptor from Bologna) and her "Last Song of Sappho", along with Mary Robinson's set of sonnets *Sappho and Phaon.* A later generation of female poets – including Elizabeth Barrett and Christina Rossetti – resumed this motif of the talented woman. Indeed, Letitia Elizabeth Landon herself – because of her unusual life and mysterious death in Africa – was to become the protagonist of poems by Barrett and Rossetti.

The figure of the *improvvisatrice* or *improvvisatore* was inherited from the Italian tradition of reciting scenes from the past in public spaces. Such performances were originally carried out in Latin, and later in vulgar Italian. This oral genre flourished during the Renaissance, but survived long after, so much so that such performers could still be found during the nineteenth century. In Italy the *improvvisatore* or *improvvisatrice* was a hybrid persona: an improvising actor who was often also the author of what he or she was staging, and associated with a prolific genius for both the content and the performance of the recited work of art. The presentation was supposedly spontaneous and melodramatic, and usually consisted of a song accompanied by an instrument: violin, lute or guitar. The public, who paid the artist at the end of the recitation, usually requested the topic of the entertainment at the beginning, since it was easy for the performer to satisfy whatever request was made of him or her. The *New Monthly Magazine* described the extempore talent of such a performer in 1824, the same year that Landon's poem came out:

> Poured forth at the impulse of the moment, and under the influence of an excitement over which the will can have but little control, the distinguishing characters of extempore compositions are rather bold and nervous figure, than correctness or precision. The very attempt to subject them to any but metrical restriction would require an intensity and coolness of consideration which is quite foreign to the spirit of an Improvisatore. The few who have aspired to immortality by giving stability to their imaginations, have uniformly failed in the attempt; but most of them have prudently abstained from the hazardous

> enterprise of publication. Improvisation is a talent rather natural than acquired.[5]

It is noteworthy that this passage specifically portrays the Italian literary figure of the *improvvisatore* or *improvvisatrice*, but it also corresponds to the canonical perception of English women poets during the nineteenth century: spontaneous, untamed, natural but slightly hysterical. The woman poet's talent in this case could be exhibited in public spaces, as a theatrical performance, whereas poetry was dictated by natural genius, which did not need the support of a playwright. This method of oral composition, in association with the female gender, attracted much public and literary attention outside the Italian geographical borders. In fact, women writers of the Romantic period frequently employed the figure of the Italian *improvvisatrice* in order to attain more freedom in public expression as women, and to use different genres of poetry mixing together spontaneous versification and oral improvisation.

However, while the talents of an English female writer and of an Italian *improvvisatrice* alike could be accepted as spontaneous and natural, both kinds of artist expressed a certain apprehensiveness regarding publication. In the case of women writers there was a general anxiety of having to compete with male writers, and as regards improvisation, being a traditionally oral and spontaneous art, this genre was not considered suitable for transcription. In employing such a model, women poets usually took some risks, since this figure had a mixed reception on English soil, as Oriane Smith affirms in her article on British women writers and eighteenth-century representations of the improvisatrice:

> Although positioning themselves as improvisatrice established a precedent for their public endeavours, this model of spontaneous public performance also exposed British women writers such as Hester Lynch Piozzi, Mary Robinson, and Letitia Landon to accusations of immorality and enthusiasm. In a time of political and social instability, the idea of the improvisatrice, when translated into a

---

[5] *New Monthly Magazine*, XI (1824), 202.

> British idiom, brought with it uncomfortable memories of a less benign precedent for women's contributions to public life.[6]

Despite this risk, Landon creates her own version of an Italian *improvvisatrice*, inscribing this character within her traditional role. Romantic women writers such as Landon tried to communicate something more than delicate feelings and shyness of public performance, pushing their poems towards the political sphere: "In spite of its ostensibly apolitical and pagan roots, during 1790's, the model of the improvisatrice became overtly politicized, and linked to what was perceived as a plague of dangerous precedents for female literary authority in the eighteenth century which threatened to undermine the moral and social stability in England."[7]

Indeed, Letitia Elizabeth Landon skilfully goes further than the original stereotype of the Italian improvisatrice, adding many other attributes to her heroine, in order to give life to her own version of the part:

> My power was but a woman's power;
> Yet, in that great and glorious dower
> Which Genius gives, I had my part:
> I poured my full and burning heart
> In song, and on the canvass made
> My dreams of beauty visible;
> I know not which I loved the most –
> Pencil or lute, – both loved so well.[8]

This revised version of the improvisatrice role not only incorporates its original qualities. She is also a new Romantic heroine, acclaimed and happy to be so; she falls in love and she does not change heart in spite of adversities. In her poem Letitia Elizabeth Landon exploits conventional feminine themes, such as love and beauty, but takes them beyond the confines of domestic affections. In doing so she breaks the traditional female canon with its own tools. As Glennis Stephenson suggests, she "struggles to resist conventional gender

---

[6] Oriane Smith, "British Women Writers and Eighteenth-Century Representations of the Improvisatrice", *Corvey Journal*, 2 (Winter 2004), Sheffield Hullam University, http://www2.shu.ac.uk/corvey/CW3journal/issue%20two/smith.html, 1.
[7] *Ibid.*, 2.
[8] L.E.L., *The Improvisatrice*, 3.

ideology, and to transform constraint into opportunity, creating L.E.L. that overwhelms the conventions which are its foundation".[9] And this tension between public space, politics and acclamation, together with a desolate private life, is well staged by Landon's Improvisatrice:

> I ever thought that poet's fate
> Utterly lone and desolate.
> It is the spirit's bitterest pain
> To love, to be beloved again;
> And yet between a gulf which ever
> The hearts that burn to meet must sever.[10]

Landon is quite categorical in representing the dichotomies between private/public, anonymity/celebrity, and home/stage. As Germaine Greer observes:

> The artist, especially the romantic artist, does exhibit himself with a view to obtaining fame and honour and love, but he is not often satisfied either with his achievement or with his reward. He has two love affairs going on at once, one with his medium and the other with his public, and neither results in a stable or contented relationship.[11]

The female talent has, therefore, to wear a mask in order to adjust herself to the many situations of the writer's life, since the role of literary genius was usually a male one. Thus Landon writes: "Corinne / Is but another name for her who wrote, / Who felt, and poured her spirit on her lay / What are the feelings but her own."[12] In Landon's poem the woman of genius is not able to reconcile the free exercise of art with that of happiness within the domestic sphere. In order to find her own inner balance, the Improvisatrice loses something of her personality every time she puts herself on the stage. Inscribing herself in a new character as first-person narrator, she shares with the public her struggles to find her real self. Especially when she presents the

---

[9] Glennis Stephenson, "Poetic Construction: Mrs Hemans, L.E.L., and the Image of the Nineteenth-Century Woman Poet", in *Reimagining Women: Representations of Women in Culture*, eds Shirley Neuman and Glennis Stephenson, Toronto, 1994, 62.
[10] L.E.L., *The Improvisatrice*, 6.
[11] Germaine Greer, *Slip-Shod Sibyls: Recognition, Rejection and the Woman Poet*, London, 1995, 278.
[12] Glennis Stephenson, *Letitia Landon: The Woman behind L.E.L.*, Manchester, 1995, 55.

histories of different women, she herself represents a part of her own story, mixed with the performance. This is one of the main differences between the male and the female protagonists in the poem: the hero will always affirm his own personality in every encounter with others, especially when struck by a beautiful woman of talent. In contrast, the Improvisatrice will share her happiness and sorrows with her public and fail to impose her gaze on the one she loves. She needs public acclaim to feel alive, to be recognized as an artist.

By the same token, however, the Improvisatrice finds in the public the source of her genius as well as of her own identity. This is not presumption or aimless ambition; the woman needs to be acknowledged by society in order not to be overwhelmed or marginalized by it. She needs the gaze of the other, the attention of the public; she performs so that they may see her, at last. What Landon is claiming in this poem is something more than fame for its own sake: a notoriety not only related to economic reward, but which endures after the death of the artist. In order to establish a special link with the public, the Improvisatrice turns poetry into a drama, in which she plays the main role. The page of the written poem becomes the stage of a play, but it is not a theatre of the mind: on the contrary, it is necessarily a public performance in an open space where the audience is as important as the main actor.

This kind of interaction has been defined as a "theatrical identity" found and displayed within the time/space of the performance: it is the present time, without past, without future:[13]

> They [the public] stole me from my lulling dream,
> And said they knew that such an hour
> Had ever influence on my soul,
> And raised my sweetest minstrel power.[14]

The woman is simultaneously the subject and the object of art. In this way she is mirrored by her own art as well as by the audience's perception. As in most of Landon's poems, *The Improvisatrice* ends with the heroine's death; however, this sudden ending does not mean that a woman of fame should surrender to the rules of society. Instead,

---

[13] Maddalena Pennacchia Punzi, *Il mito di Corinne: Viaggio in Italia e genio femminile in Anna Jameson, Margaret Fuller e George Eliot*, Rome, 2001, 23.
[14] L.E.L., *The Improvisatrice*, 14.

Landon uses death to affirm the woman's right to a role in society, even if it comes at a very high cost.

The contradiction between public fame and private life in this poem represents the split that often took place in the nineteenth century between famous women and the society they frequented. Women's artistic will and domestic duty have always been antagonists, especially in the case of celebrated and talented women; genius and fame were seen as incompatible with domestic affections. Letitia Elizabeth Landon tried to find a compromise within this dichotomy, as we can see in her life as well as in her poems, including *The Improvisatrice*. Here she stages the drama of the female genius, but transported to another place, another tradition, far from England. Moving her character away from an English background she distances herself from the society that censured her poetic imagination and especially her public identity as a single woman.

Romantic exile was often associated with Italy, a land where manners and literary expression were seen (realistically or not) as freer than in England. Behind the dislocation of her heroine, Landon shows her unwillingness to face openly the role imposed on English women like herself, who lived alone, unmarried and economically independent from a father, a brother or a husband. The poet clearly imagined Italy as a land of opportunity, a place free from rules imposed by the British middle-class tradition. Not by chance, the poem opens with these lines:

> I am a daughter of that land,
> Where the poet's lip and the painter's hand
> Are most divine, – where earth and sky,
> Are picture both and poetry –
> I am of Florence.[15]

In this metaphorical journey – not least because it is more a movement of the mind than a physical one, considering that the author never went to Italy – L.E.L. has the chance to express her dissent towards the restrictions of English patriarchal society. Italy was considered an ideal place where freedom and art were joined together in mutual symbiosis. As Moers declares in her analysis of Mme de Staël's Corinne: "In Italy there is no hypocrisy about morals, as in England,

---

[15] *Ibid.*, 1.

no malicious gossip, as in France; no false modesty or artifice; no obsession with rank or convention; but only spontaneity in love and art."[16] Moving her heroine outside the English arena, as Mme de Staël did in her novel, Landon found a free expressive space. Italy is rather an ideal space than a geographical reference in most English poems and novels published in the nineteenth century; it represents a rite of passage rather than a real nation with a defined culture and politics. As Landon writes in a letter dated 1837 to Mrs S.C. Hall, recalling her youthful readings:

> I especially remember a Life of Petrarch which perhaps first threw round Italy that ideal charm it has always retained in my eyes. The scene of his being crowned at the Capitol was always present to my mind, and gave me the most picturesque notion of the glory of poetry.[17]

Time and place find a conjunction in the Italian surroundings, since every reader will immediately associate history, tradition, landscape, scents and moods without requiring further information. For the English audience of the nineteenth century, Italy is already a space-time where nature and culture become one.[18]

As Mme de Staël had done in her novel, Letitia Elizabeth Landon stages in her poem certain differences between Italy and England, underlining the distinction between the people and culture of Northern and Southern Europe respectively. The Improvisatrice, like Corinne, is a typical Latin character from the South with dark eyes, dark hair and healthy constitution; she is passionate and talented, uninhibited in public, ready to fall in love. But Ianthe (Lorenzo's wife) embodies the Northern type: pale, blonde, delicate and especially reluctant to appear

---

[16] Moers, *Literary Women*, 203.

[17] *Letters by Letitia Elizabeth Landon*, ed. Francis J. Sypher, Scholar's Facsimiles and Reprints, Ann Arbor, 2001, 167.

[18] On the reciprocal influence between Italian and English literature and culture during the nineteenth century, see these recent studies: *Immaginando l'Italia: Itinerari letterari del Romanticismo inglese/Imagining Italy: Literary Itineraries in British Romanticism*, ed. Lilla Maria Crisafulli, Bologna, 2002; *British Romanticism and Italian Literature: Translating, Reviewing, Rewriting*, eds Laura Bandiera and Diego Saglia, Amsterdam and New York, 2005.

and speak in public.[19] Also, Landon opposes and intermingles the physical features of her women protagonists and their personalities, in order to underline a cross-cultural clash and intersection between tradition and modernity, Classicism and Romanticism. As Carla L. Peterson affirms in her study on nineteenth-century readers and their books, with reference to Mme de Staël's Corinne:

> Her heroine embodies and synthesizes aspects of both English and Italian, Northern and Southern, cultures. She is thus interpreting Corinne in light of the Romantic myth that defines European civilization as composed of two distinct cultures, that of the South and that of the North. According to this myth, the South is primarily represented by the Classical cultures of Greece and Rome. In these pagan cultures, people led simple lives, identified with nature, were given to the sensuous and materialistic aspects of existence, and devoted little time to reflection. Passionate and enthusiastic, people of the North possessed a gloomy imagination and were prone to melancholy and suffering.[20]

Following Mme de Staël's example, L.E.L. also fuses in her Improvisatrice different personal features both from the South (physical appearance and naturalness in artistic expression) and from the North (strong imagination, melancholic disposition). The poet underlines these dichotomies in order to find a compromise between fame and female genius, joining in a single female character both Italian and English qualities.

On a literary and linguistic level this split is expressed through the familiar literary genre of the dramatic monologue. Here the narrator, who lends her voice to a different woman character every time, finally takes possession of it again in telling the final act of the main story. The significant association between the woman and her voice, in this case between poet and poem, symbolizes the only way out for her

---

[19] The same parallel has been suggested by Ellen Moers when discussing Mme de Staël's female characters: "In *Corinne*, hair color is momentous: Corinne represents the passionate exuberance of dark-haired Latin culture, and Lucile, her blond rival, stands for the subdued and inhibited sensibility of Nordic culture, along with all that is implied by the home, the wife, and the private virtue in English society" (Moers, *Literary Women*, 175).

[20] Carla L. Peterson, *The Determined Reader; Gender and Culture in the Novel from Napoleon to Victoria*, New Brunswick and London, 1987, 42.

ultimate affirmation. As soon as the female artist escapes from the narrow activity of oral performance, however, she has to face the consequences of an enlarged public, which she has reached through the publication of her work. As Elaine Showalter observes with reference to Letitia Elizabeth Landon: "The early women writers refused to deal with a professional role, or had a negative orientation toward it."[21] L.E.L. was often praised for her poetry, but she was well aware of critics' opinions of her personal life-style. This is why she repeats so many times in her poems how dangerous fame can be, especially for a woman. The coupling of female/fame always made men feel uneasy.

In 1835 – and this was during the peak years of her career – she wrote in the *New Monthly Magazine*: "Genius places a woman in an unnatural position; notoriety frightens away affection; and superiority has for its attendant, fear, not love."[22] But while here she denies her interest in a literary vocation, she nevertheless establishes through her writings a new epic for women's history, as opposed to the Romantic epic usually narrated from a male point of view. She does so by using a single female character who speaks for many others, as well as for herself. On different occasions Letitia Elizabeth Landon repeats the necessity of retelling a story from a female standpoint. In *The Improvisatrice*, the author's means for telling her epic is that of a public performance, which turns, at the end, into an interior monologue. The poet continually shifts her perspective from public to private and vice versa. In this regard, Glennis Stephenson remarks "we are taken from written text (Landon) to the spoken (improvisatrice), to the visual (Sappho herself), to, at the centre, music (Sappho's song), and then abruptly back out into the primary spoken narrative".[23]

In this way, Letitia Elizabeth Landon employs three different genres simultaneously in the same long poem: the epic, the lyric and the drama. This multiplicity of genres testifies to the fact that the female literary outlook is not static, but is always changing from one angle to the other with regard to the object observed and described by the author. Landon is employing a mode of literary hybridism in order

---

[21] Elaine Showalter, *A Literature of Her Own*, London, 1982, 18.

[22] *New Monthly Magazine*, August 1835, quoted in Greer, *Slip-Shod Sibyls*, 444.

[23] Stephenson, "Poetic Construction …", 69.

to underline the play of voices staged in her dramatic poems. In *The Improvisatrice*, as well as in many other long poems, Landon mingles together the voice of the narrator with that to character described, and that of the writer herself. Her multiplied and shifting perspective is successfully represented for the reader by this kind of genre alternation.

Love, as we have seen, is the prevailing agent pushing the Improvisatrice towards death. Love and artistic performance are always strictly interconnected and, without the former, the woman artist stops singing, stops performing or painting. As we read in the "Sappho's Song":

> I should have been the wretch I am,
> Had every chord of thine been mute.
>
> I was my evil star above,
> Not my sweet lute, that wrought me wrong:
> It was not song that taught me love,
> But it was love that taught me song.[24]

In Landon's poem female genius is the natural link between world, nature and human heart. But in the case of the Improvisatrice, as with Corinne before her, or even Sappho, the creative mind cannot altogether bear the passions, since love dries up a woman's heart and with it her literary achievement. Love and the lover are like paralysing agents for improvisation: as soon as the Improvisatrice meets Lorenzo her gaze is monopolized by his, her tongue cannot express her feelings as before and she is completely seized by this new experience.

> There are some moments in our fate
> That stamp the colour of our days;
> As, till then, life had not been felt, –
> And mine was sealed in the slight gaze
> Which fixed my eye, and fired my brain,
> And bowed my heart beneath the chain.[25]

It may be recalled that the same thing happened to Corinne, who, as soon as she is left by her lover, is no longer able to improvise, and

[24] L.E.L., *The Improvisatrice*, 10-11.
[25] *Ibid.*, 28-29.

immediately loses her will and inspiration for public performance. The Improvisatrice's reaction is similar:

But his dark eyes kept fixed on mine,
    Which sank beneath their burning gaze.
Mine sank – but yet I felt the thrill
Of that look burning on me still.
I heard no word that others said –
    Heard nothing, save one low-breathed sigh.
My hand kept wandering on my lute,
    In music, but unconsciously.[26]

If the male Romantic hero is capable of uniting the two spheres of artistic creation and love – or better still, if love reinforces his own ego – the woman is incapable of such reconciliation. In Landon's poem the male character uses the written word, which is originally limited, static, and male gendered, while the female protagonist abounds with oral expression, which is unstable but free. This means that she will not lose her power, but, unable to sustain her incompatible public and private roles, she will bind them together in death, in a final, decisive and everlasting self-affirmation:

It is deep happiness to die,
Yet live in Love's dear memory.
Thou wilt remember me, – my name
Is linked with beauty and with fame.[27]

Then she will part from this world only physically, since her art, her melodies, her fame, and her lute will represent her for all time:

        I worshipped thee,
My beautiful, bright deity!
Worshipped thee as a sacred thing
Of Genius' high imagining; –[28]

As for the protagonist of her long poem, and indeed for Landon herself, the art of performance is something that goes behind her will:

---

[26] *Ibid.*, 31.
[27] *Ibid.*, 101.
[28] *Ibid.*, 95.

the poet feels a compulsion towards composing poems that drives her out of her mind and leaves her without physical and mental strength:

> Poetry always carries me out of myself. I forget everything in the world but the subject which has interested my imagination. It is the most subtle and interesting of pleasures, but, like all pleasures, it is dearly bought; it is always succeeded by extreme depression of spirits, and an overpowering sense of bodily fatigue.[29]

The last image of the Improvisatrice is represented through a painting, observed by an external narrator, who finds herself in the house where the portrait is hung. The Improvisatrice is contemplated as the human incarnation of naturally talented beauty. She recalls once more, in a single image, Corinne at the cape of Misena, Sappho on the rock before the river, and a Priestess of Apollo:

> Dark flashing eyes, like the deep stars,
> Lighting the azure brow of night;
> A blush like sunrise o'er the rose;
> A cloud of raven hair, whose shade
> Was sweet as evening's, and whose curls
> Clustered beneath a laurel braid.[30]

Here again the artist becomes a silent and motionless object of art, ready to be admired, without a proper name, and to be fitted to the audience's will. At the same time, if she gives what the public requests of her, she will never be an exclusive male property, since she will be remembered and admired by a large audience. From Lorenzo's point of view, the woman's performance now gives way to nostalgic thoughts recollected after the death of the artist: a melancholic identification with a lost material object turned into an immortal piece of art.

Landon's poems clearly wish to break from the limits of her time, those imposed by her society and linked to the gender of the writer. She is well aware of her literary genius and expresses it using different masks for every poem. She displays a female power unusual for her time, challenging her male counterparts in the literary field. Therefore, she destabilizes the other, using, in Mary Jacobus' words, "a textual or

---

[29] *Letters by Letitia Elizabeth Landon*, 168.
[30] L.E.L., *The Improvisatrice*, 104.

epistemological unconscious that occupies the ambiguous space where genre and gender collide".[31] Landon skilfully manipulates poetical genres in one single long poem, showing a sequence of many women artists at the centre of a stage, and unveiling her willingness to be observed and applauded as a talented writer who can were different masks and play different tunes all together.

[31] Tilottama Rajan and Julia M. Wright, *Romanticism, History, and the Possibility of Genre: Re-forming Literature 1789-1837*, Cambridge, 1998, 242.

ANNA LAETITIA BARBAULD'S ETHICS OF SENTIMENT

DONATELLA MONTINI

> For few can reason, but all can feel, and many who cannot enter into an argument, may yet listen to a tale.[1]

There is a significant continuity between Anna Laetitia Barbauld's poetical writing and her editorial commitment to the English novel. Both share an interest in the Romantic issue of moral teaching and in fostering the reader's understanding and growth. Barbauld, whose father had taught alongside Joseph Priestly at Warrington Academy, never lost her dissenter's vocation for "freedom of the mind",[2] which characterizes her moral and aesthetic approaches to femininity, politics and domesticity. Her voice kept its non-conformist tone, evident in all her writings, whatever the matter at stake.

In the debate over the freedom of women, for instance, she held an absolutely personal stance. When Mary Wollstonecraft, who admired Barbauld as an intellectual and a teacher, argued against her alleged capitulation to a "supposed sexual character",[3] Barbauld answered in favour of good mothers and wives rather than *femmes savantes*. Maternity ("To a Little Invisible Being who is Expected Soon to

---

I would like to thank Rosy Colombo for our stimulating conversations about Anna Laetitia Barbauld's poetical writing. Rosy's committed passion for Barbauld as a poet inspired my interest in her as a literary critic.

[1] Anna Laetitia Barbauld, "On Romances: An Imitation", in *The Works of Anna Laetitia Barbauld: With a Memoir by Lucy Aikin*, 2 vols, London, 1825, II, 172.

[2] Anna Laetitia Barbauld, "Corsica", in *Eighteenth-Century Women Poets*, ed. Roger Lonsdale, Oxford, 1990, 302.

[3] Mary Wollstonecraft, A *Vindication of the Rights of Woman*, ed. Miriam Kramnick, Harmondsworth, 1975, 143.

become Visible", 1795) and domesticity ("Washing Day", 1797)[4] are amongst her favourite topics.

From her early poems onwards the language of domestic life, with its dignity and joys, runs alongside poems on human and political rights[5] or against war. Among her more political poems, "Corsica" (1773), for example, pleads on behalf of the "Corsican struggle for Liberty", supporting the campaign of the Corsican refugee Pasquale Paoli. Elsewhere she tells the poor not to "fear the God whom priests and kings have made" ("To the Poor", 1795).[6]

Barbauld's literary career enhanced the dialogic dimension of the public sphere. Her mind was dedicated to the rights of the individual and to the assessment of civil values. Within this framework she set up her modern role as a Romantic literary critic, addressing and creating a new readership that the establishment would not take into consideration. Unlike Coleridge, however, she intended to cultivate her readers by working on their emotions rather than persuading their minds. In the poem dedicated to Coleridge himself ("To Coleridge", 1799) she suggests that "The hill of science … / A grove extends; / … while things of life, / Obvious to sight and touch, all glowing round, / Fade to the hue of shadows".[7] She claims that the writer of fiction can be a strong agent of enchantment and education, "for few can reason, but all can feel, and many who can not enter into an argument, may yet listen to a tale". Barbauld maintains that a dynamics of emotions can take over the aridity of logic, because tales "teach us to think by inuring us to feel".[8]

One of the most troublesome points of discussion in the conflict-ridden dialogue between Coleridge and Barbauld – a dialogue that outlasted their lives – concerned the form of the novel. Barbauld's critical treatises on this genre, which attempted a systematic overview of extant works, were her most voluminous, as well as her best: these writings dealt with problems regarding the form and definition of the

[4] *Eighteenth-Century Women Poets*, 307-308 and 308-10

[5] Barbauld contributed to the campaigns in 1790 for the repeal of the Corporation and Test Acts that excluded Dissenters from public office, and in 1791 for the bill to abolish the slave trade.

[6] *Eighteenth-Century Women Poets*, 307.

[7] *Ibid.*, 310

[8] Barbauld, "On Romances: An Imitation", 172 and 175.

novel and its characters, and the relationship between novelists and reading public.

Barbauld's literary criticism, written in the first decade of the 1800s (*The Correspondence of Samuel Richardson*, 1804; *Selections from the Spectator, Tatler, Guardian, and Freeholder*, 1804; *British Novelists*, 1810; *The Female Speaker*, 1811), stemmed from a precise professional choice. As literature was becoming a job, a new social class of *gens des lettres* had risen: Dr Johnson himself had outlined how criticism had taken the form of a new discipline, a profession which aimed to arrange and proclaim the transmission of knowledge and of a national canon. The professional critic, even more than the author, was now in the position to legitimize the literary product with reference to the reader's taste.

A few decades earlier, in the 1770s, Barbauld had contributed to the collections of critical essays edited by her brother John Aikin, with short articles on romance and comedy, on *The Arabian Nights* and on *The Castle of Otranto*. But she had never laid claim to her authorship, and her signature at the top of the page was "A.L. Aikin". What happened at the beginning of the new century was quite different, a turning point as far as genre is concerned, from more than one point of view. First, Barbauld, in a Johnsonian mode,[9] chose to write almost exclusively prefaces, and second, she identified herself as an editor, a subject who takes care of, arranges and comments on texts written by someone else. Readers of the time were familiar with this figure, not only as the editor of journals, or of classics, but also as the nameless "editor" – in reality a fictional persona, deputy of the author – that eighteenth-century novels had regularly adopted as part of an aesthetic strategy designed to create the effect of verisimilitude.[10]

Barbauld inherits this legacy and reinvents it by renouncing the mask of anonymity and by exposing herself unhesitatingly to an explicitly ideological dimension. This was an unavoidable dimension in any attempt at definition of the canon: the conventional eighteenth-century editor had anticipated it, and by electing the authors to edit had become the mediator between producer and consumer, between

---

[9] See K.M. Rogers, "Anne Barbauld's Criticism of Fiction: Johnsonian Mode, Female Vision", *Studies in Eighteenth-Century Literature*, XXI (1991), 27-42.

[10] See Robert Iliffe, "Author-mongering: The 'Editor' between Producer and Consumer", in *The Consumption of Culture 1600-1800 – Image, Object, Text*, eds Ann Bermingham and John Brewer, London, 1997, 166-92.

literary creation and the market, between readership and an aesthetic taste to be moulded and oriented. Barbauld was determined to create her own list of names and she did so by founding precise aesthetic criteria and rules.

The two main critical works authored by Barbauld were her edition of Samuel Richardson's private correspondence (1804), in six volumes "*To which are prefixed*", says the frontispiece, "*A Biographical Account of that Author and Observations on his Writings*", and, six years later, in 1810, the fifty volumes dedicated to a selection of *British Novelists*. This is the overall title of the anthology including twenty-eight novels (twelve by women writers) that Barbauld systematically prefaces with a historical and formal comment. Each author is introduced, her or his life and works are described, and each novel is summed up and carefully evaluated. A long essay, "On the Origin and Progress of Novel-Writing",[11] precedes the anthology as a whole.

In both these works it is the novel that is subjected to examination: the genre that the major Romantic poets were contemporarily devaluating was Barbauld's object of discourse. What is certain is that the canonization of the novel coincides metonymically with a precise name and life, those of Samuel Richardson. Richardson stands for the novel, or at least this is what Barbauld believed, and it is with this opinion that Coleridge will take issue not only in his 1808 *Lectures* but also in 1811-12 when he wonders how that "amiable lady" can even think of comparing Shakespeare to Richardson who "is *only* interesting. Shakespeare on the contrary elevates and instructs", and,

---

[11] Authors and novels chosen by Barbauld for her selection are in the following order: Richardson, *The History of Clarissa Harlow*, *The History of Sir Charles Grandison*; Defoe, *Robinson Crusoe*; Fielding, *Joseph Andrews*, *Tom Jones*; Clara Reeve, *The Old English Baron*; Horace Walpole, *The Castle of Otranto*; Coventry, *The History of Pompey the Little*; Goldsmith, *The Vicar of Wakefield*; Lennox, *The Female Quixote*; Johnson, *Rasselas, Prince of Abissinia*; Hawkesworth, *Almoran and Hamet*; Inchbald, *Nature and Art*, *A Simple Story*; Mackenzie, *Julia de Roubigné*, *The Man of Feeling*; Smollett, *Humphry Clinker*; Graves, *The Spiritual Quixote*; Moore, *Zeluco*; Smith, *The Old Manor House*; Burney, *Evelina*, *Cecilia*; Radcliffe, *Romance of the Forest*, *The Mysteries of Udolpho*; Bage, *Hermsprong, or Man as He Is Not*; and Edgeworth, *Belinda*, *Modern Griselda*. All the novels, except the last two by Edgeworth, date from the eighteenth century.

what is more important, emancipates us from "ordinary situations and common feelings".[12]

However, it is not clear to Barbauld – as she declares in the Preface to Richardson's *Correspondence* – why the poet has been set on such a high pedestal in the temple of fame, and the novelist on such a low one: the latter's control over form, but especially over reader response, "the pleasures he affords to his readers .... the power exercised over the reader's heart",[13] require the greatest talent and therefore merit our warmest praise.

A form whose rise reveals a process of agglutination, whose development trails along transformations and condensations, is assigned a father and an origin by Barbauld: Richardson may be said to be the father of the modern novel with regard both to its content ("serious and pathetic": to Barbauld serious insofar as it is pathetic) and its form: "he was also original in the mode of epistolary writing by which he carried on the story",[14] a form possessing, as one of its privileged aspects, an unobtrusive authorial voice.

The same ideological standpoint is expressed through the historical sequence chosen for the *British Novelists* – a collection that follows a simple chronological order but significantly assigns first place to Samuel Richardson's *Clarissa* and *Sir Charles Grandison* (*Pamela* is not included because of the protagonist's acquisitive morals); Defoe comes second with *Robinson Crusoe.* Perhaps Barbauld mistakes here a beginning for the origin, a particular form for the originating form, sharing the Romantic vision of the artist infusing the creative spark like a God. Or perhaps this perception of her ideological stance stems from our present-day perspective that tends to compare the novel not to a single root sucking its life out of the soil, but to a rizomatic root horizontally expanding and encapsulating different forms.

After the originating moment Barbauld sees a "progress", as the title of the Introduction to *British Novelists* states: "On the Origin and Progress of Novel Writing." Along the path of its historical development, the genre achieves continuity by advancing through

---

[12] Samuel Taylor Coleridge, *Lectures 1808-1819 on Literature*, ed. R.A. Foakes, London, 1987, 118.

[13] Mrs A.L. Barbauld, Preface to *The Correspondence of Samuel Richardson, to which are prefixed A Biographical Account of that Author and Observations on his Writings*, 6 vols, London, 1804, I, ix-x.

[14] Barbauld, Preface to *The Correspondence of Samuel Richardson*, xi.

continuous original metamorphoses and by renewing itself in ever different forms. In this way progress encloses endless regeneration, ever new beginnings, whereby the canon may come to include quite different forms, even the works of Mother Radcliffe. From this perspective the pre-eminent title among the excluded works is surely that of *Tristram Shandy*, parodic *monstrum* that pulverizes the very idea of an origin and relies on a merely casual beginning of writing.

What Barbauld prefers is realistic writing: the picture of domestic life as a setting, people of our acquaintance as the characters, as she never tires of saying. This results in, among other things, a radical distinction between Richardson the realist and Mme LaFayette, in whose novels "the heroes and heroines are princes and princesses …. The scene is perhaps in Spain, or among the Moors, it does not reflect the picture of domestic life, they are not men and women we see about every day."[15]

Entering into the long-running dispute over the distinction between novel and romance, Barbauld seems to take up the tradition inaugurated by the well-known Preface to *Incognita* (1691) by William Congreve and resumed by Clara Reeve a century later both in the Preface to *The Old English Baron* (1778) and then in *The Progress of Romance* (1785). In these texts the two authors draw clear boundaries between the two forms: "The Romance is an heroic fable, which treats of fabulous persons and things. – The Novel is a picture of real life and manners, and of the time in which it is written. The Novel gives a familiar relation of such things, as pass everyday before our eyes, such as may happen to our friends, or to ourselves."[16]

Barbauld proceeds in this direction and even quotes Fielding in claiming that "a good novel is an epic in prose, with more of character and less (indeed in modern novels nothing) of the supernatural machinery".[17] Such a work leads to pleasure that does not derive from the emotions of the sublime, but which rather recalls the didactic scope of moral teaching, because realistic writing augments the ethic dimension of literature "by filling the reader's heart with the successive emotions of love, pity, joy, anguish, transport, or

---

[15] Barbauld, "On the Origin and Progress of Novel-Writing", in *The British Novelists; with an Essay; and Prefaces Biographical and Critical*, 50 vols, London, 1810, I, 16.
[16] Clara Reeve, *The Progress of Romance*, 2 vols, Colchester, 1785, I, 111.
[17] Barbauld, "On the Origin and Progress of Novel-Writing", 1.

indignation", in order to get to "virtuous and noble sentiments".[18] What makes the novel dangerous is whatever makes it deviate from its realistic vocation. Barbauld does not forget the well-known caveat to the female readership: "Love is a passion particularly exaggerated in novels …. In order to increase this interest, a false idea is given of the importance of the passion" and girls will improperly consider their life monotonous once compared to "scenes of perpetual courtship and passion."[19]

Barbauld calls for, and at the same time sanctions, a style of writing "with characters moving *in the same sphere of life with ourselves*, and brought into action by incidents of daily occurrence".[20] In an exemplary page from the Preface to the *Correspondence*, Barbauld focuses on and sums up her idea of Richardson:

> Richardson was the man who was to introduce a new kind of moral painting; he drew equally from nature and from his own ideas. From the world about him he took the incidents, manners, and general character, of the times in which he lived, and from his own beautiful ideas he copied that sublime of virtue which charms us in his Clarissa, and that sublime of passion which interests us in Clementina. *That kind of fictitious writing of which he has set the example, disclaims all assistance from giants and genii. The moated castle is changed to a modern parlour; the princess and her pages to a lady and her domestics, or even to a simple maiden, without birth or fortune; we are not called on to wonder at improbable events, but to be moved by natural passions, and impressed by salutary maxims.* The pathos of the story, and the dignity of the sentiments, interest and charm us; simplicity is warned, vice rebuked, and, from the perusal of a novel, we rise better prepared to meet the ills of life with firmness, and to perform our respective parts on the great theatre of life.[21]

The new forms of writing take shape in a two-fold mode, either by analogy or by opposition. "Moated castle" turns into a "modern parlour", the "princess" into a "maiden", while the reader provoked to astonishment by uncanny events is now excited in his "natural passions and impressed by salutary maxims".

---

[18] Barbauld, Preface to *The Correspondence of Samuel Richardson*, xx.

[19] Barbauld, "On the Origin and Progress of Novel-Writing", 50 and 52.

[20] Barbauld, Preface to *The Correspondence of Samuel Richardson*, xvii (my emphasis).

[21] *Ibid.*, xxii (my emphasis).

Such realism is even more significant when it becomes the realism of conscience explored by narrative in the form of the domestic novel. So it happens that Barbauld collects the legacy of eighteenth-century female writing, which always emphasizes the world of interiority with respect to the experience of social life (Fanny Burney's *Cecilia* is preferred to the more brilliant *Evelina*), the quest for reasons with respect to the descriptions of actions. Barbauld thus confirms Joanna Baillie's idea of tragic heroes (1798): "the chief antagonists they contend with must be the other passions and propensities of the heart, not outward circumstances and events."[22] The tragic hero is not put to the test by the external world but by his own passions. Barbauld, like Baillie, prefers character to plot and events. This is why Clarissa, who champions the freedom of the mind, is Barbauld's favourite character, and why Richardson precedes Defoe and is placed at the origin of the modern novel: Richardson stages and exalts the interior life where active virtue, moral conduct and sensibility join aesthetic aims, resulting in the novel form.

When writing unites fact and fiction, life and fiction, furthermore, it inevitably evokes Samuel Richardson, who had deliberately selected and arranged his private *Correspondence* with a view to offering it to his reading public. These very letters are collected and edited by Barbauld for the radical publisher Richard Phillips. She does not seem unduly worried about philological accuracy: she shortens the texts, modifies the spelling of some words, omits dates and attributes others without good reason. She cuts and pastes arbitrarily. Publication of the collection began at the beginning of 1804 and the *The Edinburgh Review*, certainly the most influential journal of literary criticism in the nineteenth century, did not fail to review the first six volumes. The reviewer was Francis Jeffrey, the editor of the journal. Although radical in politics, *The Edinburgh Review* supported and spread strong conservative and traditional views on literary innovations. Barbauld's work is ironically introduced and illustrated: not only is the corpus of Richardson's private letters dull and boring, full of petty details of everyday life, "a melancholy farrago", but also the critical preface does not express "the general character of her genius; and it must be acknowledged, that she has a tone and manner which is something

---

[22] Joanna Baillie, "Introductory Discourse", in *A Series of Plays: in which it is attempted to delineate The Stronger Passions of the Mind. Each passion being the subject of A Tragedy and A Comedy*, London, 1798, 59.

formal and heavy; that she occasionally delivers trite and obvious truths with the pomp and solemnity of important discoveries, and sometimes attempts to exalt and magnify her subject by a very clumsy kind of declamation".[23]

The reviewer's pitiless remarks seem purposely to neglect the question of the affirmation of authorship through the form of the letter, the "familiar letter", which is the emblem of private and of public as the same time. The familiar eighteenth-century letter unites entertainment and education in which the self emerges, in an artless and natural mode, but at the same time it is an instrument of "fallacy and sophistication",[24] and Barbauld is aware of the embedded ambiguity when she defines letter writing as "the most natural and the least probable way of telling a story".[25] Richardson's life told in letters is a literary composition in itself, a novel without adventures whose protagonist plays the role of eyewitness to his own interiority. Conventions of the time distinguished between letters of conversation and letters of feeling, and Richardson takes on the task of linking these two modes of communication.

From this perspective *Clarissa* is the text which will transmit Richardson's work to future generations: after a dull start in the first volumes, in which writing follows meandering petty details, the story proceeds and the characters become "real personages". There is a single unifying plot, there are no sub-plots, "no digressions, no episodes .... With Clarissa it begins, with Clarissa it ends."[26] Getting to Clarissa, both novel and character, is like walking along an avenue towards an ancient mansion:

> We do not come upon unexpected adventures and wonderful recognitions, by quick turns and surprises: we see her fate from afar, *as it were from a long avenue, the gradual approach to which, without ever losing sight of the object, has more of simplicity and grandeur than the most cunning labyrinth that can be contrived by art.* In the approach to the modern country seat, we are made to catch transiently a side-view of it through an opening in the trees, or to burst upon it from a sudden turning in the road; *but the old mansion stood full in the*

[23] *The Edinburgh Review*, IV (1804), 23.
[24] Samuel Johnson, *Prefaces, Biographical Critical, to the Works of the English Poets*, 10 vols, London, 1779-1781, VII, 238.
[25] Barbauld, Preface to *The Correspondence of Samuel Richardson*, xxvii.
[26] *Ibid.*, lxxxiii.

> *eye of the traveller, as he drew near it, contemplating its turrets, which grew larger and more distinct every step that he advanced; and leisurely filling his eye and his imagination with still increasing ideas of its magnificence.*[27]

Barbauld has clearly not forgotten Addison's lesson in his "Pleasures of Imagination", according to which the aesthetic experience is essentially visual through the contact with "visible Objects".[28] The plain, domestic analogy Barbauld establishes between the journey to the text and the journey to the house, between the novel and an old mansion, is not to be underestimated. Not only does she distance herself from the pleasures of the picturesque, but she also reaffirms a devotion to the pleasures of sight, typical of the eighteenth-century artist, by exploring the encounter between visual arts and fiction that women Romantic poets, including Barbauld herself, had been cultivating.[29] So to the contemporary Gothic journeys, *à la* Radcliffe, full of wild and inaccessible sites, steep ridges and precipices hiding black castles, or to the ironic Austenian journeys towards fake medieval abbeys, Barbauld prefers "a public road", open and straight, "without ever losing sight of the object", but no less sensual for that.[30] The pleasure of the eye becomes a full vision, "as it were from a long avenue" to "an old mansion" whose architectural traits enlarge, as does the reader's pleasure, enriching both sight and imagination. The landscape is Augustan, devoid of any Hogarthian serpentine disturbances: the sight is full and sunlit, totally exposed to the traveller's eye and maintaining constant contact with the object: the "inward eye", the transcendental vision, is left to Coleridge.

And then the sad closure. *The British Novelists* was published in 1810. In 1812 Barbauld published her last poem, "Eighteen Hundred and Eleven", against the war. More than an anti-war cry, the poem sounded to the English ear like a powerful prophesy of the passing away of British imperial power. Barbauld published nothing further in the remaining thirteen years of her life.

---

[27] *Ibid.*, lxxxiii-lxxxiv (my emphasis).
[28] Joseph Addison, *The Spectator*, CCCCXI (Saturday, June 21, 1712), 411.
[29] Jane Stabler, "'Know me what I paint': Women Poets and the Aesthetics of the Sketch 1770-1830" (see pages 27-40 of the present volume).
[30] See Carole Fabricant, "Binding and Dressing Nature's Loose Tresses: The Ideology of Augustan Landscape Design", *Studies in Eighteenth Century Culture*, VIII (1979), 109-35.

Romantic Female and Male Poets: Dialogue and Revision

WOMEN ROMANCE WRITERS: MARY TIGHE AND MARY HAYS

CECILIA PIETROPOLI

The second half of the 1700s saw the rediscovery of the literature of the Middle Ages and, with it, of the romance; its *matière* was, however, adapted to the culture and tastes of the time, creating a genre with both ancient and modern characteristics. As Rita Copeland observes: "The words 'romance' and 'romantic' as used in the seventeenth century and later imply a certain retrospective construction of the Middle Ages as archaic and exotic, but the Middle Ages used the term 'roman' to characterize its own modernity, its vernacularity and institution of new literary genres."[1] In the late Middle Ages, the romance was still the innovative genre *par excellence* that, in using the vernacular and adopting a new form, broke new ground. But the approach to chivalry and romance radically changed in the fifteenth century, when they were seen as the offspring of a past golden age. As a consequence, when towards the end of the century William Caxton decided to revive and publish the English chivalric romances, he amended and adapted them to the aesthetic and moral conventions of a transnational aristocratic literary movement that had its cradle in Burgundy.[2] When in 1485 Caxton edited and printed Thomas Malory's *Le Morte Darthur* for an upper-class reading public, he presented it as a "noble" as well as "joyous" book:[3]

---

[1] Rita Copeland, "Between Romans and Romantic", *Texas Studies in Literature and Language*, XXXIII (1991), 215.
[2] Diane Borstein, "William Caxton's Chivalric Romances and the Burgundian Renaissance in England", *English Studies*, LVII (1976), 1.
[3] William Caxton, Final Note to *Le Morte Darthur*, 2 vols, Harmondsworth, 1969, II, 532.

> And for to pass the time this book shall be pleasant to read in; but for to give faith and believe that all is true that is contained herein, ye be at your liberty. But all is written for our doctrine, and for to beware that we fall not to vice ne sin, but to exercise and follow virtue, by which we may come and attain to good fame and renown in this life, and after this short and transitory life, to come unto everlasting bliss in heaven, the which he grant us that reigneth in heaven, the blessed Trinity. Amen.[4]

But when the Italian Renaissance took over, the English romances were again considered the offspring of a local, and therefore minor, tradition. In the second half of the sixteenth century, while Edmund Spenser was again resorting to the moral and didactic function of the local chivalric romance for his *Faerie Queene,* Roger Ascham wrote in *The Schoolmaster*:

> In our forefathers' time, when papistry as a standing pool covered and overflowed all England, few books were read in our tongue, saving certain books of chivalry, as they said, for pastime and pleasure, which, as some say, were made in monasteries by idle monks or wanton canons; as one, for example, *Morte Darthur*, the whole pleasure of which book standeth in two special points – in open manslaughter and bold bawdry ….[5]

The English Renaissance ended up by excluding the romance from the canon of approved literature, considering it a rough and popular genre, and as such void of aesthetic or moral validity. The stories of knights in courtly literature were therefore adapted to suit a popular audience,[6] so much so that in the seventeenth century the word "romance" had come to allude to an archaic world, where love and adventure reigned supreme, that set itself apart as an alternative to daily life.

Kevin Morris dates back to 1724 the beginnings of the eighteenth-century comeback of the genre within the canon of high literature: "The traces of this agitation can be found as early as Allen Ramsey's *Ever Green* collection (1724), with interest in the primitive and the

---

[4] Caxton's Original Preface to *Le Morte Darthur*, I, 6.

[5] Roger Ascham, *The Schoolmaster* (1570), Ithaca and New York, 1967, 68-69.

[6] *Le Morte Darthur* can again be taken as an example: between 1485 and 1634 Malory's work was re-published in six different editions, but all of them catering for a popular reading public and with aims utterly different from Caxton's.

titillation of fancy."[7] In the 1600s popular use of the term had accentuated the fantastic and the magical aspects of the adventure romance: paradoxically, it is precisely the presence of the mythical and marvellous that fascinated writers of a strictly enlightenment mould like Richard Hurd, author in 1762 of *Letters on Chivalry and Romance*, or Thomas Percy, who, in his collection the *Reliques of Ancient English Poetry* (1765), made available works from the past that otherwise would have remained inaccessible. A few years later, James Beattie – although of the conventional persuasion that the Middle Ages were a dark and culturally arid period – affirmed in *On Fable and Romance* that no poetry managed better than that of the Middle Ages to give expression to the supernatural. In this context the essay by Thomas Warton, *Observations on the Faerie Queene of Spenser* (1754), assumes particular importance since he introduces the idea that it is possible to attribute to the great vernacular works the same dignity as to the Classics.

Within the Romantic comeback of late medieval literature, the romance is the privileged genre, due to its organic nature and to the fact that it is best suited to accomplish the much-sought combination of the physical and the metaphysical. Essentially dynamic, it interacts with the sentimental, the realistic and the historical novel, but above all it is coloured with Gothic tones in its search for recurring and universal themes, such as the conflict between good and evil and the struggle between vice and virtue. In the Gothic novel, the marvellous – the distinctive sign of the genre – becomes uncanny, or macabre and threatening. This happens, according to Gillian Beer, whenever romance writers, rather than rise towards the world of imagination, choose to drag it into daily reality, thereby transforming the space given over to the fulfilment of desires into one given over to disillusionment.[8] Already by the end of the 1700s, precisely at the time it was becoming increasingly popular in England, the Gothic novel was being critically attacked. Wordsworth condemned it in his Preface to *Lyrical Ballads*, while Coleridge stigmatized its excesses and manifest vulgarity, complaining that it had abandoned the original

[7] Kevin L. Morris, *The Image of the Middle Ages in Romantic and Victorian Literature*, London, 1984, 35-36.
[8] Gillian Beer, *The Romance*, London, 1970, 40-41.

educational and moral function of the courtly romance.[9] It was also noted that the fantastic potentialities of the legends of knights errant had been exploited to the extreme, so that it appeared opportune to reset such tales in their historical context, allowing a clear distinction to be made between history and fiction. Since only men could access historical truth, the world of imaginative history, by now denatured and deprived of its lifeblood from excessive use, was the domain of women novelists and poets.

Therefore, romance took on the new connotations of an uncultured genre, suited only to poorly educated people with plenty of free time: "The romance in their eyes was always bound up with the primitivistic idea of the untaught minstrel, the natural genius who with unsophisticated feeling and inborn imagination told stories about the real world and his own fantasy worlds."[10] And who better than women, whether as writers or as readers, to incorporate such a paradoxical symbiosis as that of natural genius and ignorance? It served little purpose that Maria Edgeworth pointed out how even historians lacked objectivity, defending the right of women to mix history and fiction and to include in their romances not only public events and characters of great importance but also facts of daily life.[11] Since history remained a male domain and women were limited to the romance, they put themselves to the test in various sub-genres that today, however, are placed alongside the names and works of some of the most famous poets in the canon of English Romantic literature. The best example is provided by the tale in verse in Gothic style, whose fame is linked to Coleridge's "Christabel". And yet Coleridge used the *topoi* of the Gothic novel in a completely untypical way, creating the suspicion that in "Christabel" he did not wish so much to propose a Gothic poem as to create a parody of the Gothic style.[12]

The two works I wish to use as examples in this essay – by the aristocrat Mary Tighe and the radical Mary Hays – date back to the last decade of the eighteenth century, the period of maximum

---

[9] *Coleridge's Miscellaneous Criticism*, ed. Thomas Middleton Raysor, London, 1936, 370-74.

[10] Hermann Fischer, *Romantic Verse Narrative: The History of a Genre*, Cambridge, 1991, 27.

[11] Michael Gamer, "Confounding Present with Past", *Poetica*, XXXIX-XL (1994), 113.

[12] Edward Dramin, "'Amid the Jagged Shadows': Christabel and the Gothic Tradition", *The Wordsworth Circle*, XIII (1982), 221.

feminization of the romance. In these texts the genre was revised in different ways by two women writers whose cultural and ideological motivations were diametrically opposed. Stuart Curran underlines the importance of women in the creation of the eighteenth-century cult of Sensibility that had great bearing on Romantic poetry.[13] The male literary world reacted to the quantity and quality of their works by classifying them according to cultural stereotypes ranging from the modest and uncultured imitator devoid of genius or original ideas to that of the arrogant and presumptuous – and sometimes even immoral – female. This did not, however, prevent women from expressing themselves with original voices and from creating their own tradition, so much so that numerous male colleagues, especially from the second Romantic generation, were not able to rid themselves of the annoying feeling that women had laid deep tracks in national literature that could not be easily ignored. Both Tighe and Hays use in their works, by way of a metaphor of the relationship with the male literary world, the figure of a courtly knight who places himself at the service of the two female protagonists.

Psyche, a poem in six cantos by the Irish poet Mary Tighe, is inspired in its structure and versification by Spenser's *Faerie Queene*. In the eighteenth century Spenser's work was considered a source of the great tradition of British poetry; even Spenser's poetry, however, ended up being considered excessively feminine. Mary Tighe is listed among the followers of Spenser for her interpretation, from a moral angle, of the legend of Cupid and Psyche, giving her characters an allegorical appearance. *Psyche* was written around 1795 and printed in fifty copies, which were first circulated among a rather restricted circle of literary friends. It was then reprinted in 1815, after the premature death of the author from tuberculosis. The work met with great success both in Britain and the United States, a success that lasted up to the middle of the century. Then *Psyche* was forgotten and, until the recent reappraisal of female Romantic poetry, was cited almost exclusively because of its similarities with John Keats' "Lamia". Keats himself had a contradictory attitude towards Mary Tighe, initially declaring himself attracted by her "enchanting imagery" and extolling her qualities in "To Some Ladies" in 1815 and then repudiating what he considered the superficial beauty of her

[13] Stuart Curran, "Romantic Poetry: The I Altered", in *Romanticism and Feminism*, ed. Anne K. Mellor, Bloomington: IN, 1988, 195.

verses in favour of poetry of greater intellectual and psychological depth. In 1817 he included her in a list of uninteresting bluestocking intellectuals. And yet traces of the influence of *Psyche* can be found in "The Eve of St Agnes".[14]

Mary Tighe applied the new aesthetics of sensibility to her revision of the *topoi* of the romance, especially to the motifs of the progress of the hero in search of his own identity and of love as the final prize for his knightly quest. When Mary decided to move woman from her traditional role as the inspiration of the adventure, or as the passive reward for it, and to make her the protagonist, she took to an extreme the process of rewriting the genre from a feminine viewpoint and at the same time signalled the fragility of the genre's rules, undermining the foundations of its rhetoric. In the first two cantos of her poem, Tighe draws on Apuleius' version of the Cupid and Psyche legend. Love is sent by his mother Venus to punish Psyche, whose crime is that of being a mortal who is so beautiful that she puts Venus' position as goddess of beauty at risk. He falls in love with Psyche and takes her to the luxurious Palace of Love, where he will be able to spend his nights with her but without ever showing his face. Psyche regrets being so lonely and, ill advised by her jealous sisters, one night decides to illuminate the face of Love. Thrown out of the luxurious palace, she is forced to abandon both the Island of Pleasure and her aristocratic isolation and come face to face with the outside world. As she wanders alone in despair in the forest, a dove appears offering her food and making her feel "still protected by a power so great, / His tenderness her toils will mitigate" (II, 400-401).[15] The dove is the dove of Innocence, sent by Love to protect her. A little further on she lies down to rest and thinks of her lost love. When she wakes up "A knight all armed appears close mid the embowering shade" which "Tempering with mildest courtesy, the awe / Which majesty inspired, low in her sight / Obeisance made" (III, 36, 38-40). Then conquering her fear and natural shyness,

> Gently approaching then with fairest speech
> He proffered service to the lonely dame,
> And prayed her that she might not so impeach

[14] Greg Kucich, "Gender Crossings: Keats and Tighe", *Keats-Shelley Journal*, XLIV (1995), 31.
[15] Mary Tighe, *Psyche, with Other Poems*, London, 1811, 67.

The honour of his youth's yet spotless fame,
As aught to fear which might his knighthood shame;
But if her unprotected steps to guard,
The glory of her champion he might claim,
He asked no other guerdon or reward,
Than what bright honour's self might to his deeds award.
(III, 46-54)[16]

The ritual of the meeting between lady and knight is perfectly respected in every detail. As Psyche's wanderings continue she comes across a series of allegorical figures, such as Passion, Ambition, Vanity, Jealousy and Credulity, which are as fascinating as they are perilous and which provide her with different and dangerous temptations. She is often on the point of giving in to their flattery and falling into perdition without redemption, but her knight, who follows her silently and attentively, manages each time to save her from danger. The Courtly Knight is none other than Love, who aspires to help her pass the trial and then, once she is more mature and wiser from the experience, take her back. Psyche's ordeal strictly adheres to the conventions of the romance as outlined by Northrop Frye.[17] She first moves along a downward curve that leads her to touch the depths of despair, and once she overcomes various obstacles and the enemy is defeated, she can then begin the upward curve that will enable her to regain her original place in the Palace of Love.

The obstacles facing Psyche are allegories of the dangers that threaten even the most intense of loves. In Mary Tighe's hands, Psyche's quest takes on the moral significance and tones of her own intimate suffering. The combat between moral precepts and profane temptations, another paradigm of the medieval romance that Mary does not renounce but rather adapts to her own ends, is an experience that she lives in her own mind and that constitutes the foundation on which her growth and maturity were based. In the first part of the poem Psyche, closed within an enchanted world with her lover, is shy and subdued, but once she has abandoned her private world and faces up to the outside world, she becomes more self-assured and independent and seems in fact to be indifferent to the attentions of men, causing her Courtly Knight much pain. In the end, however,

---

[16] *Ibid.*, 77-78.

[17] Northrop Frye, *The Secular Scripture: A Study of the Structure of Romance*, Cambridge: MA, 1976, 53 *et passim*.

Mary Tighe chooses for Psyche the tranquillity of married life with Love, an option that could appear too easy an option, considering the difficulties and dangers the protagonist has encountered in the story up to that point. This choice corresponds, however, to the principle shared by numerous Romantic women writers that the greatest reward for a woman's virtue lies in a peaceful domestic life. Such a transposition of the romance to the level of daily life implies a further significant change to the rules of the genre, since traditionally, in the world of knights, love was the initial reason for the quest rather than its end, and any eventual bond of marriage was seen as a major obstacle in the way of the knight to obtaining glory and honour.

The final part of *Psyche* suggests that, far from being a radical writer, Mary Tighe ignored the political potential of the romance which, in her hands, could have upset social conventions, and not only narrative ones, by giving women a public platform. Her life seems to have been guided by discipline and the acceptance of traditional roles,[18] which has led critics to describe Mary as a woman incapable of rebelling against family ties and control,[19] as well as being a poet incapable of creating original forms. She complied passively, according to this view, with conventions belonging to a patriarchal tradition, restricting herself to readapting them in order to make them suitable to the expression of female emotions.

But Harriet Kramer Linkin invites us to look at another possible interpretation of *Psyche* suggested by Mary Tighe's exploiting of the implicit ambiguity in the syntax of the English language, and to reflect carefully on the initial verses of the poem's Proem:

> Let not the rugged brow the rhymes accuse,
> Which speak of gentle knights and ladies fair,
> Nor scorn the lighter labours of the muse,
> Who yet, for cruel battles would not dare
> The low-strung chords of her weak lyre prepare ….
>
> (Proem, 1-5)[20]

---

[18] Marlon B. Ross, *The Contour of Masculine Desire*, New York and Oxford, 1989, 157.

[19] It would appear that the marriage in 1793 with a cousin on the mother's side, Henry Tighe, was something desired by the family rather than by Mary and that she was in reality always attracted to her brother-in-law William who was also a poet.

[20] Tighe, *Psyche*, 5.

At a first reading, it seems evident that the author feared an adverse reaction from her readers, a feeling reinforced by the Preface Mary wrote for *Psyche* in which, by reminding her readers that she wrote exclusively "for the more interested eye of friendship",[21] foresaw and responded to potential accusations of artificiality and immorality from her male readers. Yet, the ambiguity of the syntactic function of "the rugged brow" and "the rhymes", which can both be subjects or direct objects, suggests that it may be the writer who had doubts as to whether readers would be equal to a work like hers.[22] Marlon Ross also reveals an underlying tension in the versification of *Psyche*, which now and then appears on the surface of a work otherwise openly derivative. He concludes that "Tighe is hesitant, and yet desirous, to claim originality in versification and voice";[23] and for an educated woman, with her family background and character, such a tension could never be resolved through rebellion. In a metapoetic key, the relationship between Psyche and her knight becomes representative of the interaction between the writer and her literary progenitor. Mary Tighe modified the rules of the romance by making them suited to feminine adaptation, but at the same time she always had before her the mirror of the work by her knight Edmund Spenser, whose guidance she needed in order to curb her imagination, at times too free, and in order to give authority to her poem. After all, is it not the courtly knight who, after having put her through a difficult quest and a brave struggle, makes the lady he is protecting a goddess and bestows immortality on her?

The work by Mary Hays, a writer often listed among the great revolutionaries of the end of the century, is of a different tenor. In her *Letters and Essays, Moral and Miscellaneous*, published in 1793, Mary Hays includes a brief tale in prose titled "A Fragment. In the Manner of the Old Romances", in which she tells the story of a girl who, wandering rather imprudently in a forest, finds herself having to face up to a series of adventures which appear to be metaphors of sexual experiences. The pseudo-medieval fragment had made its first appearance in English literature a few years earlier in the form of a tale entitled "Sir Bertrand: A Fragment". Given that it is impossible to

---

21 *Ibid.*, Preface, ix.

22 Harriet Kramer Linkin, "Romanticism and Mary Tighe's Psyche: Peering at the Hem of Her Blue Stockings", *Studies in Romanticism*, XXXV (1996), 63.

23 Ross, *The Contour of Masculine Desire*, 162.

attribute with any degree of certainty this tale either to John Aikin or Anna Laetitia Aiken, it is difficult to say whether the invention of this sub-genre of the romance is due to a man or a woman. What is certain, instead, is that the Gothic fragment entered the canon of English Romantic literature through Coleridge's unfinished poem "Christabel". What interests me here, however, is not to make a questionable comparison of the revisions made to the romance by male and female writers respectively, but to highlight the variations women writers in particular brought to the conventions of the genre.

In Mary Hays' fragment, the female protagonist, Cleanthe, abandons, just as Coleridge's Christabel was to do, her father's house, symbol of oppression but also of paternal protection, in order to follow a path that would lead her from innocence towards experience. The beginning of the story – "The sun was sinking in the bosom of the Western Ocean, when after a bright day in the autumnal season, the young and beauteous Cleanthe strayed into a thick forest, that spread its solemn shade behind the stately castle of the baron her father" – introduces the archetypal Gothic elements: the father's castle, the forest, the evening hour and shadows. But Cleanthe is in fact a young woman of the Romantic generation, and so

> The faint hints of gold and purple that streaked the varying clouds, the last sighs of the sinking breeze, the variegated hues of the fading foliage, the plaintive cooings of the wood-pigeon, and the hollow murmurs of a distant torrent – conspired to soothe her soul into a tender and pleasing melancholy; and awaken those lively and vivid trains of fancy, that by degrees abstract the mind from sensible objects, and bewilder it amid distant and visionary pursuits.

While wandering, she stops near an ancient oak tree, realizing she has "wandered out of her knowledge". While Cleanthe is meditating on what to do next, two knights come by locked in "a fierce and desperate combat".[24] Frightened, she hides in the ruins of an abbey where a woman, who had been stabbed to death for having surrendered to the attraction of pleasure, suggests she should learn from her mistakes. Having recovered after fainting, she finds herself

---

[24] Mary Hays, "A Fragment. In the Manner of the Old Romances", in *Letters and Essays, Moral and Miscellaneous*, New York and London, 1974, 212-14.

in a flowery meadow and the colours and fragrances reawaken her senses. Immediately afterwards

> she saw advancing towards her, arrayed in flowing vestments, and crowned with immortal amaranths, the brave and beauteous Alcanzor; (for whom she had long cherished a tender an faithful affection,) grace and sprightliness animated his form, and more than mortal beauty glowed in his face: – drawing near he knelt at her feet.[25]

However, Alcanzor, rather than protecting her from the dangers of desire, becomes himself a potential temptation. In spite of the attraction she feels towards him, Cleanthe rejects him and shuts herself away again in her father's house. In this way she abandons the road to experience and transition from adolescence to adulthood.

It would appear then, that in an age when the romance tends to be placed in the sphere of home life, Cleanthe, by making her choice – the apparently easy one of chastity – refuses to be part of the outside world in order to remain anchored to the world of innocence.[26] Yet her return to the family home is the opposite turn of events compared to the return of Psyche into the arms of Love. In fact, while Psyche accepted the heroism, protection and the command of her knight, Mary Hays was using the conventions of the romance to overturn its traditional function and bring into question the passivity of the woman as reward for the knight's adventures.[27] To a greater degree than Mary Tighe, who was mainly interested in influences and conflicts of an aesthetic nature, Mary Hays recognized the political potential of the romance, just as she noticed that knights were historically oppressors and symbols of war rather than love. The fact that the romance, in spite of its apparent escapist and consolatory functions, hid marked ambiguities and was potentially subversive and violent was already implicit in criticisms made of the genre during the Renaissance. Such potentiality is made explicit by the Romantic version of the genre,[28] even though it conceals cruder political manifestations under the guise

---

[25] *Ibid.*, 217.

[26] Edward W. Pitcher, "Eighteenth-Century Gothic Fragments and the Paradigm of Violation and Repair", *Studies in Short Fiction*, XXXIII (1996), 37.

[27] Allen W. Grove, "To Make a Long Story Short: Gothic Fragments and the Gender Politics of Incompleteness", *Studies in Short Fiction*, XXXIV (1997), 3.

[28] Jacqueline M. Labbe, *The Romantic Paradox: Love, Violence and the Uses of Romance, 1760-1830*, Basingstoke, 2000, 3.

of dreams and nightmares. The Romantic heroine can, therefore, hardly feel protected by the chivalric code, but appears to be the victim of blind chivalry that metaphorically reproduces the oppression carried out by end-of-century society towards women. Her refusing to step out into the outside world and to grow up is not for Cleanthe the result of excessive fear but rather a refusal of the ideology borne by the romance. Despite her evident attraction towards Alcanzor, Cleanthe prefers not to have a courtly knight at her side, choosing instead to be her own protector.

With the male world in general Mary Hays entertained a quite ambiguous relationship: in her private life she overturned traditional roles when she openly declared, in the face of convention, her love for William Frend, only to have her dignity as a woman offended when he rejected her love. Relationships with the literary world and the men which dominated it were equally complex: she displayed at times attitudes of authentic idolatry towards her mentors, while on other occasions she would face up to them in open controversy.

The literary paths taken by both the writers considered here, created feelings of ecstasy and torment in them. Mary Tighe, following a period of intense involvement in London's literary world, retired, like her Psyche, to the elitist and sophisticated haven of her Dublin circle, where she enjoyed intense, albeit short-lived, popularity. The revolutionary and assertive Mary Hays risked, like Cleanthe, ending up in hell and, again like her, shunned conflict and distanced herself from her friends and erstwhile protectors due to personal and ideological differences: she went on to live an intensely private life. By giving two quite different meanings to the genre, the two writers obtained opposing results: paradoxically, it was Mary Tighe who managed to tame the romance, by making it a docile tool of expression of her own poetical style, while the radical Hays, in the face of the potential dangers inherent in the genre, preferred to renounce all activity and retire quietly to the private sphere.

Felicia Hemans, Letitia Landon, and "Lady's Rule"

Richard Cronin

From the death of Byron until the publication of *In Memoriam* – for a period, that is, of more than twenty-five years – Felicia Hemans was the most successful poet in Britain. In 1829, reviewing *The Forest Sanctuary* and *Records of Woman*, Francis Jeffrey offered an elegiac survey of the literary landscape:

> The tuneful quartos of Southey are already little better than lumber: – and the rich melodies of Keats and Shelley, – and the fantastical emphasis of Wordsworth, – and the plebeian pathos of Crabbe, are melting fast from the fields of our vision. The novels of Scott have put out his poetry. Even the splendid strains of Moore are fading into distance and dimness, except where they have been married to immortal music; and the blazing star of Byron himself is receding from its place of pride.[1]

His implication is clear. The figure who has trampled out the bright stars of Romanticism is Felicia Hemans. In the years from 1825 when she published *The Forest Sanctuary* and *Lays of Many Lands* until her death in 1835, Hemans effected a more radical reconformation of English poetry than had been contrived by any woman poet before her, or has been since.

This is a fact so embarrassing that, until 1989, when it was pointed out by Marlon Ross,[2] it was passed over in almost complete silence by academic literary historians. Since then, a formidable group of critics,

[1] *The Edinburgh Review*, L (1829-30), 32.
[2] See Marlon B. Ross, *The Contours of Masculine Desire: Romanticism and the Rise of Women's Poetry*, New York and Oxford, 1989, 267-309.

amongst them Anne Mellor, Stuart Curran, Angela Leighton, Isobel Armstrong and Susan Wolfson, have recognized Hemans' importance, and have begun the task of re-writing literary history in order to accommodate it.[3] But their work, too, is not free from embarrassment. Curran, for example, boldly identifies Hemans as the "major figure" in the forging of the bourgeois or liberal literary culture that was to dominate Victorian England, but he cannot control his impatience with Hemans' sentimentality and her celebration of domesticity. For him, Hemans is, "above all, the creator and enforcer of ideological control masking itself as praise for feminine instinct and female duty".[4]

It seems almost churlish to insist that Hemans be accorded her rightful place in literary history only to lambast her for having chosen to occupy it. The problem is that Hemans, as Mellor points out, "constructed her self and poetry as the icon of female domesticity",[5] and it is not an icon that many modern critics are prepared to reverence. The common response is to argue that Hemans in fact subverts the values that she seems to celebrate. So, Mellor finds that "Having accepted her culture's hegemonic inscription of the woman within the domestic sphere, Hemans' poetry subtly and painfully explored the ways in which that construction of gender finally collapses upon itself, bringing nothing but suffering, and the void of nothingness, to both men and women".[6] Wolfson agrees that the presiding theme of Hemans' most popular volume, *Records of Woman*, is "the failure of domestic ideals, in whatever cultural variety, to sustain and fulfil women's lives".[7] The problem here is obvious enough. Mellor, Wolfson and Leighton rescue Hemans from Curran's

---

[3] Isobel Armstrong, *Victorian Poetry: Poetry, Poetics and Politics*, London, 1993, 318-32; Stuart Curran, "Women Writers, Women Readers", in *Cambridge Companion to British Romanticism*, ed. Stuart Curran, Cambridge, 1993, 177-95; Angela Leighton, *Victorian Women Poets: Writing Against the Heart*, London and New York, 1992; Anne K. Mellor, *Romanticism and Gender*, London and New York, 1993; Susan J. Wolfson "'Domestic Affections' and 'The Spear of Minerva': Felicia Hemans and the Dilemma of Gender", in *Re-Visioning Romanticism: British Women Writers, 1776-1837*, eds Carol Shiner Wilson and Joel Haefner, Philadelphia, 1994, 128-66; and *Felicia Hemans: Selected Poems, Letters, Reception Material*, ed. Susan J. Wolfson, Princeton and Oxford, 2000.

[4] Curran, "Women Writers, Women Readers", 190.

[5] Mellor, *Romanticism and Gender*, 123.

[6] *Ibid.*, 142.

[7] Wolfson, "'Domestic Affections' and 'The Spear of Minerva'", 145.

disparaging description of her work, but only by making the fact of her enormous popularity either inexplicable or the product of a grotesque misreading. Is it really credible that Hemans could have contrived to win her place as the most successful poet in Britain by the production of poems that expose the destructive hollowness of the values that her readers held most dear?[8]

Such critical contortions are produced by a desire to reclaim the work of a poet whose poems seem, on the face of it, to celebrate an ideology that most modern critics, for perfectly good reasons, find distasteful. Hemans celebrates both domesticity and heroism, she pays her devotion, as her memorialist and daughter, Harriet Owen, notes, at once to "the chivalrous and the tender",[9] and modern critics are no happier with her cult of heroism than they are with her cult of domesticity. Her most famous poem, "Casabianca" ("The boy stood on the burning deck") celebrates the staunchness of a boy who will not abandon a burning ship, because his father is unconscious below deck, and so unable to respond to the boy's pleas that he be permitted to leave his station. It is impossible for a reader now not to respond queasily to the boy's increasingly panicky appeals to his father before he and the ship are blown to smithereens, and the poem reaches its conclusion: "But the noblest thing that perished there, / Was that young faithful heart" (ll. 39-40).[10]

Nevertheless, when Armstrong offers the poem as "a violent elegy about the way phallic law destroys itself", or Mellor insists that the boy's "filial fidelity" is shown to be "not only futile but counter-productive" and that "'The noblest thing which perished there' was perhaps not Casabianca's 'young faithful heart' so much as the domestic values to which that heart foolishly adhered", then, surely, the poem is reclaimed only by being wilfully misread.[11] The boy's conduct is represented as heroic rather than foolish, and the readership

---

[8] Mellor confronts the problem directly, and boldly insists that "Hemans' popularity rested on a broader social recognition of the general truth of her vision" (*Romanticism and Gender*, 142), her demonstration, that is, of the destructive nullity of the domestic ideal, but, for all its boldness this is unpersuasive.

[9] Harriet Owen, *Memoir of the Life and Writings of Mrs Hemans*, Edinburgh, 1844, 56.

[10] *The Poetical Works of Mrs Felicia Hemans*, London, 1873, 398. All references are to this edition in which the lines are not numbered. Line numbers are supplied for ease of reference from the Chadwyck-Healy English Poetry Database.

[11] Armstrong, *Victorian Poetry*, 331; Mellor, *Romanticism and Gender*, 142.

that made the poem famous, we must assume, found that heroism underscored rather than undermined by the manner in which his appeals to his father invite the reader to register the full pathos of his situation.

But modern critics, one suspects, are not simply responding to ideological pressures. Hemans' poems present to the reader a glassy surface that seems to offer no crevice to which the critical intelligence can cling. Jerome McGann, in a characteristically independent intervention in Hemans studies, points out how her poetry "covets an undisturbed appearance", that it registers "no apparent divorce between form and content", and that it was precisely this characteristic of poems that are "finished throughout with an exquisite delicacy, and even serenity of execution" that Jeffrey admired and that makes them seem to modern readers merely "bland".[12] It is, of course, discrepancies between form and content, between the formal characteristics and the expressive qualities of a poem, on which all critics educated under the auspices of New Criticism have been trained to focus. Hemans characteristically offers no such discrepancies, and the critical response has been to locate an ideological complexity that can stand in for the complex relationship between form and content that is felt to be disablingly absent. If, as Paula Feldman suggests, Hemans' poetry "undercuts, even while it reinforces, conventional views of women",[13] then the critic is freed to trace a complex relationship, not between form and content, but between text and sub-text, so that the critical argument, even though it may lack the substance, can comfortingly retain the structure of the kind of argument that New Criticism represented as distinguishing literary studies.

Hemans' first volume was published in 1808, when she was only fifteen. Her career began, then, just a year after Byron's and pre-dated Shelley's and Keats'. Early poems such as *The Restoration of the Works of Art to Italy* (1816) and the prize-winning "The Meeting of Wallace and Bruce on the Banks of the Carron" (1819) secured her a

---

[12] Jerome J. McGann, *The Poetics of Sensibility: A Revolution in Literary Style*, Oxford and New York, 1996, 218-19. McGann misquotes Jeffrey's "serenity of expression" as "severity of expression", a less accurate and hence less interesting description.

[13] Introduction, in Felicia Hemans, *Records of Woman: With Other Poems*, ed. Paula R. Feldman, Lexington: KY, 1999, xx.

solid reputation, but in a review of her work in 1819 the *Edinburgh Magazine* notes that she has few readers, and asks "Why are they so few?"[14] It was only with the publication of *The Forest Sanctuary*, and *Lays of Many Lands* both in 1825, *Records of Woman* in 1828, and *Songs of the Affections* in 1830 that she secured her place as the pre-eminent British poet, and it was in these volumes that she developed the poetic form with which she was always most closely associated, her own version of the lyrical ballad.

The *Edinburgh Magazine* had in fact identified her failure to offer the public the narrative poems that they craved as the principal reason for her lack of popularity, but it is a want that in her later poems she amply supplies. The poems may tighten towards the lyric, though still retaining a narrative character, or they may expand towards the romance, while still preserving their concentration on states of feeling rather than patterns of event. The states of feeling deployed are most commonly melancholic, and the response insistently demanded of the reader is sympathetic pity. In other words, the poems are characteristically sentimental. The poems are rhymed: couplets and quatrains are the commonest schemes, but there is great variety, Spenserian stanzas, for example, in *The Forest Sanctuary*. Metrically, there is even greater diversity – iambs and anapaests, pentameter lines and stanzas in common measure, even experiments in classical metre – but in all cases the intonations of the speaking voice are subordinated to the flow of the metre. Angela Leighton is right to point out that in some of the *Records of Woman* the movement of the couplets is more fluid, but even in "Properzia Rossi", where the fluidity is at its most extreme, and more than half the poem's iambic pentameter couplets are enjambed, the couplet form continues to superimpose itself on Properzia's voice in a manner far removed from Browning's in a poem like "My Last Duchess". The diction is chastely ornate. Neologism and archaism are avoided, and the vocabulary selected from a stock of words that had been familiar in poetry for many years.

Jeffrey offers the most exact description of this style, which "would strike us, perhaps, as more impassioned and exalted, if it were not regulated and harmonized by the most beautiful taste":

---

[14] *Edinburgh Magazine*, III (1819), 443.

> It is infinitely sweet, elegant, and tender – touching, perhaps, and contemplative, rather than vehement and overpowering; and not only finished throughout with an exquisite delicacy, and even serenity of execution, but informed with a purity and loftiness of feeling, and a certain sober and humble tone of indulgence and piety, which must satisfy all judgements, and allay the apprehensions of those who are most afraid of the passionate exaggerations of poetry.[15]

Jeffrey is equally exact in defining the dominant characteristic of such a style: it is "feminine", and establishes Hemans' work as "a fine exemplification of Female Poetry". Jeffrey makes this seem not only a modest achievement, but an achievement of modesty. Hemans' poems are as "perfect" as they are because she accepts rather than rebels against the limitations of her gender: "the delicacy of [women's] habits, and the still more disabling delicacy which pervades their conceptions and feelings", which prevent them from delineating "the fierce and sullen passions of men", and limit them to representations of that area of life which is woman's proper concern, "the practical regulation of the private life in all its bearings, affections, and concerns".

It is significant that this ideally feminine style was not developed by Hemans until she was in her thirties. In 1819, reviewing her prize poem on Wallace, the *Edinburgh Magazine* could still describe her poetry as "by far the most *manly* which ever came from a female pen".[16] Two oddities remain. First, there is an odd discrepancy between the modesty of the achievement that Jeffrey describes and the power that he attributes to it: it has forced from "its place of pride" even "the blazing star of Byron himself". There is an equally odd discrepancy between Jeffrey's insistence that women writers must confine themselves to the private life, and the content of the poems themselves. It is easier to address the second point first.

Hemans' poems range further from home both in time and in space than those of any of her male predecessors with the possible exception of Southey. She outdoes even Baillie's *Plays of the Passions*, which

---

[15] *The Edinburgh Review*, L (1829-30), 47.

[16] *Edinburgh Magazine*, III (1819), 576. Byron thought Hemans' poetry manly enough to prompt feeble plays on her name; "Mrs Hewoman", "I do not despise Mrs Heman – but if she knit blue stockings instead of wearing them it would be better", "your feminine He-Man" (*Letters and Journals of Lord Byron*, London, 1977, VII, 158, 182, 183).

she so much admired, in appropriating all human history and the whole of the known world to provide the subject matter for her poems. She speaks as Sappho in the sixth century BC, as the wife of Hasdrubal at the end of the third, as the wife of Rudolph von Wart in the fourteenth century, the wife of Charles V in the sixteenth, and as Arabella Stuart in the seventeenth. The geographical range is equally wide, from American Indians to those of the sub-continent, from the Russia of "Ivan the Czar" to the tropical island home that the exile dreams of in "The Palm Tree". Jeffrey does not neglect this characteristic of her poems, but singles it out for praise. She has taken her themes "from the legends of different nations, and the most opposite states of society; and has contrived to retain much of what is interesting and peculiar in each of them, without adopting along with it, any of the revolting or extravagant excesses which may characterise the taste or manners of the people or the age from which it has been derived".[17] She shares with Southey an imperial imagination,[18] but for Jeffrey she can do so without compromising her femininity, which requires her to restrict her sphere to "private life" and not to venture on "affairs of moment as they are conducted in the great theatre of the world". Her ingenious solution, as Tricia Lootens shows, is to expand the domestic sphere, the sphere of private life, until it becomes co-extensive with the globe. In one of her most popular poems, "The Graves of a Household", she seems to mourn a family that, even in death, is dispersed around the world. The children over whom the "same fond mother bent" (l. 5)[19] each night now lie in distant graves, one in America, another committed to the sea, one in Spain, and the last, a daughter, in an Italian grave. The poem apparently mourns their dispersal, and yet it is infused too with a proud sense that the most intimate of domestic spaces, the English country churchyard, has become as wide as the world. As she puts it in another poem, "England's Dead": "Wave may not foam, nor wild wind sweep, / Where rest not England's dead" (ll. 7-8).[20]

[17] *The Edinburgh Review*, L (1829-30), 47.

[18] For a condensed statement of Southey's imperialist aspirations, see "The Vision", the second part of *The Poet's Pilgrimage to Waterloo*. On Hemans and imperialism, see Tricia Lootens, "Hemans and Home: Victorianism, Feminine 'Internal Enemies', and the Domestication of National Identity", in *Victorian Women Poets: A Critical Reader*, ed. Angela Leighton, Oxford, 1996, 3-23.

[19] *The Poetical Works of Mrs Felicia Hemans*, 437.

[20] *Ibid.*, 355.

Jeffrey insists that Hemans' verse shows an "exquisite delicacy", which seems to be at once a delicacy of execution and a delicacy of sentiment, and he praises her tenderness and her purity. He has in mind, one assumes, a poem such as "The Memorial Pillar" which celebrates the piety of the Countess of Pembroke who erected the pillar in 1656 at the place where she had last parted from her mother more than forty years before:

> Can I, while yet these tokens wear
> The impress of the dead,
> Think of the love embodied there,
> As of a vision fled?
>
> (ll. 49-52)[21]

The answer, of course, is no, and the poem ends by imagining the reunion of mother and child in Heaven: "Surely your hearts have met at last!" (l. 60). "Edith, A Tale of the Woods" tells the story of a young woman who is left alone in the wilds of America when her whole party, including her young husband, are slaughtered. Edith is fostered by an old Indian and his wife, who have lost their own daughter. Cared for by them, she recovers, and gradually leads the Indians towards Christ until "their prayers were one" (ll. 132 and 137).[22] She feels then that her work is done, and the poem closes when the old warrior sings over her dying body a tender but pious lament.

Jeffrey's description perfectly accommodates both poems. But there are an equally large number of poems by Hemans that seem on the face of it neither delicate, nor tender, nor, at any rate from a Christian point of view, edifying. A substantial group of poems, for example, commemorates women whose passions erupt into suicidal and/or murderous violence. As early as 1819 in *Tales and Historic Scenes*, there is "The Wife of Asdrubal", in which the wife bitterly denounces her husband's ignoble capitulation to the Romans before stabbing her children to death and throwing herself into the flames of the burning citadel,[23] and "The Widow of Crescentius" who disguises herself as a minstrel boy in order to poison the Emperor Otho, avenging his execution of her husband. As she watches Otho expire in

---

[21] *Ibid.*, 307.
[22] *Ibid.*, 285.
[23] *Ibid.*, 32-33.

agony a "feverish glow of triumph dyed" her cheek (l. 255).[24] In *Lays of Many Lands*, "The Suliote Mother" hurls herself and her children from a precipice rather than be taken captive.[25] In *Records of Woman* Maimuna avenges the murder of her son by raising a Muslim army to burn to the ground "The Indian City" of her son's killers after putting its inhabitants to the sword;[26] and the "Indian Woman's Death Song" is sung as she paddles her canoe towards the cataract over which she and her baby will plunge to their deaths. She has been deserted by her husband, but as she paddles:

> upon her Indian brow
> Sat a strange gladness, and her dark hair wav'd
> As if triumphantly.
>
> (ll. 9-11)[27]

It is the same triumph with which Sappho throws herself from the cliff in "The Last Song of Sappho".[28]

Jeffrey quite fails to register a recognition that Hemans' poems are divided in their character, and he is, I think, right. Edith and Maimuna are violently contrasting types of womanhood, but they are accommodated within poems that very clearly share a style, and it is Hemans' style that acts for Jeffrey as the guarantee of her tenderness and delicacy, of her femininity. This remains the case almost without reference to the content of the poems. It is what gives Hemans' mature verse the quality that W.M. Rossetti tartly describes as "the monotone of mere sex",[29] but it is the construction of that monotone that is her more powerful achievement. Jeffrey alludes, I think, to the same quality, when he refers to her "serenity of expression", a serenity that remains quite undisturbed by even the most sensational and violent subject matter. Both Jeffrey and Rossetti recognize that serenity as the badge of her femininity, but it works to project femininity as something both theatrical and, for all its sentimentality, incongruously cold.

---

[24] *Ibid.*,26.
[25] *Ibid.*, 261-62.
[26] *Ibid.*, 287-89.
[27] *Ibid.*, 293.
[28] *Ibid.*, 532.
[29] Introduction, *The Poetical Works of Mrs Felicia Hemans*, ed. W.M. Rossetti, London and New York, 1873, xxvii.

Hemans was a much sought after contributor to the annuals that began to dominate the poetry market in the later 1820s, and was, unlike Landon, powerful enough to dictate her own terms. She was not reduced, like Landon, to the composition of hasty verses to accompany whatever plates the publisher had selected for the volume. But from the mid-1820s her own poems become increasingly pictorial, so that to read one of her volumes is like being conducted through a gallery of pictures, pictures most often of women who are placed in a rich variety of postures that have in common a certain extravagance and theatricality. The reader is invited to respond sentimentally to these pictures, but also coolly, rather as the Soul walks through her gallery in Tennyson's "The Palace of Art". As I shall argue, this is not a coincidence, for Hemans and L.E.L. were two of the principal, if largely unacknowledged, influences on the early Tennyson.

It is her unfaltering "serenity of expression" that persuades her contemporaries that her poems remain properly enclosed within the feminine sphere of private, domestic affections, and that continues to persuade many of her modern readers of the same thing. Marlon Ross, for example, is a careful reader of Hemans, and yet he offers her essay on Goethe's *Tasso* as an exploration of the irreconcilability of "the realm of the romantic, of sentiment and affection" and the masculine world, "the outer struggle for worldly quest and conquest",[30] and he does this despite Hemans' italicized insistence that Tasso, one of the major figures in her own pantheon, was at once a poet and a warrior, "*superior with the sword and the pen to all men*", and by her vigorous translation of Goethe's lines:

Not steel to steel
Is bound more closely by the magnet's power
Than the same striving after lofty things
Doth bind the Bard and Warrior.

In fact, the narratives to which Hemans consistently turns are those in which the domestic and the chivalrous, the inner world of the affections and the outer world of conquest, the feminine and the masculine, are brought together.

[30] Ross, *The Contours of Masculine Desire*, 267. Hemans' essay appeared in *The New Monthly Magazine and Literary Journal*, n.s., III (1834), 1-5.

Her demonic women erupt into masculine violence, even if often their violence is directed only against themselves and their children. Her angelic women are given to frequenting battlefields, most often in search of a lover's body. "Woman on the Field of Battle" is for Hemans a defining icon, though in the poem of that name, the woman, who has followed her lover to the wars, is herself among the slain:

> Why camest thou here?
> Why? – ask the true heart why
> Women hath been
> Ever where brave men die,
> Unshrinking seen?
>
> (ll. 36-40)[31]

Edith sits by her young husband as he dies "… and vainly bound / With her torn robe and hair the streaming wound" (ll. 29-30).[32] In "Joan of Arc, in Rheims" roles are reversed. It is Joan's moment of triumph as she stands helmeted in the cathedral, carrying the banner of France that is witnessed by her menfolk, her father and her two brothers, and it is the woman whose thoughts are recalled to the domestic paradise that she has left.[33] "Marguerite of France" compacts within herself both the masculine and feminine ideals when she rallies the cowardly troops by threatening to don armour and herself attack the besieging Muslims, carrying her infant son in her arms:

> And I will gird my woman's form,
> And on the ramparts die!
> And the boy whom I have borne for woe,
> But never for disgrace,
> Shall go within mine arms to death
> Meet for his royal race.
>
> (ll. 89-96)[34]

But more often it is femininity itself that is transformed into armour, as when in *The Siege of Valencia* Gonzalo praises his daughter:

---

[31] *The Poetical Works of Mrs Felicia Hemans*, 338-39.
[32] *Ibid.*, 283.
[33] *Ibid.*, 294-96.
[34] *Ibid.*, 495.

> She hath put on
> Courage, and faith, and generous constancy
> E'en as a breastplate.
>
> (I, 382-84)[35]

Or in *The Forest Sanctuary*, when a young woman goes valiantly to her death strengthened by her love for her brother, "The perfect image of affection, pressed / Like armour to [her] bosom" (ll. 355-56).[36]

Far from segregating it from the masculine sphere, Hemans consistently suggests that it is only in its relationship with the masculine that the feminine is defined or valorized. Her representative women are those like "Gertrude" who sits by her husband, wiping his brow, as he suffers his last ordeal, being broken on the wheel,[37] or, in a less ghastly manifestation of the type, "The Switzer's Wife", who sends her husband from home to fight for his nation's freedom with her blessing:

> I know what thou wouldst do, – and be it done!
> Thy soul is darken'd with its fears for me,
> Trust me to Heaven, my husband, – this, thy son,
> The Babe whom I have borne thee, must be free!
> And the sweet memory of our pleasant hearth
> May well give strength – if aught be strong on earth.
>
> (ll. 79-84)[38]

Here, as in almost all her poems, Hemans reinforces conventional notions that woman finds her best fulfilment in selfless service of a man, and of the masculine values that he represents. Her willingness to do so was, of course, one of the grounds of her huge popularity. The patriotic Swiss is named in the poem as Werner, and in Hemans' headnote identified as Werner Stauffacher, but the woman is identified only as his wife – appropriately, it might seem, because her virtue is that she finds her only being in him. But this is to ignore the fact that his masculinity finds its only expression through her. The code of values that defines him as a man can only be articulated by a woman. The same is true in all Hemans' mature poems, for, whether or not

[35] *Ibid.*, 76.
[36] *Ibid.*, 16-17.
[37] *Ibid.*, 279-80.
[38] *Ibid.*, 275.

they give voice to a woman character, the sentiments of the poems are the expression of a voice that is the product of Hemans' style, a style that Jeffrey correctly read as definitively feminine.

Angela Leighton, in a fine reading of "The Chamois Hunter's Love", points out that the chamois hunter, who loves the perilous, stormy heights, is almost a metonym for the Byronic, that is, the Romantic Byron of *Manfred.*[39] The young woman who loves him must abandon for him her "blessed home" in the valley, and she anticipates that her married life will be "mournful" (ll. 13 and 21),[40] a life spent waiting fearfully for her husband to return from one of his perilous expeditions. Leighton is right to point out that she repudiates her own life in a gesture that is at once dutiful and exhilarated, but it is even more significant that the male Romanticism to which she surrenders her independence is itself the product of her own voice. She at once subordinates herself to it, and fully accommodates it within herself.

Landon creates a somewhat similar effect in *The Improvisatrice*. Lorenzo, the object of the Improvisatrice's passion is described at the moment that she first sees him, with his "dark and flashing eye" that yet betrayed an "almost female softness", his pale cheek, "raven curls", "high and haughty brow" as white as the mountain snow, and his heart-stopping eloquence (ll. 422-39).[41] We learn later that he has "thick-clustering curls" and a "smile which past like lightning o'er / The curved lip" (ll. 938-41).[42] It is a description that, as all of her early readers would have recognized, is derived directly from the idealized prints of Byron's portraits that were so popular in the years immediately following his death. The Improvisatrice is utterly in thrall to the dark charms of her Byronic hero, and yet the poem, from another point of view quite disempowers him, reduces him to the status of a character in a poem by L.E.L., a prop in a feminine fantasy.

Hemans, like Landon, found in Scott the most powerful model for her own poems, although, again like Landon, Scott's influence is often mediated through that of Byron. But Scott's manner, and, to a large

---

[39] Leighton, *Victorian Women Poets: Writing Against the Heart*, 24-25.

[40] *The Poetical Works of Mrs Felicia Hemans*, 320.

[41] L.E.L., *The Improvisatrice; and Other Poems*, London, 1825, 29-30. All references are to this edition in which the lines are not numbered. For ease of reference, line numbers have been supplied from the Chadwyck-Healy English Poetry Database.

[42] *Ibid.*, 63.

extent, his values, are transformed when she mimics them in her own voice, or rather in the voice that she developed in the mid-1820s, when her literary career was already far into its second decade. Ross scarcely overstates the case when he claims that "Hemans sees her goal as the feminization of culture at large".[43] At least one part of that goal she achieved. When, late in her life, she visited Scott at Abbotsford, she was pleased with her reception, and, as a farewell gift, left Scott a poem. She insists emphatically on Scott's masculinity, his voice is

> Like a chieftain's gathering-cry;
> While its deep master-tones hold sway
> As a king's o'er every breast ….
>
> (ll. 12-14)[44]

But by 1829, when Hemans wrote this poem, "deep master-tones" already seemed both odd and antiquated, and it was Hemans who, more than anyone, had made them seem so. L.E.L. was her chief assistant in the work, and it is significant that at the time of her death Landon was working on a study of Scott's female characters, as though her project was to appropriate for women not only Scott's poetic manner but even his robustly masculine novels.

The two women never met, and yet it might be argued that each produced the other. Both women, as Mellor points out, constructed themselves as icons, and, since there were only two niches available, the choice one made in large part determined the choice of the other. The names under which they published are themselves indicative. After 1812, when she married, Felicia Browne became "Mrs Hemans", and retained that style long after her death, in the many editions of her poems throughout the nineteenth century. She presented her work to her readers as the poetry of a wife and mother, despite the fact that, in 1818, after she had borne him four sons and was pregnant with a fifth, Captain Hemans departed for Italy and never saw his wife again. Her most successful predecessor, Charlotte Smith, had made from a similar predicament the signature tune of all her poems, in which a domestic calamity, though never explained, is alluded to repeatedly. Hemans seems to have turned her misfortune to

---

43 Ross, *The Contours of Masculine Desire*, 292.
44 *The Poetical Works of Mrs Felicia Hemans*, 481.

social advantage – Wordsworth admired her "above all, for her delicate and irreproachable conduct during her long separation from an unfeeling husband"[45] – but she allows no trace of her domestic circumstances to seep into poems that maintain her privacy quite intact. Until the death of her mother she lived in Wales, moving to Wavertree near Liverpool in 1828, thus by her choice of residence avoiding any role within the London literary scene. She remained for almost all her readers a name on a title page, and the name she chose, "Mrs Hemans", she donned in the same way that Ximena dons her virtues, as "a breastplate", as a hard, protective surface that allows no chink through which the reader's prying gaze can penetrate.

Landon, who lived her whole life in London and was so enamoured of society that she insisted, as her one-time friend Rosina Bulwer records, on going to a ball even when ill with the flu, published under the three letters, L.E.L.[46] The tactic may first have been suggested by her mentor, William Jerdan, her next-door neighbour and the astute editor of *The Literary Gazette*, who first ushered her into fame by making her the most regular contributor of "Original Poetry" to his journal. Edward Bulwer remembered the effect on him and his fellow undergraduates at Cambridge:

> At that time, poetry was not yet out of fashion, at least with us of the cloister; and there was always, in the Reading Room of the Union, a rush every Saturday afternoon for "The Literary Gazette", and an impatient anxiety to hasten at once to that corner of the sheet which contained the three magical letters of "L.E.L.". And all of us praised the verse, and all of us guessed at the author. We soon learned it was a female, and our admiration was doubled, and our conjectures tripled. Was she young? Was she pretty? and – for there were some embryo fortune-hunters among us – was she rich?[47]

"L.E.L." was a device that from the first invited the reader to decode the poem and reveal the poet, to pry beneath the text, which is conceived as a somewhat diaphanous material scarcely obscuring the

---

[45] *The Poetical Works of William Wordsworth*, eds E. de Selincourt and Helen Darbishire, 5 vols, Oxford, 1947, IV, 461.

[46] The best introduction to Landon and her work is by Glennis Stephenson, *Letitia Landon: The Woman Behind L.E.L.*, Manchester, 1995.

[47] *New Monthly Magazine*, XXXII (1831), 546. From Bulwer's review of Landon's *Romance and Reality*.

warm and palpitating body of the woman who wrote it. All the six volumes of Landon's poetry can be read as a large expansion of the invitation compressed into the "three magical letters of 'L.E.L.'".

Hemans was interested in the figure of the woman poet, whose verses won her fame, but who found at last that this was no compensation for her failure in love. Germaine de Staël's *Corinne, or Italy* was, in many ways, the founding text of nineteenth-century women's poetry. "C'est moi", Hemans wrote in the margin, and Landon contributed the verse to the 1833 translation.[48] Hemans explores the topic in poems such as "Corinne at the Capitol", "The Last Song of Sappho", and, most powerfully, in the monologue, "Properzia Rossi" in *Records of Woman*. But for Hemans the Corinne figure is just one of her large gallery of female types: for Landon she is the controlling figure of all her poetry. It is a theme that she addresses directly in "Corinna" from her first volume, *The Fate of Adelaide and Other Poems*, in the title poem of the second volume that made her famous, *The Improvisatrice and Other Poems*, in "Erinna" from *The Golden Violet and Other Poems*, and in "A History of the Lyre" from *The Venetian Bracelet*, Landon's finest poem, in which she tells the story of a second Italian Improvisatrice, Eulalia. But it is a story implicit in all Landon's major poems.

At the end of *The Golden Violet* she turns, as she several times does at the conclusion of her longer poems, to address the reader directly. "My power", she writes "is but a woman's power" (l. 3525).[49] This is at once a confession, and a quotation, from her own *The Improvisatrice*, where it is the character rather than her creator who concedes "My power was but a woman's power" (l. 25).[50] The quotation reveals belatedly, as it were, that the Italian woman poet of *The Improvisatrice* was only ever a mask for L.E.L. herself, except

[48] The importance of *Corinne*, like many other things, was first pointed out by Ellen Moers, *Literary Women*, New York, 1976, 173-210. On Madame de Staël's reclamation of the figure of Sappho, see Margaret Reynolds, " 'I lived for art, I lived for love': The Woman Poet Sings Sappho's Last Song", in *Victorian Women Poets: A Critical Reader*, 277-306.

[49] L.E.L., *The Golden Violet, with Its Tales of Romance and Chivalry, and Other Poems*, London, 1827, 238. Lines in this edition are not numbered. For ease of reference line numbers have been supplied from the Chadwyck-Healy English Poetry Database.

[50] *The Improvisatrice*, 3.

that it is not really a revelation because her readers had never doubted it.

Landon offers the subjects of her poems as the evidence that hers is only a woman's power. She writes almost exclusively of love:

> If that I know myself what keys
> Yield to my hand their sympathies,
> I should say it is those whose tone
> Is woman's love and sorrow's own …
>
> (ll. 3529-32)[51]

She knew herself very well, as does her character, "Erinna", whose topics are indistinguishable from Landon's:

> I have told passionate tales of breaking hearts,
> Of young cheeks fading even before the rose;
> My songs have been the mournful history
> Of woman's tenderness and woman's tears …
>
> (ll. 375-78)[52]

Landon's poems tell over and over again the same story. A young woman is loved, returns the love, is abandoned, and dies. The abandonment may be by betrayal or by accident, the errant lover may never come back in which case the lady will die of grief, but even if he should return it will only be in time to catch the woman's body as she falls. In *The Troubadour* the framing tale is of exactly this kind, and embedded within it are a variety of smaller narratives that almost without exception repeat the same story. In "Rosalie" she compresses into just three lines the story that, expanded and repeated, fills all six volumes of her verse:

> Alas! alas! hers is a common tale: –
> She trusted, – as youth ever has believed; –
> She heard Love's vows – confided – was deceived!
>
> (ll. 134-36)[53]

But these are not really stories about the sorrows of love. The women in them function simply as surrogates of the poet, and that is

[51] *The Golden Violet*, 238.
[52] *Ibid.*, 266-67.
[53] *The Improvisatrice*, 118.

why they have to be abandoned. Mutual love, fulfilled love, is for Landon an impossible topic, as she several times recognizes, for example in *The Troubadour*:

> But what has minstrel left to tell
> When love has not an obstacle?
> My lute is hush'd, and mute its chords,
> The heart and happiness have no words![54]

Or earlier, and with a more charming brusqueness, in "Roland's Tower: A Legend of the Rhine":

> They loved; – they were beloved. Oh, happiness!
> I have said all that can be said of bliss,
> In saying that they loved.
>
> (ll. 93-95)[55]

Happiness in love is a heresy against Landon's "woman's creed of suffering" (l. 367),[56] but, much more importantly, it allows an intrusive interloper into the relationship that remains central in all of Landon's poems, the relationship between herself and her reader. These are stories of "woman's tears", and tears, for Landon, dissolve the distinction between poet and character. Her characters weep, and she represents the verse that records their tears as itself a kind of weeping. Poetry came to her, she tells us, just as it came to Erinna for whom "song came gushing, like the natural tears, / To check whose current does not rest with us" (ll. 121-22).[57] The weeping woman, the woman abandoned and fast dwindling into death, exerts over the reader a powerful sentimental appeal, but her true function within the poems is to figure the appeal that the poems themselves make to their reader, who is himself the chivalrous man who, by reading Landon's poems, rescues her from her desolate loneliness. It is very knowingly done.

[54] L.E.L., *The Troubadour, Catalogue of Pictures and Historical Sketches*, London, 1825, 244. All subsequent references are to this edition. This volume has been omitted from the Chadwyck-Healy database so line numbers are not given. Numbers in brackets refer to pages of this volume.
[55] *The Improvisatrice*, 135.
[56] *The Golden Violet*, 25.
[57] *Ibid.*, 250.

Landon's style is at once utterly natural and extremely artificial.[58] She represents poetry as a spontaneous overflow of emotional fluid, as tears. She weeps onto paper, like the aged mother of "The Sailor":

> … The Bible lay
> Open beside, but blistered were the leaves
> With two or three large tears, which had dried in.
>
> (ll. 99-101)[59]

But here the tears are realized with an awkward precision that sharpens melancholy into pain, an effect that Landon is usually anxious to avoid. Hence her reliance on a narrow and cosseted diction, much of which is merely conventional – the roses, stars, violets and nightingales, the pale cheeks over which blushes come and go, the miraculously white hands – but which is nevertheless stamped with her own mark. If a tree is to be rested under, it is likely to be a chestnut, often "chestnut"; if there is a dance it will probably be the saraband; the conventional roses, lilies and violets are variegated by flowers that seem personal favourites, the tulip and the laburnum; women are like flowers, and flowers are like women; verbs are active, especially when they are describing plants, which are much given to flinging. So, the "wilding broom" of "Gladesmuir" "gracefully / Flings its long tresses like a maiden's hair / Waving in yellow beauty" (ll. 14-16).[60]

The landscapes that this style is peculiarly adapted to describe are like those of *The Golden Violet*, where the poems on the first day are spoken in a "spacious hall" that shuttles between being an outdoors and an indoors place:

> The dome above like a glory shone
> Or a cloud which the sunset lingers upon,
> While the tinted pane seem'd the bright resort,
> Where Iris' self held her minstrel court …
>
> (ll. 317-20)[61]

---

[58] McGann and Riess offer a wittily perceptive description of the style: "It is cold and sentimental at the same time, flat and intense, like the photographs of Cindy Sherman" (Introduction, *Letitia Elizabeth Landon: Selected Writings*, eds Jerome McGann and Daniel Riess, Peterborough, Ontario, 1997, 29).

[59] *The Improvisatrice*, 226.

[60] *Ibid.*, 194.

[61] *The Golden Violet*, 21.

On the second day the contest moves outside into the gardens, but the gardens offer a "carpet meet" of flowers, and the mossy tree on which the Countess takes her seat accommodates her like a chaise longue:

> And at her feet, as if from air
> A purple cloud had fallen there,
> Grew thousand violets, whose sighs
> Breathed forth an Eastern sacrifice …[62]

It is peculiarly appropriate that the prize for which the poets compete, the golden violet, is itself insecurely placed, seeming sometimes a flower and sometimes a jewel.

That odd union of the natural and the artificial is Landon's special mark, and it seeps into her representation of human relationships. Her verse is a natural outpouring that is also and always self-consciously poetic. She presents it as unpremeditated song, and yet there is always implicit in it a sidelong glance at the reader. Her women characters, too, are at once unselfconscious, and tremblingly sensitive to the presence of young men. Hence, she is particularly fond of representing her women at moments when they are conscious of someone looking at them: "There was a blush, as if she knew / Whose look was fixed on her …" (ll. 62-63).[63] It is an often repeated moment. When the Improvisatrice arrives at the costumed ball dressed as "a Hindoo girl", the thought of Lorenzo's eyes on her makes her blush: "For well my conscious cheek betrayed / Whose eye was gazing on me too!" (ll. 755-56).[64]

The power of these moments is in the precision with which they echo that distinctive relationship with the reader that is Landon's special mark. Her poems, more often than they are tears, are the blush, the rush of blood to the face with which she like her heroines signals her consciousness of the beloved, who is for her not Lorenzo but the reader.

Landon writes about love in poems the real subject of which is her own poetry. Hence the association she repeatedly insists on between love and poetry. When the Improvisatrice paints Sappho it is at the moment when she takes farewell of "lyre, life, and love" (l. 137).[65]

---

[62] *Ibid.*, 165.
[63] *The Improvisatrice*, 5.
[64] *Ibid.*, 50.
[65] *Ibid.*, 10.

Life, as it is represented by Landon, is only constituted by poetry and love, and the two are scarcely distinguishable, as in *The Troubadour*:

> I know not whether love can fling
> A deeper witchery from his wing
> Than falls sweet Power of Song from thine.[66]

The central character of the poem, Raymond, a man more errant than knightly, is enraged by the caprices of his mistress, and loses in his anger the complexion proper to all Landon's heroes and heroines: "Not his the paleness that may streak / The lover's or the minstrel's cheek".[67] But in the end it is love that figures poetry, rather than vice versa. The unhappy love careers that she so consistently ascribes to her heroines are moulded to echo her understanding of the poet's career, a career that she repeatedly charts. First, there is the youthful poet's dizzy rise to fame, a period in the poet's career which is exactly analogous to the first rapture of young love. Raymond is an unlikely poet, but Landon makes him one, it seems, only so that she can allow him to enjoy:

> The loveliest part
> Of the young poet's life, when first,
> In solitude and silence nurst,
> His genius rises like a spring ...[68]

Erinna triumphs in her first success: "I felt immortal, for my brain / Was drunk with its first draught of fame" (ll. 42-43).[69] Even the still more mournful Eulalia joyfully remembers her poetic youth:

> The flowers were full of song: – upon the rose
> I read the crimson annals of true love;
> The violet flung me back an old romance ...[70]

First poems are like first love. It is impossible to tell

---

[66] *The Troubadour*, 10-11.
[67] *Ibid.*, 108.
[68] *Ibid.*, 10.
[69] *The Golden Violet*, 245.
[70] "A History of the Lyre", ll. 211-13, in *The Venetian Bracelet*, London, 1829, 87-115. This volume is quoted here and subsequently from the Chadwyck-Healy Poetry Database.

What the young minstrel feels, when first the song
Has been rewarded by the thrilling praise
Of one too partial, but whose lightest word
Can bid the heart beat quick with happiness.

(ll. 231-34)[71]

The triumphant peak of the poet's career is the supreme moment of erotic consummation, the moment when "Corinna" stands crowned on the Capitol, and responds to her coronation with a triumphant blush "Such as young Psyche wore, when love first taught / His own sweet language" (ll. 27-28).[72] Afterwards, as for all Landon's women, comes abandonment, not by a lover, not even by her readers (though that may be the concealed fear), but the poet loses her pleasure in the fame that she has won. Raymond is warned that though his "songs be on every tongue, / And wealth and honours round him flung", he will at the last own that his fame has been "dearly bought". Erinna casts aside her lyre in disillusion, and Eulalia, too, acknowledges that the exercise of her talents has not compensated her for her loneliness. In the poem in which she memorializes Hemans, Landon asks "Was not this [her fame] purchased all too dearly?" (l. 33).[73] In "A History of the Lyre" in particular the familiar story has a deeper resonance. The poem is marked by the sad self-knowledge of a poet who had to make a living, and hence had to make a compromise with "worldliness", not being able to afford the idealism of the unknown poet (Landon, I suspect, is thinking of Keats) who is commemorated by the Countess of *The Golden Violet*: he "fondly woos / The world without that worldliness / Which wanting, there is no success" (ll. 247-48).[74] Eulalia's complaint seems to figure Landon's sense that she has not fulfilled her talent, and that her failure is in part a consequence of having to write for an inadequate readership, winning praise that a "passing moment might light up my cheek, / But haunted not my solitude" (ll. 352-53).[75]

really?

[71] L.E.L., *The Fate of Adelaide, a Swiss Romantic Tale, and Other Poems*, London, 1827, 100. All subsequent references are to this edition in which the lines are not numbered. For ease of reference line numbers are taken from the Chadwyck-Healy Poetry Database.
[72] *Ibid.*, 98.
[73] "Felicia Hemans", in L.E.L., *The Zenana and Minor Poems*, London, 1839, 248.
[74] *The Golden Violet*, 17.
[75] *The Venetian Bracelet*, 109.

However, in the earlier poems, the trajectory of the poet's career seems not so much a product of self-knowledge, still less a surrender to the view that a woman's proper role is as wife and mother rather than as poet, but rather a kind of flirtation. It is a career that enables her to assume the position of her own abandoned women, making an identical claim on the chivalrous, protective instincts of her reader. The technique is at its most transparent at the conclusion of *The Troubadour*, when, after thanking the reviewers for their kind treatment of her, she ends the poem by paying a heartfelt tribute to her father. It was a very widely admired passage. As she writes, she tells us, her "page is wet with bitter tears", for no success, however triumphant, can console her for the loss of her father:

> But never will thy name depart
> Until thy orphan girl may share
> The grave where her best feelings are.
> Never, dear father, love can be,
> Like the dear love I had for thee![76]

The self-presentation as an "orphan girl" may be the most flagrant bid for a sympathetic reading that any poet has ever dared: it is a very knowing passage, and yet also, one feels, entirely sincere.

Landon consistently represents the poet as both subject and object, as seeing eye and as object of another, always male, gaze. Her attempt is to dissolve the distinction between poet and poem, so that she becomes herself the object of the reader's admiring attention. Again her lovelorn women echo her. In abandonment, and in death, their bodies petrify until they become statues of themselves, "... like to marble, when the sculptor's skill / Has trac'd each charm of beauty, save the blush" ("Fragment – Is not this grove", ll. 59-60).[77] The Queen of Cyprus appals her heartless husband by dropping dead in front of him:

> The brow was set
> In its last mould; that marble cheek,
> Fair as if death were loth to break
> Its spell of beauty . . .
>
> (ll. 1893-96)[78]

---

[76] *The Troubadour*, 254.

[77] *The Fate of Adelaide, a Swiss Romantic Tale, and Other Poems*, 152.

[78] *The Golden Violet*, 123-24.

Mirza, on being abandoned, is transformed even before she dies: "your sculptors never wrought / A form in monumental stone / So cold, so pale" (ll. 3326-28).[79] Leila, who is rash enough to fall for Raymond, is found dead by a pool, gazing at her own reflection. She is transformed into a garden statue, and the red light of the setting sun eerily preserves in the reflection the tints of living flesh that have drained from her skin:

> 'Twas strange to look upon her face,
> Then turn and see its shadowy trace
> Within the fountain; one like stone,
> So cold, so colourless, so lone, –
> A statue nymph, placed there to show
> How far the sculptor's art could go.
> The other, and that too the shade,
> In light and crimson warmth array'd …[80]

The melancholy of these moments does not quite efface their triumphant quality, which celebrates a woman's release from transient flesh into enduring marble, and from the painful subjectivity of experience into the cold objectivity of art. Once again, the dead lovers are sculpted only as figures of the dead poets. Poets, of course, have traditionally claimed the power to bestow immortality, so that to be celebrated in a poem is to be granted a memorial that will outlive marble and gilded monuments, but Landon's distinction is that her poet frankly confesses that the monument she builds is a monument to herself. It is a gesture performed most extravagantly by Eulalia, when, very shortly before her death, she takes her visiting English friends into the garden, and poses for them beside a statue of herself:

> And in the midst
> A large old cypress stood, beneath whose shade
> There was a sculptured form; the feet were placed
> Upon a finely-carved rose wreath; the arms
> Were raised to Heaven, as if to clasp the stars
> Eulalia leant beside; 'twas hard to say
> Which was the actual marble …
>
> (ll. 430-36)[81]

[79] *Ibid.*, 224.
[80] *The Troubadour*, 205.
[81] "A History of the Lyre" (*The Venetian Bracelet*, 114).

Eulalia identifies the statue as her "emblem", and within a few months she dies, finally eliminating the distinction between herself and the sculptured form she so closely resembles.

All of Landon's poetry returns obsessively to a tightly bunched arrangement of a small group of motifs, all of them already deployed in the poem that first made her famous, *The Improvisatrice*. This is the figure, the Italian woman who wins fame through her talent at poetic improvisation, that Landon found in *Corinne*, and that underlies all her poems. It sufficed her so completely because it allowed the most complete possible identification between poet and poem, both because the Italian woman could be understood, and was always understood by her contemporaries, as a transparent mask for L.E.L. herself, and because improvisation is a performance in which the poet and the poem are equally and indistinguishably the object of the audience's regard.

The verse form that she employs here, and in most of her poems not written in blank verse, had been developed by Hemans, but Landon's use of it is distinctive. Couplets are interrupted at irregular intervals by quatrains, but, unlike Hemans, Landon prefers quatrains in which the first and third lines are unrhymed, allowing her verse to seem far less controlled, more spontaneously improvised than Hemans'. Again as with Hemans, the iambic beat is interspersed with anapaests, but far more unpredictably, so that one often has to correct a misconception of a line's metre as one reads. Hemans' verse is remarkable for it technical assurance, Landon's for a technical uncertainty so marked that metre and syntax are likely at any time to collapse. Both seem to founder in lines describing Petrarch as first glimpsed by Laura: "Pale, dark-eyed, beautiful, and young / Such as he had shone o'er my slumbers" (ll. 53-54). This is the Improvisatrice's first painting. Petrarch is depicted standing in a "gorgeous hall", the accoutrements of which are even more awkwardly described: "Censers of roses, vases of light / Like what the moon sheds on a summer night" (ll. 45-46).[82]

Such lines are indications, I suppose, that the poem was written at high speed – Landon claimed to have completed it in a month – but they are also curiously functional. First, they lend the verse its improvisational quality, and second, and more importantly, they foster

[82] *The Improvisatrice*, 4.

in the sympathetic reader an anxious tenderness for the poet, working almost like the heart-stopping wobble that the accomplished tightrope artist builds into her performance. They create the illusion that one is not reading a poem but listening to a live performance, an improvisation, and the illusion is more powerful, of course, in a poem that centres on descriptions of exactly such performances. The improviser is so potent a figure for Landon precisely because she is a performer, in intimate contact with an audience, and it is a similar intimacy that Landon's poetry works towards, so that the poem becomes "a sweet and breathing bond / Between me and my kind" (ll. 71-72).[83]

The story of the poem is quickly told, and closely based on *Corinne*. Lorenzo sees the Improvisatrice in Florence, and at once loves her as she loves him. They meet in a flowery alcove, he presses one burning kiss upon her hand, and then he disappears. She next sees him in church, at his marriage ceremony. Years later he returns and explains that he had been from childhood betrothed to Ianthe, a young orphan adopted by his father and brought up with him. He "loved her as a brother loves / His favourite sister" (ll. 1387-88),[84] and felt unable to break off the engagement. Ianthe was a delicate consumptive woman, and despite Lorenzo's tender care of her, she has died, freeing him to return to Florence and the Improvisatrice. But it is too late. She is herself about to die of a broken heart.

As usual, echoing tales are woven into the narrative – a Moorish woman helps the Christian captive that she has fallen for to escape, but both are drowned at sea; Ida administers a love potion to Julian in a desperate attempt to revive the love he once felt for her, and inadvertently poisons him; an Indian bride joins her young groom on his funeral pyre. After Lorenzo abandons her the Improvisatrice can only sing songs that reflect her own predicament:

> And lays which only told of love
> In all its varied sorrowing,
> The echoes of the broken heart,
> Were all the songs I now could sing.
>
> (ll. 1067-70)[85]

---

[83] "Erinna" (*The Golden Violet*, 247).
[84] *The Improvisatrice*, 93.
[85] *Ibid.*, 71.

But all the previous examples given of her work are similar. It is the same with her paintings. After she has witnessed Lorenzo's marriage she paints herself as Ariadne deserted by Theseus in the hope that, after she has died, "Lorenzo might these tints behold, / And find my grief; – think – see – feel all / I felt, in this memorial!" (ll. 1346-48).[86] But before ever she had met Lorenzo she had painted Sappho abandoned by Phaon and taking her last farewell of "lyre, life, and love". The impulse that drives the whole poem is not the Improvisatrice's desire for Lorenzo, but her desire to become herself a work of art, to transform herself into her own painting of Ariadne –

> I drew her on a rocky shore: –
> Her black hair loose, and sprinkled o'er
> With white sea-foam; – her arms were bare,
> Flung upwards in their last despair.
> Her naked feet the pebbles prest;
> The tempest-wind sang in her vest:
> A wild stare in her glassy eyes;
> White lips, as parched by their hot sighs;
> And cheek more pallid than the spray,
> Which cold and colourless on it lay: –
>
> (ll. 1325-34)[87]

– which is why Lorenzo's return works only to precipitate her death. At the end of the poem Lorenzo has become a man prematurely aged with grief, living alone in a "stately hall" (l. 1531)[88] amongst his pictures and statues amongst which there is "One picture brightest of all there!", showing the Improvisatrice playing at her harp, apotheosized, seeming like Sappho or the Pythian priestess, beside which is placed her funeral urn (1551-78).[89]

This is alarming, as if the fate of Browning's "My Last Duchess" should be represented not as a consequence of the Duke's monstrous perversity, but as the goal to which the Duchess all her life aspired. Landon, like Hemans, self-consciously transforms herself into a cultural icon of womanhood. She constructs herself as the icon of feminine vulnerability just as self-consciously as Hemans constructed

[86] *Ibid.*, 90.
[87] *Ibid.*, 89.
[88] *Ibid.*, 102.
[89] *Ibid.*, 103-105.

herself as the icon of rooted, feminine domesticity. Neither icon is likely to find modern favour, but it is at least as important to recognize the power that they once exerted, a power that enabled two women, for the first and only time in the history of English poetry, quite to eclipse in popularity and prestige the work of their male contemporaries. Hemans, by making women the guardians and the mouthpieces of masculine values, transformed masculinity into an idea that depended on women for its stability and its articulation.

Landon's achievement is odder. Much more insistently than Hemans she insists on her own vulnerability. She does not, like Hemans, negotiate energetically between genders, but seems content to remain "A woman in her woman's sphere / Of joy and grief, of hope and fear".[90] She insists, or seems to, on a woman's utter dependence on and vulnerability to a man, and yet, when she insists on women's capacity to love with an utter selflessness that is unknown to men, the word she chooses to describe that quality is odd, "self devotedness",[91] a phrase in which the complete devotedness of the self seems insecurely distinguished from a complete devotion to the self.[92] It is the second, disguised meaning that dominates a body of work in which a rhetoric that seems wholly designed to figure the vulnerability of a woman to a man, and of a poet to a reader, work in which feminine vulnerability is extended from a social posture until it becomes a poetic style, can nevertheless drive repeatedly towards a vision in which victimhood becomes apotheosis, in which abandonment frees a woman from the flesh, transforming her into a marble monument that commands the male gaze, but remains itself as coolly impervious to the existence of its male worshippers as is the Improvisatrice to Lorenzo, when he is reduced to musing "his weary life away" (l. 1546), gazing forlornly on a woman who, because she has become a painting, is forever removed from him.

Landon writes a poetry that seems to exhibit throughout a servile dependence on its readership that is presented as a guarantee of its authentic femininity, and yet the poems drive towards climaxes in which the woman frees herself from dependence on her male lover, and the poet frees herself from dependence on the reader. These are

[90] *The Troubadour*, 195.

[91] *Ibid.*, 116.

[92] One recalls the monster's address to the body of the dead Frankenstein, in which the word has a similar ambiguity, "generous and self-devoted being".

moments in which the poet disappears into the poem, but the poem is itself only a representation of the poet. The distinction between the two disappears, and they are fused together in a gesture that is mournful, because it always signals the poet's death, and yet triumphant, because in death the poet can at last celebrate the autonomy of her art.

The nineteenth of April 1824 was for Tennyson "a day when the whole world seemed to be darkened for me". On a rock, close to his home, he carved the words "Byron is dead".[93] The death of Byron marked in the poetic realm what the death of William IV was to mark in the national realm, the beginning of an era of "woman's rule". Tennyson's *Poems, Chiefly Lyrical* of 1830, and *Poems* of 1832 are most remarkable for a group of poems that concern enclosed or secluded women, poems such as "Mariana", "The Lady of Shalott", "The Palace of Art", "Oenone", "Fatima" and "The Sleeping Beauty".[94] In an influential article Lionel Stevenson derived these enclosed maidens from Shelley's "To a Skylark", in which the skylark is first compared to the "poet hidden / In the light of thought", and is then said to be

> Like a high-born maiden
> In a palace tower,
> Soothing her love-laden
> Soul in secret hour
> With music sweet as love, which overflows her bower.[95]

Stevenson concludes that for Tennyson the enclosed woman figures the poet, and in this group of poems Tennyson explores his own predicament as a poet isolated by his calling from the busy world around him. It is not just for ideological reasons that I share Carl Plasa's suspicion of a reading that so "blithely turns the 'she' of the text into the 'he' of its poet".[96] All of Tennyson's poems, even "The Palace of Art" which immures a feminized "Soul" rather than a

---

[93] Hallam Tennyson, *Alfred Lord Tennyson: A Memoir*, 4 vols, London, 1897, I, 4.
[94] Published after 1832 in a revised form under the title "The Day-Dream".
[95] Percy Bysshe Shelley, "To a Skylark", ll. 41-45 (see Lionel Stevenson, "The 'High-Born Maiden' Symbol in Tennyson", in *Critical Essays on the Poetry of Tennyson*, ed. John Killham, London, 1960, 113-25).
[96] Carl Plasa, "'Cracked from side to side': Sexual Politics in 'The Lady Of Shalott'", *Victorian Poetry*, XXX (1992), 247.

woman, seem fraught with a distinctively female experience of a kind that never intrudes into Shelley's stanza. Stevenson's failure, and one that is replicated by all his successors, with the single exception of Herbert F. Tucker,[97] is that he does not attend to the poems that intervened between Tennyson and Shelley's ode, and in particular that he does not attend to the poems of Mrs Hemans and L.E.L., for if Tennyson's poems derive ultimately from Shelley it seems clear that he reads Shelley through poems written by the women poets who succeeded him.

Hemans treats the topic of the enclosed maiden in poems such as "Arabella Stuart", spoken by Arabella in the prison cell in which she has been enclosed since her frustrated elopement with William Seymour. She speaks her poem to a lover, who, she fears, has already forgotten her, "Dost thou forget me, Seymour?":

> My friend! My friend! Where art thou? Day by day,
> Gliding like some dark mournful stream away,
> My silent youth flows from me.
>
> (ll. 125-27)[98]

She is surely one of the prototypes of Tennyson's Mariana, as is Landon's *The Improvisatrice*, when Lorenzo marries his betrothed and abandons her: "He came not! Then the heart's decay / Wasted her silently away" (ll. 1162-63).[99]

Oenone resembles these women, too, abandoned by Paris, but by the end of the poem, when "fiery thoughts" "shape themselves" within her, and she leaves her valley bent on the vengeful destruction of Troy she has become like one of Hemans' more savage heroines, "The Widow of Crescentius" or the mother who burns down "The Indian City" in revenge for the killing of her sons. "The Lady of Shalott" who gives up her art, "left the web" and "left the loom", and, enthralled by her vision of Lancelot, floats singing down the river into Camelot, is transformed by the end of her voyage from an artist into a work of art, a funeral sculpture of herself. It is the metamorphosis that L.E.L. treats in poem after poem. Landon, as Armstrong remarks,

---

[97] See Herbert F. Tucker, "House Arrest: The Domestication of English Poetry in the 1820s", *New Literary History*, XXV (1995), 442, where Tucker describes Tennyson as "this studious son of Hemans".

[98] *The Poetical Works of Mrs Felicia Hemans*, 266.

[99] *The Improvisatrice*, 78.

prefers to describe an action "not *as* it happens, but when it is either just over or just about to happen".[100] "How the pulses will beat, and the cheeks will be dyed" (l. 821),[101] the Improvisatrice sings of "The Indian Bride". In "Fatima" Tennyson, like Hemans and Landon before him, looks back to Sappho and writes a love song of erotic anticipation so complete that it seems to render it unnecessary that Fatima's lover should ever in person arrive. The Soul in *The Palace of Art* at the end of the poem abandons her gorgeous palace for a humble cottage in the vale, in a gesture that, not least in its ambivalence, closely echoes the self-abnegating eagerness with which Hemans and Landon imagine women poets such as "Properzia Rossi" and "Eulalia" ready to surrender their fame for a life of humble, loving domesticity.

In this group of poems, Tennyson writes quite uninhibitedly as a woman. It is not to be imagined that he was unmoved by commercial considerations. Unlike Browning, he had no private income and no expectations. The market for poetry had collapsed, and Hemans and Landon were the two poets who had most conspicuously managed to resist the market trend. But I doubt if it was just this. Masculinity no longer seemed capable of housing the life of the affections. Tennyson turns away from this to a female experience that seems more vital even if, like Mariana's, it is an experience that is rich only in its atrophy. It was a time, even a male poet such as Tennyson was forced to recognize, of "lady's rule".

[100] Armstrong, *Victorian Poetry*, 327.
[101] *The Improvisatrice*, 55.

WOMEN RE-WRITING MEN: THE EXAMPLES OF ANNA SEWARD AND LADY CAROLINE LAMB

GIOIA ANGELETTI

In their Introduction to *Romantic Women Writers: Voices and Countervoices*, Theresa Kelley and Paula Feldman point out the two main directions along which feminist criticism of Romantic women's writing has developed:

> Some argue that writing by Romantic women should be read on its own terms and situated in its own contexts so that its assessment will not be contaminated by critical predispositions derived from the traditional Romantic canon. Others contend rather that the voices of Romantic women writers gain their fullest resonance when read within and against that traditional canon.[1]

The present reading of two Romantic women writers is in line with the second critical trend. It starts from the idea of the appropriation of male literary texts and models in order to highlight the revisionist practice involved in an apparently simple emulation. As Paul Keen argues, "women writers implicitly revised, rather than directly challenged, established cultural assumptions by encoding subversive arguments about sexual politics within accepted literary genres and styles".[2]

Both Anna Seward and Lady Caroline Lamb, though resorting to different modes of appropriation of images, themes and styles of earlier or contemporary male writers, and though establishing

---

[1] *Romantic Women Writers: Voices and Countervoices*, eds Paula R. Feldman and Theresa M. Kelley, Hanover: NH, 1995, 6-7.

[2] Paul Keen, *The Crisis of Literature in the 1790s: Print Culture and the Public Sphere*, Cambridge, 1999, 173.

distinctive relationships with the masculine literary tradition, succeeded in asserting their own voices as female, feminine, and, in some respects, feminist writers. The difference in their individual responses to and exploitations of the possibilities offered by eighteenth-century and early nineteenth-century patriarchal culture was determined partly by their dissimilar temperaments and partly by the different households and social environments in which they grew up.

Anna Seward's education in the small yet influential cultural centre of Lichfield was arranged by her austere father, the town's Anglican Canon. Though he encouraged her to read the English classics, he was so strict in grounding her upbringing on the moral codes of contemporary conduct books that Seward temporarily forfeited her literary ambitions to devote herself to more innocuous feminine occupations. Despite her later defiant decision to become a professional writer and even remain a literary spinster, Seward's long-suppressed instinctive nature never surfaced so violently as to represent a real threat to the strict manners of an often hypocritical cultural establishment. More effectively, and somehow more wisely, than Caroline Lamb, she managed to encapsulate her critique of male literary models or of contemporary social issues within an articulation and defence of domestic ideology and beneath the mask of an apparently harmless femininity. As Mitzi Myers observes, "Domestic ideology could be read as a programme for female empowerment rather than for female subordination",[3] and in this light Seward's treatment of domestic, local and occasional themes within perfectly acceptable feminine genres can be interpreted as a strategic way of accessing the literary market.

Lady Caroline Lamb, on the other hand, was brought up in the Whig aristocratic society of Devonshire House in London under the aegis of three powerful women who did not care much for her education (in fact she was almost illiterate till she was ten).[4] The dandy habits of the Devonshire household must partly account for Caroline's impetuous temper, moodiness, emotional fluctuations and irritability, which offers a fascinating contrast to the more balanced

---

[3] Mitzi Myers, "Reform and Ruin: a Revolution in Female Manners", *Studies in Eighteenth-Century Culture*, XI (1982), 199.

[4] Henrietta Frances Spencer, who became Lady Bessborough (Caroline's mother), Georgiana Spencer (her aunt), and Lady Elizabeth Foster (her aunt's friend).

character of Anna Seward. Curiously enough the two women also exemplified two antithetical female icons: while Seward matched the classical canon of fleshy and healthy female beauty, Lamb was almost a tomboy, so pale and anorexic that Lord Byron once thought, on seeing her, he was being haunted by a skeleton.

Their ways of appropriating and re-writing antecedent male texts were also different. For Seward, such re-writing involved a re-interpretation or feminization of some forms and themes typical of her literary models, in particular Erasmus Darwin, Pope, Prior and Rousseau; for Lamb, appropriation expressly meant re-visiting and re-writing Byron's style, dramatis personae and motifs by means of parodic overturning and impersonation.

Anna Seward's absorption and re-positioning of male literary models involves her appropriation of Erasmus Darwin's language and style in connection with her representation of nature; her re-moulding of the stereotyped Romantic heroine created by men; and her feminization of typically masculine genres and themes. While in her letters Seward openly admits her manipulation of male sources, in her poems it remains a "subterranean challenge[s]",[5] to use Patricia Meyer's term, hidden under the veil of domesticity and sentimentality.

In 1777 Erasmus Darwin, the eminent polymath of Lichfield who, since their first meeting in 1756, had become Seward's mentor, editor and adviser, bought "a little wild umbrageous valley"[6] a mile from Lichfield to plant an elaborate garden with botanical specimens. He immediately invited Anna Seward to visit it. One year later, moved by the scene, she wrote a seventy-line panegyric to celebrate it. Darwin appreciated it and suggested she should expand it into a work propounding Linneus' binomial system for classifying plants: "You should make flowers, plants, and trees, into men and women. I … will write the notes, which must be scientific", he said to her.[7] Seward, however, declined the assignment.

---

[5] Elizabeth A. Fay, *A Feminist Introduction to Romanticism*, London, 1998, 24.

[6] Margaret Ashmun, *The Singing Swan: An Account of Anna Seward and Her Acquaintance with Dr Johnson, Boswell and Others of Their Time*, New Haven and Oxford, 1931, 66.

[7] *Bluestocking Feminism: Writings of the Bluestocking Circle, 1738-1785*, ed. Gary Kelly, 6 vols, London, 1999, IV, 299.

Five years later Darwin sent her lines (fixed, or mutilated) to *The Gentleman's Magazine*, and then used them (further amended) as the exordium of his book-length poem in heroic couplets, *The Botanic Garden* (1791). His failure to acknowledge the original author of those lines aroused Seward's and, subsequently, Walter Scott's indignation.[8]

Why did Seward refuse Darwin's proposal? Her own explanation that she was not sufficiently knowledgeable to engage in a work implying a scientific competence is hardly believable. In her *Memoirs of the Life of Dr Darwin* (1804) she clearly reveals an interest in and a familiarity with science and the subjects of Darwin's works.[9] The truth is that, despite the influence that his style, diction and imagery exerted on her, she distanced herself from some specific aspects of his writing, as can be deduced by comparing Seward's 1778 juvenile poem and Darwin's altered version of this text included in *The Botanic Garden*.

Both versions present a similar idiosyncratic and hybrid subject matter, eccentrically mingling mythological, botanical and religious images, while their stylistic affinity consists in a similar use of the emphatic imperative at the beginning of the line. On the whole, however, not only is Darwin's poetic diction more rhetorical in its frequent use of the capitalization and personification of abstract nouns, but, somewhat surprisingly, his natural images are more ornate, affected and less realistic than Seward's. For example, Seward's line "My choral birds their vivid plumes unfold",[10] is replaced by Darwin with "My plumy pairs in gay embroidery dres'd" (l. 21),[11] and her impressionistic line "And insect-armies wave their wings of gold" is supplanted in Darwin's version by "And Echo sounds her soft

---

[8] Scott was the first important editor of Seward's poetical works (*The Poetical Works of Anna Seward; with Extracts from Her Literary Correspondence*, ed. Walter Scott, 3 vols, Edinburgh and London, 1810).

[9] Seward's interest for science and her concern with industrial progress is particularly evident in her poem "Colebrook Dale" (1781), in which she refers to the Lunar Society of Birmingham, the most important Midland scientific society, including such eminent members as Erasmus Darwin, James Watt, James Keir, Matthew Boulton and Joseph Priestley. See Jenny Uglow, *The Lunar Men: The Friends Who Made the Future 1730-1810*, London, 2002, where Anna Seward's connection with the "Lunar Men" is several times referred to.

[10] Seward's poem appeared in *The Gentleman's Magazine*, LVIII, (1783), 428.

[11] Erasmus Darwin, *The Botanic Garden; A Poem, in Two Parts*, London, 1791, 2.

symphonious shell" (l. 24).[12] In sum, the master and his pupil resorted to a different rhetoric of poetic naturalism, which proves that Seward did not simply emulate her mentor but very often revised and re-worked his language and imagery under new guises.

Undoubtedly Seward was attracted to a style characterized by what, in the Preface to *Lyrical Ballads*, Wordsworth and Coleridge disparagingly defined as "gaudiness",[13] a style Walter Scott regarded as "remote from common life and natural expression", essentially informed by "florid description", "lofty metaphor[s]", "bold personification", "inversion" and "compound epithets".[14] Seward tested good poetry according to whether or not it respected such neoclassical canons as *ut pictura poesis*. It was her contention that, as in Salvator Rosa's and Claude's paintings, in poetry "lovely and terrible objects" must be "brought to the eye"[15] by means of a rhetorical style and a musical, harmonious verse.

Darwin adopts the heroic couplet in *The Botanic Garden* to talk about the life of plants in physiological and mythical terms; Seward makes use of the same neoclassical metre in some of her works, for example in her Monody "An Elegy on Captain Cook" (1780) and in her epistolary verse narrative *Louisa* (1784). However, her adoption of Johnson, Pope and Dryden's favoured form hides no satirical intent but simply depends on its aesthetic rigour, decorum and regularity. Other conspicuous Darwinian aspects of her writing – particularly in the poems written after 1780[16] – are the frequent use of the anthropomorphism of abstract qualities and natural phenomena, an embellished style full of descriptive epithets and multiple periphrases, sensuous and synaesthetic expressions, elegant and archaic words, the persistent use of alliteration and a language much indebted to the literature of sensibility and the Della Cruscans. In both Darwin's and Seward's works one cannot avoid noticing the recurrence of verbs and

---

[12] *Ibid.*, 3.

[13] Preface to *Lyrical Ballads*, in *William Wordsworth*, ed. Stephen Gill, Oxford, 1984, 596.

[14] *The Poetical Works of Anna Seward*, I, xxiv.

[15] S.H. Monk, "Anna Seward and the Romantic Poets: A Study in Taste", in *Wordsworth and Coleridge: Studies in Honor of George McLean Harper*, ed. Earl Leslie Griggs, Princeton, 1939, 123.

[16] In this year Seward published "An Elegy on Captain Cook", which, together with her success among the bluestocking ladies of Lady Anna Miller's circle at Batheaston, marked the beginning of her literary career and fame.

epithets emphasizing sensations and emotions, such as “throbbing”, “thrilling”, “sympathy”, “tender”, “sweet”, “fragrant”, and so on.

Seward’s imitative and revisionist practice especially concerns her personal response to the pseudo-scientific language and hybrid subject matter characterizing *The Botanic Garden*. As revealed by her letter to Darwin dated 29 May 1789, she admired his “highly picturesque descriptions of mechanic construction, and process of various arts, and of mythological marvels”, his depiction of landscapes as if they were painted by Lorrain Claude and by Salvator Rosa, his ornamental diction and his “instructive” notes[17] – all characteristics that also recur in Seward’s poems. For example in “Llangollen Vale” (1796)[18] the notes provide information about the etymology of certain toponyms, while in “An Elegy on Captain Cook” they accurately supply scientific, ethnological and anecdotic facts concerning the famous explorer’s voyages.

In some poems, including the sonnets, Seward appropriates Darwin’s habit of assigning emotions and sensations to plants, yet, at the same time, she revises it by shifting the focus from the vegetable to the human world. Her purpose is to show that the plants are endowed with human feelings only because men project their inner life onto them and see it reflected in natural phenomena. Whenever she paints nature, either in its minutiae or in its sublime quality, Seward invests it with a sentiment and passion that are hardly separable from her own feelings or those of her dramatis personae. In her poetry human beings and nature correspond with, and live alongside, each other.

Sometimes she emulates the botanical and ornithological terminology of *The Botanic Garden*, as when she holds a magnifying glass to nature and focuses her poetic lenses on the minutiae of the natural world, like the sonorous flight of the “insect armies” with “wings of gold” depicted in her juvenile poem or the multitudinous tiny creatures and plants populating her lyrics and sonnets. This concern for the minute description of nature explains why Seward may have developed a growing scepticism about Darwin’s empirical

---

[17] *Bluestocking Feminism*, IV, 259.

[18] “Llangollen Vale” (1796) was dedicated to Lady Eleanor Butler and Sarah Ponsonby, two of the most transgressive women of their time: they dared to defy social conventions by spending their life together in a sort of Arcadian Welsh hermitage.

observation, tending to identify physics and metaphysics, to "enlist Imagination under the banner of science",[19] and to universalize and objectify natural phenomena by deploying the rhetoric of myth.

Seward's letters and poems show us that while she accepted the combination of art and science in poetic composition, she objected to the former being eclipsed by the latter, and although she admired Darwin's vision of nature, she distanced herself from the low emotional intensity of his imagery. In his verse, she wrote, "the passions are generally asleep, and seldom are the nerves thrilled by his imagery, impressive and beauteous as it is, or by his landscapes, with all their vividness".[20]

Seward's picture of nature occupies a peculiar halfway-house position between Burke's philosophical and aesthetic notions of the Beautiful and the Sublime. Though agreeing with Darwin and Shelley on the existence of dynamic links uniting all living beings and forming a biological organic whole, Seward sets aside all transcendental discourse and focuses instead on the physical and sensuous empathy between man and nature. As in Dorothy Wordsworth's verse, in her poems the natural world is mostly depicted as a parallel dimension to the human in which the observers can mirror themselves and satisfy their need to empathize.

Much like other women Romantic poets, Seward had a literal and concrete interest in the natural world and its minutiae, often regardless of its latent divinity. As Stuart Curran points out, these writers use "the quotidian and localized as instruments of [their] representation".[21] So in her "Ode to the Sun" (1780) the "LORD of the Planets" is evoked not as a symbol of God but simply as the ultimate physical source of life, sensuously linked to the earth by its "mild prolific beam" and "all-cheering light".[22]

This almost scientific scrutiny of nature is what Judith Pascoe defines, with reference to Charlotte Smith's poetry, as the "earth-bound aesthetic"[23] of women Romantic poets, and what Curran calls

---

[19] See Darwin's Advertisement to *The Botanic Garden* (Unnumbered page).

[20] *Bluestocking Feminism*, IV, 302.

[21] Stuart Curran, "Women Readers, Women Writers", in *The Cambridge Companion to British Romanticism*, ed. Stuart Curran, Cambridge, 1993, 192.

[22] *Bluestocking Feminism*, IV, 46.

[23] Judith Pascoe, "Female Botanists and the Poetry of Charlotte Smith", in *Re-visioning Romanticism: British Women Writers, 1776-1837*, eds Carol Shiner Wilson and Joel Haefner, Philadelphia, 1994, 193.

an "alternate Romanticism that seeks not to transcend or to absorb nature but to contemplate and honor its irreducible alterity".[24] In the quotidian, localized natural Other, Seward also seems to look for a sympathetic world in which she can mirror and even inscribe herself, in other words a world which may become a vehicle of self-representation. For example, the eponymous heroine of *Louisa* perceives a mysterious empathy between her inner vibrations and the sound produced by the "mountain Bee", which "from flower to flower, / Seem'd to prolong, with her assiduous wing, / The soft vibration of the tuneful string".[25] Likewise in "Epistle To Miss Honora Sneyd" the poet hears her sadness echoed in the song of "the sweet linnets … on the bough" and of the "tender ringdoves" that "languishly coo".[26] Finally, in "Sonnet XCII" the little "weak, deserted leaves forlorn"[27] on the naked tree become an emblem of the fleetingness and stoicism of human life.

In *Louisa* the English rural landscape is identified with a feminized domestic space of durable human affections opposed to a male world of transient values, trade and colonial expansion. The heroine is beautiful and stoic like the countryside surrounding her. She is the central conscience of this hybrid poem – a pastoral romance in the form of an epistolary sentimental novel in verse. In a sense, she is a hybrid too, since, as Seward explains in the Preface, she derives from the union of "the impassion'd fondness of Pope's Eloisa, with the chaster tenderness of Prior's Emma; avoiding the voluptuousness of the first, and the too conceding softness of the second".[28] Inevitably she also recalls Rousseau's *Nouvelle Héloïse*, but from this combination of various feminine icons, Seward manages to construct a new image of femininity that does not exclude conventionally masculine traits, such as the heroine's self-conscious rational scrutiny of her own feelings and her fleeting moments of rage and rebelliousness. Louisa is Anna Seward since, although she is respectful of the behavioural codes established by conduct books, she

---

[24] *The Poems of Charlotte Smith*, ed. Stuart Curran, Oxford, 1993, xxvii-xxviii.
[25] *The Romantics: Women Poets 1770-1830*, ed. C. Franklin, London, 1996, 6.
[26] *The Swan at Lichfield: Poems of Anna Seward*, ed. Margaret Williams, Lichfield, 1994, 17.
[27] *Bluestocking Feminism*, IV, 203.
[28] *The Romantics: Women Poets 1770-1830* (the Preface has no page numbers).

displays a strong and independent spirit, at times prone to melancholy yet never yielding to despair.

Like her author, who could never accept the idea of becoming what was then called a "femme covert" – that is, socially and financially covered by marriage – Louisa is a woman of high-minded passion yet also of rational self-determination, distancing herself both from the icon of the courtly woman, personified in the poem by Emira, and from the Rousseauesque image of the angel-in-the-house, the submissive and sentimental heroine. Though in love with Eugenio, who seems to be able to see only her virtuousness and gracefulness, she is not subservient to him. Unlike Pope's Eloisa, she never writes to her lover but chooses as her only correspondent her friend Emma, thus establishing a private sphere of sympathetic exchange safeguarded from public display and interference.[29] Indeed her love for Eugenio is almost a secondary theme in the poem, providing only the stimulus for passion, whereas its pivotal motif is the deep "sympathy of soul"[30] existing between the two women, a radical change from the traditional heterosexual relationship at the heart of Pope's and Rousseau's texts.

This difference introduces us to the third aspect of Seward's appropriation of male models: her feminization of conventionally male themes and motifs. Significant examples occur in three of her major works: "An Elegy on Captain Cook", *Louisa*, and "Llangollen Vale". In both *Louisa* and "An Elegy on Captain Cook", Seward addresses contemporary issues, such as industrial and commercial growth, colonial and economic expansion, from the viewpoint of those women who regard them as a threat against the civilizing function of love and other domestic forces, like family affections and friendship. Thus, without talking overtly about the disastrous consequences of the contemporary gold rush and hunting for success, Seward hints at them by focusing on the effects they have on domestic affections. For example "An Elegy on Captain Cook" ends with the poignant image of the hero's melancholy widow, left alone to contemplate her destiny

[29] This is also how Seward saw her own correspondence, as a private exchange within the domestic sphere. Indeed she refused to publish her political letters, which appeared only after her death, therefore casting light on aspects of her personality and thought that had been totally ignored till then.

[30] *The Romantics: Women Poets 1770-1830*, 2.

in front of a tempestuous sea, symbolizing the menace and danger confronted by those who live far from home.

Likewise, in *Louisa* Seward tackles the national theme of colonial expansion and financial success from the heroine's point of view, so that both her friendship with Emma and her love for Eugenio are seen as seriously threatened by their exile in foreign countries. Emira, the rich Lamia-like serpent-woman Eugenio marries in order to save his father from bankruptcy, personifies both the seducing Other and the injustice of the marriage market. The domestic, private scene of authentic affections is set against the wider world of false values and corrupt morality. Seward reaches a similar conclusion in her other long poem, "Llangollen Vale". From the grand scene of Welsh history and myth, she gradually zooms in on the local love legends of the Vale and finally on the private secluded dwelling of the two eccentric ladies, whose "sacred friendship" contrasts with the coldness and harshness of the "stern Authorities".[31] Their intimate world, subversive and scornful of conventions, is for Seward a subtle vehicle for denouncing the hypocrisy and single-mindedness of the larger outside world.

In conclusion, Seward revises the values of the patriarchal world and the male literary tradition by subjecting them to a process of feminization that aims to create new forms and themes. In other words, she is able to find a lady-like, seemingly innocuous, way of criticizing those values that allows her to avoid public censorship while remaining true to herself and resolute in her intentions.

Caroline Lamb's revisionist practice is closely related to her personal life. Therefore it is much more than a mere appropriation and re-writing of male predecessors. Duncan Wu has observed that Caroline Lamb's relationship with Byron is the "unifying principle"[32] shaping her whole work. In fact, the obsessive affair she had with Lord Byron between March and November 1812 had an enormous impact both on her literary output and on her personality. Two of her works particularly exemplify the complex process whereby she either impersonates Byron or mimics and transfigures his themes, forms and characters to give rise to an original composition: her novel *Glenarvon*

---

[31] Anna Seward, *Llangollen Vale* (1796), Oxford and New York, 1994, 6.

[32] Duncan Wu, "Appropriating Byron", *The Wordsworth Circle*, XXVI (Summer 1995), 141.

(1816) and her poem *A New Canto* (1819). For reasons of space, the present analysis will focus on the latter.

After Byron left her she was maddeningly divided between the overwhelming desire to get him back and the equally strong yearning to take revenge for his unfair, sometimes cruel, treatment of her obsessive need for attention. Since her real-life melodramas – her fits of insanity, her self-injuring acts, and her Gothic erotic letters – did not produce the desired effect of regaining his affections, she constructed fictional worlds mingling history and romance into which she could incorporate and possess Byron either by "trans-figuring" his identity,[33] or by re-producing and re-shaping his poetic modes and tones. In other words, an essential motivation behind the composition of both *Glenarvon* and *A New Canto* is that they represented for her ways of pursuing her relationship with Byron: the novel by revising and re-writing the story of their tempestuous affair and *A New Canto* by offering a travesty and parody of Byron's own writing. As Lamb's biographer, Henry Blyth, wrote, Byron remained "a romantic dream always to be pursued",[34] although Lamb once told her friend Lady Morgan that the relationship "destroyed [her]", that she "lost [her] brain … was bled, leeched",[35] just like the dashing heroine of *Glenarvon*, vampirized by the fascinating villain.

Glenarvon was published three years before Lamb's mock-heroic parody, but its intent is the same. "To write this novel was then my sole comfort",[36] confessed Lamb to Lord Granville, because it provided her with a fictional space in which to carry out her revenge on Byron and on the society which was gradually ostracizing her because of her unfeminine conduct. More importantly, though, the novel turned into a masochistic re-enactment of the most powerful and painful experience of her life, which thus she could explore again and understand better through a sort of self-exorcism and self-introspection. As Frances Wilson underlines, "Glenarvon isn't the story of Lamb's jealous vindication of her behaviour" but "an

[33] Nicola J. Watson, "Transfiguring Byronic Identity", in *At the Limits of Romanticism: Essays in Cultural, Feminist and Materialist Criticism*, eds Mary A. Favret and Nicola J. Watson, Bloomington and Indianopolis, 1994, 1.

[34] Henry Edward Blyth, *The Fatal Passion: The Life of Lady Caroline Lamb*, London, 1972, 175.

[35] *Lady Morgan's Memoirs: Autobiography, Diaries and Correspondence*, ed. W.H. Dixon, 2 vols, London, 1862, II, 201.

[36] Elizabeth Jenkins, *Lady Caroline Lamb*, London, 1932, 184.

unresolved account of the pleasures … resulting from dangerous and self-destructive desires",[37] desires which, however disastrous, Lamb intended to re-enact and keep somehow alive rather than suppress.[38]

The same combination of revengeful feelings and the desire of re-living, from an ironic distance, her ruthless relationship with Byron, characterizes Lamb's parodic experiment. If *A New Canto* was in part an attempt to ruin Byron's reputation in England while he was an exile in Italy, oddly enough it was also another means, after *Glenarvon*, of keeping his memory alive and securing the continuity of her relationship with him. *A New Canto* is supposed to be the Third Canto of *Don Juan*, in octava rima like the previous two (Byron had already published the first two cantos in 1819). Lamb wanted the poem to appear anonymously, so as to fool the audience into believing that it was by Byron himself, thus perfectly succeeding in her impersonation (as when she used to disguise herself as Byron's page or one of his characters, including Don Juan himself). She certainly envied and wanted to ape Byron's chameleon-like skill, his ability to adapt his personality to different circumstances, perhaps realizing how similar she and he were in their confusing good and bad, fact and fiction, heaven and hell.

When Lamb wrote *A New Canto* her affair with Byron had already been over for seven years, which again confirms both her compulsive need to keep it alive and the influence that Byron continued to exert on her.[39] In imitating and at the same time criticizing Byron, in particular the Byronic narrator of *Don Juan*, Lamb seems to look forward to the post-modern and feminist appraisal of parody as a "double-voiced" and dialogic discourse aiming at both identifying with and distancing the object of parody. *A New Canto* appropriates her ex-lover's motifs, metres and styles while encoding, at the same time, a cultural and literary critique of the parodied author and text. Almost foreshadowing Adrienne Rich's notion of writing as revision, Caroline Lamb takes the Byronic text not so much to mock and ridicule it as to deconstruct its foundations and open it to new

[37] Caroline Lamb, *Glenarvon*, ed. Frances Wilson, London, 1995, xxvi.
[38] In *Glenarvon* she even inserted the letter that Byron wrote to her to put an end to their affair passing it off as a letter from the dark hero Glenarvon to his deserted lover Calantha.
[39] As late as 1824, after Byron's death, she could still admit to Medwin, "He broke my heart and still I love him" (Jenkins, *Lady Caroline Lamb*, 249).

elements which can revitalize and position it under a new light. Indeed in twenty-one of the 27 stanzas of the poem Lamb seems to pay homage to Byron's mock-epic and satire by poking fun at contemporary society, but then, still speaking through the same narrative persona, she deploys his satirical style in order to turn it against him.

The complexity of Lamb's parody lies first of all in the fact that she is re-writing a text that, in many respects, is itself a parodic revisiting of both the epic tradition and Byron's own romantic drama and Prometheanism. Therefore, in *A New Canto* she is mimicking Byron's own caricaturing, parodying practice and impersonation strategy. Just as Byron adopts personae in order to (pretend to) distance himself from what the poem describes, so Caroline Lamb adopts the persona of the narrator of *Don Juan* with the double purpose of imitating his satiric-comic vein and of turning his banter against himself. Moreover, speaking as Byron's persona also meant taking off Byron himself, since she, like most readers, used to identify him with his own characters or other authors' Byronic heroes.

The first time Caroline Lamb wrote to Byron she addressed him as Childe Harold, and in a letter of June 1814 as "Mefistocles [*sic*] Luke Makey, De la Touche, Richard the 3rd, Valmont, Machiavelli, Prevost, the wicked Duke of Orleans".[40] Posing as Byron also meant questioning his identity, presenting the audience with a different version of the notorious poet, a new public persona, by ridiculing his linguistic and stylistic idiosyncrasies. Byron felt threatened by Lamb's audacious masquerades and forgeries, because they risked disfiguring his authentic ego. As a result, he dedicated to her hostile poems such as "To Lady Caroline Lamb" (1812) and "Remember Me" (1812) in both of which she is condemned as an adulteress. He felt "ravished",[41] he once wrote to Lamb's mother-in-law, which is partly what she desired to achieve by aping him.

A New Canto apparently describes Doomsday with the apocalyptic scene of a London shaken by general chaos and agony, but one immediately realizes that the portentous paraphernalia are only a strategy to attack contemporary degeneracy and futility. With a tone that recalls Byron's sardonic wit in the Dedication to *Don Juan*, the

---

[40] Lamb, *Glenarvon*, 35.

[41] Leslie A. Marchand, *Byron's Letters and Journals*, 12 vols, London, 1973-1982, III, 12.

narrator of *A New Canto* draws up an indictment against the representatives of the intelligentsia and almost all social and political parties: "impudent"[42] reviewers – including, of course, Jeffrey –, the mad Prince Regent (with the satirist Thomas Moore "chuckling at his pain"[43]), "Vile cheats" and "coward sinners"[44] (recalling the "Cold-blooded, smooth-faced, placid miscreant!" in Stanza XII of the Dedication), ministers, lawyers (whose language is "obscure and circumspect", says Byron in Canto I), Napoleon (here contravening Byron), Turkish infidels, "skulkers",[45] contemporary playwrights and so forth. She, or better the narrator, spares no one, not even him or herself.

Lamb exaggerates Byron's self-mocking and self-ironic ability by having the narrator declare that he is a bold sinner, "scorning all here, nor caring for hereafter / A radical, a stubborn and an old one",[46] and that his conscience is condemnable like all those who can be "bought and sold"[47] (thereby turning against Byron his own allegation in the Dedication to *Don Juan* that the Lake Poets write to earn their salaries). But, above all, by mimicking the narrator's voice of Byron, she manages to make him pronounce a kind of self-critique, as when he admits that he writes only "to rhapsodize",[48] that his verses are a joke meant to "gull" the reader by means of "flights poetic / … eight, and ten, and twenty feet sublime"[49] and "maudlin, hey-down-derrified pathetic".[50] As Wu suggests, Lamb "makes the assured, scabrous poet of Don Juan his most acute critic".[51]

In order to ridicule Byron's style, Lamb's parody also avails itself of intertextual strategies. For example, in Stanza XXV she mimics and criticizes the motley poetic tone of *Don Juan* by means of a quotation from Byron's poem. This is how he describes his writing:

---

[42] Lady Caroline Lamb, *A New Canto*, London, 1819, l. 7.
[43] *Ibid.*, l. 31.
[44] *Ibid.*, ll. 7, 105.
[45] *Ibid.*, l. 113.
[46] *Ibid.*, ll. 106-107.
[47] *Ibid.*, l. 124.
[48] *Ibid.*, l. 162.
[49] *Ibid.*, ll. 210-11.
[50] *Ibid.*, l. 212.
[51] Wu, "Appropriating Byron", 143.

What joke? – My verses – mine, and all beside,
    Wild, foolish tales of Italy and Spain,
The gushing shrieks, the bubbling squeaks, the bride
    Of nature, blue-eyed, black-eyed, and her swain,
Kissing in grottoes, near the moon-lit tide,
    Though to all men of commonsense 'tis plain,
Except for rampant and amphibious brute,
Such damp and drizzly places would not suit.[52]

The "gushing shrieks" and "bubbling squeaks" are an echo of Byron's language in the storm scene in *Don Juan*, Canto II; whereas the "kissing in grottoes", as Wu rightly points out, recalls the cave scene in Canto II, when Haidée and her servant Zoe carry Juan to a cavern to nurse him without being discovered by her cruel father. However, Lamb's grotto is not a romantic but a "damp and drizzly" place, only suited to "rampant and amphibious brute".[53]

Lamb's attempt to forge the typical diction of *Don Juan* is evinced by the adoption of a style that mixes high and low registers, Latinate expressions and slang, climactic and bathetic effects, a style which, though uncommon among Romantic women writers, was one Lamb refined to a level of technical excellence. Nevertheless, the narrator's own comments aim at disparaging rather than extolling this mongrel poetic language; likewise, his rhetorical devices seek to arouse disgust rather than admiration for Byron's comic style. Behind such a simile,

And Norway's copper-mines about the Baltic
    Swell, heave, and rumble with their boiling ore,
Like some griped giant's motion peristaltic,
    Then burst, and to the sea vast gutters pour[54]

we can capture Lamb sneering at Byron's mock-heroic characters and their predecessors in the Italian mock epic of the Renaissance.

In addition, Lamb caricatures Byron's habit of digressing or of addressing his reader to anticipate what will come next – "We meet again, if we should understand / Each other", says Byron at the end of

[52] Lamb, *A New Canto*, ll. 193-200.

[53] According to Duncan Wu, these lines are an allusion to Byron's sexual appetites and to his Promethean acts of bravado, such as his swimming of the Hellespont in 1810.

[54] Lamb, *A New Canto*, ll. 91-94.

Canto I; and Lamb takes him off: "You shall have more of her [the Muse] another time."[55] She even seems to deride Byron's irony and use of paradox, when her Byronic narrator describes himself in these words: "I am a graceless poet, as you know, / Yet would not wish to wound a proper feeling."[56] Ironically she is here publicizing the pain Byron caused her once she realized that his outspoken adoration for her "little volcano",[57] as Byron, in his letters, defined her heart, and his promises of eternal love were just a *façon de parler* rather than sincere words. Indeed in *A New Canto*, Lamb also refers to "Strugglers with tyrant passion and its prey, / Love's single hearted victims, sacred, true",[58] which again might be an indirect allusion to herself and her turbulent love affair.

Another significant example of her parody concerns the way in which she deals with the question of public fame. In the Dedication and at the end of *Don Juan*, Canto I, Byron writes that the "end of Fame … 'tis but to fill / A certain portion of uncertain paper / … To have, when the original is dust, / A name, a wretched picture and worse bust". Lamb pokes fun at this affected humbleness and denigration of fame by having the narrator initially admit, "I'm sick of fame – I'm gorged with it"[59] and finally, "But something must be done to cure the spleen / And keep my name in capitals, like Kean".[60] After all, Byron's affair with Caroline conveniently secured him an easy access into the fashionable society of Devonshire House, a perfect springboard for his success.

In Canto II, Stanza CCI, of *Don Juan*, Byron claims that some women "play the devil, and then write a novel", an undeniable allusion to Caroline Lamb and *Glenarvon*, in which he is portrayed as a satanic hero. However, the main achievement of Lamb's two most significant works is not the revengeful destruction of Byron's reputation. In both cases she oversteps the threshold of permitted feminine genres by inscribing a transgressive femininity into a Gothic romance and by experimenting in Juvenalian satire and mock-heroic

---

[55] *Ibid.*, l. 209.
[56] *Ibid.*, ll. 45-46.
[57] *Byron's Letters and Journals*, II, 171.
[58] Lamb, *A New Canto*, ll. 181-82.
[59] *Ibid.*, l. 1.
[60] *Ibid.*, ll. 215-16. Edmund Kean was one of Byron's favourite actors.

epic.[61] In both cases she starts from a male model without, however, locking herself "into a dubious mimicry".[62] In her works, as through cross-dressing and masquerade in her life, Lamb deliberately or subconsciously destabilizes the fixity of a masculine culture that discriminates literary genre according to gender and keeps the private sphere separate from the public. To this scenario she allusively opposes a utopian society able to override all strict categorizations and dichotomies between masculinity and femininity. Therefore it is regrettable that the reckless, witty and rebellious Lamb eventually followed Foscolo's recommendation to "write a book which will offend nobody" since "women cannot afford to shock".[63] As a matter of fact, had she written just traditional feminine romances, such as *Graham Hamilton* (1822) and *Ada Reis* (1823), she would not be the object of the present reassessment.

Finally it may be speculated that Lamb's life-long attraction for Byron also depended on his living, like her, as a threshold figure, both at the heart of Regency London and marginalized because of his eccentric behaviour. This shared extravagance made them similar enough to become both accomplices and rivals. Therefore the unrealizable dream of this masculine woman was not to destroy her male rival, "mad, bad, and dangerous to know"[64] like herself, but to fuse her ambiguous femininity with his ambiguous masculinity through her androgynous writing.

Seward and Lamb stood half way between the more conservative and the more radical female voices of the time. Many of their works are grafted on the dominant male tradition but, in most cases, they used this revisionist practice as a starting-point to create then new and original compositions. Despite their different ways of realizing their works and themselves within a male-dominated cultural establishment, the ultimate achievement of their re-writing was similar. Seward was a more astute literary player, almost anticipating Emily Dickinson's dictum "tell all the truth / But tell it slant", by acting within the legitimate sphere of domestic ideology. The defiant,

---

[61] For a difference between Horatian and Juvenalian satire, see Gilbert Highet, *Anatomy of Satire*, Princeton, 1962.
[62] Watson, "Transfiguring Byronic Identity", 200.
[63] *British Women Poets of the Romantic Era*, ed. Paula R. Feldman, Baltimore and London, 1997, 363.
[64] Jenkins, *Lady Caroline Lamb*, 95.

self-expressive and melodramatic Lamb, on the other hand, found no fun in "dancing in incognita",[65] because, as her friend Bulwer Lytton once said of her, her "woes … sprung from feeling" and her "only guilt was not concealing".[66]

[65] Blyth, *The Fatal Passion: The Life of Lady Caroline Lamb*, 162.
[66] Jenkins, *Lady Caroline Lamb*, 269.

NOTES ON CONTRIBUTORS

GIOIA ANGELETTI gained her Ph.D in Scottish Literature at the University of Glasgow and presently teaches at the University of Parma. She has published articles and reviews on Romantic and Victorian literature and translations of Romantic, Victorian and contemporary British poetry. Her recent publications include *Eccentric Scotland: Three Victorian Poets. James Thomson ("B.V."), John Davidson and James Young Geddes* (2004) and *Teorie* target oriented *della traduzione poetica: trans-creazione e riscrittura dell'alterità* (2004).

SERENA BAIESI gained her Ph.D in Literatures and Culture of the English Speaking Countries at the University of Bologna, where she is presently research fellow and tutor in English Literature. She has published a study of colonial women writers in Australia (*Pioniere in Australia; diari, lettere e memoriali del periodo coloniale, 1770-1850*), and articles on colonial and postcolonial literature. She has also published several articles on English Romantic literature, paying specific attention to Letitia Elizabeth Landon, historical drama by women playwrights and the critical reception of Romantic writers and dramatists. She is currently editing a special issue of the interdisciplinary journal *La questione Romantica* on colonial literature.

BEATRICE BATTAGLIA is Associate Professor at the University of Bologna. She is the author of *La zitella illetterata: ironia e parodia nei romanzi di Jane Austen* (1983), *Nostalgia e mito nella distopia inglese* (1998), and editor of *Jane Austen Oggi e ieri* (2002) and (with Diego Saglia) of *Re-Drawing Austen* (2004). Her recent publications include *La critica alla cultura occidentale nella letteratura distopica* *inglese* (2006) and *Viaggio e paesaggio*, issue 15/16 of *La questione Romantica*. Her book *Paesaggi e misteri. Riscoprire Ann Radcliffe* is forthcoming.

LILLA MARIA CRISAFULLI is Professor of English in the Faculty of Languages, University of Bologna. She is the Director of the Interdisciplinary Centre for Romantic Studies, editor of the interdisciplinary journal *La questione Romantica* and member of the editorial board of international literary journals. She has written extensively on English Romanticism, on the cultural relations between Italy and Great Britain, and on Jacobin literature. She is the author of monographic studies on P.B. Shelley, among which *La realtà del desiderio: saggi morali, teoria estetica e prosa politica di P.B. Shelley* (1999), and has published essays on John Keats, William Godwin, Mary Shelley, Mary Wollstonecraft, Joanna Baillie, Letitia Elizabeth Landon. She has been the co-ordinator of many national and departmental research projects that deal with the wide literary production of women writers in Europe during the pre-Romantic and Romantic age. She is the editor of *Antologia delle poetesse romantiche inglesi* (2003). In recent years her research has focused on Romantic theatre and drama.

RICHARD CRONIN is Professor of English Literature at the University of Glasgow. His publications include *The Politics of Romantic Poetry: In Search of the Pure Commonwealth* (2000), *1798: The Year of the* Lyrical Ballads (1998); *Imagining India* (1989), *Colour and Experience in Nineteenth-Century Poetry* (1988), *Shelley's Poetic Thoughts* (1981). In addition, he has published articles on G.G. Byron, John Clare, William Godwin, R.P. Jhabvala, John Keats, Rudyard Kipling, R.K. Narayan, Salman Rushdie, John Ruskin, Walter Scott, Mary Shelley, P.B. Shelley, Alexander Smith, Alfred Tennyson, William Wordsworth. His most recent book is *Romantic Victorians: English Literature, 1824-1840.*

STUART CURRAN, Vartan Gregorian Professor of English and Comparative Literature at the University of Pennsylvania, has been one of the foremost scholars recovering women's voices in late-Enlightenment Britain. He is the general editor of the fourteen-volume *Works of Charlotte Smith*, the last volumes of which will appear in 2007. He is the author of two critical studies on Shelley, as well as the standard bibliography of the poet; he was also for many years the editor of the *Keats-Shelley Journal*. He has edited the *Cambridge Companion to British Romanticism* (1992).

LIA GUERRA is Associate Professor of English Literature at the University of Pavia. Her research areas include the eighteenth century, travel literature of the eighteenth and early nineteenth centuries, Romantic women writers and James Joyce. She has published books on the poets of the First World War (*La polvere e il segno: Poeti inglesi della prima guerra mondiale* in 1980), James Joyce (*Interpreting James Joyce's* Dubliners*: An Experiment in Methods* in 1992), and Mary Shelley (*Il mito nell'opera di Mary Shelley* in 1995, and Mary Wollstonecraft Shelley and Percy B. Shelley, *Storia di un viaggio di sei settimane* [1817] in 1999), as well as essays on *The Spectator*, Samuel Johnson, Edmund Burke, Mary Wollstonecraft, H.M. Williams, Mary Shelley, Mariana Starke, Isaac Rosenberg, Basil Bunting, Dylan Thomas, Samuel Beckett and Barbara Pym.

DOROTHY MCMILLAN is a Senior Lecturer in English Literature, former Head of School of English and Scottish Language and Literature and past President of the Association for Scottish Literary Studies. Currently she is working mainly on writing by women, especially Scottish women. With Douglas Gifford she has edited *A History of Scottish Women's Writing* (1997). Other volumes include her anthology *The Scotswoman at Home and Abroad: Non-fiction Writing 1700-1900* (1999), an edition of George Douglas Brown, *The House with the Green Shutters* (2005), *Queen of Science*, an edition of Mary Somerville's *Personal Recollections* (2001), an anthology *Modern Scottish Women Poets* (2003); with Richard Cronin she has edited *Emma* for the Cambridge Edition of Jane Austen's works (2005).

DONATELLA MONTINI teaches English Language and Translation at the University of Rome, "La Sapienza". She is the author of *The Language of Fiction* (2007), *I discorsi dei re. Retorica e politica in Elisabetta I e in Henry V di Shakespeare* (1999), *Le lettere di Shakespeare* (1993), co-author of *The World Wide Reader – A*

History and Anthology of Literatures in English (2001). She is currently working on epistolary language and translating Samuel Richardson's *Correspondence*.

CECILIA PIETROPOLI is Associate Professor of English Literature at the University of Bologna. She is the author of *I tipi del comico nel teatro ciclico inglese* (1982), *Havelok il Danese* (1995) and *Il teatro dei Miracoli e delle Moralità* (1996). She has published extensively on the Romantic reception of the Middle Ages, in particular in Scott's historical fiction and in Romantic poetry. She is currently working on Romantic theatre and drama. She has edited a special issue of *La questione Romantica* dedicated to *Romanticismo / Medievalismo* (7/8, 2001).

DIEGO SAGLIA is Associate Professor of English Literature at the University of Parma and his research concentrates on the Romantic period. He is the author of *Poetic Castles in Spain: British Romanticism and Figurations of Iberia* (2000) and *I discorsi dell'esotico: l'oriente nel romanticismo britannico 1780-1830* (2002), and co-editor of *Il teatro della paura: scenari gotici del romanticismo europeo* (with Giovanna Silvani, 2005), *Re-Drawing Austen: Picturesque Travels in Austenland* (with Beatrice Battaglia, 2005) and *British Romanticism and Italian Literature: Translating, Reviewing, Rewriting* (with Laura Bandiera, 2005).

JANE STABLER is Reader in Romanticism at the School of English, University of St Andrews. Her books include the Longman *Byron Critical Reader* (1998) and *Byron, Poetics and History* (2002). She is working on a study of the way the poetic conversations of the Byron-Shelley circle influenced the next generation of English poets in Italy.

TIMOTHY WEBB is Emeritus Professor and Senior Research Fellow in the Department of English at the University of Bristol. His books include *The Violet in the Crucible: Shelley and Translation* (1976), *Shelley: A Voice Not Understood* (1977), *English Romantic Hellenism: 1700-1824* (1982), *Shelley's "Devil's" Notebook* (with P.M.S. Dawson, 1993) and *Shelley's Fause Draft Notebook* (with Nora Crook, 1997). He has edited Yeats for Penguin Poetry (*Selected Poetry*, with multiple texts, 1991; reprinted with revisions and additions, 2000), and Shelley for Everyman (*Selected Poems*, 1977, and *Poems and Prose*, 1995). He has published articles on many writers, the majority of them Romantic writers, and also on such subjects as Anglo-Italian literary relations, translation, the transmission of the classics, travel and the foreign, the Romantic city, and Irish literature and history.

INDEX